A
HISTORY
OF
ALREWAS

by
Norman Stubbs
and
Roger Hailwood

First Published by R.N. Stubbs 1987

ISBN 0 9511946 0 7

First Published in this edition by
Hailwood Enterprises (Publishing)
23 Churchill Crescent
Alrewas
Burton on Trent
Staffordshire DE13 7EH

ISBN 978-0-9556685-1-7

Printed by Prontaprint Burton
77 Station Street
Burton on Trent
Staffordshire DE14 1BT

*With acknowledgement of the help received from my friend,
the late Arthur Daniels.*

Main Sources and References

Alrewas Parish Register.
Poor Law Accounts, etc. 1771 to 1817.
The Salt Collection.
Lander's Transcriptions of Manor Court Rolls.
County Directories 1831 to 1935.
Alrewas School 1855 to 1955—J. R. McKnight.
History of Croxall and Catton—Rev. Richard Usher.
Parish Magazines.
Minute Book of Parish Meetings—W. Taverner.
Sunday School Register 1890 to 1901.

To my many old scholars.

And in this revised edition,

To the late Norman Stubbs

Who continues to inspire.

ALREWAS DISTRICT
EARLY TRADING TRACKS

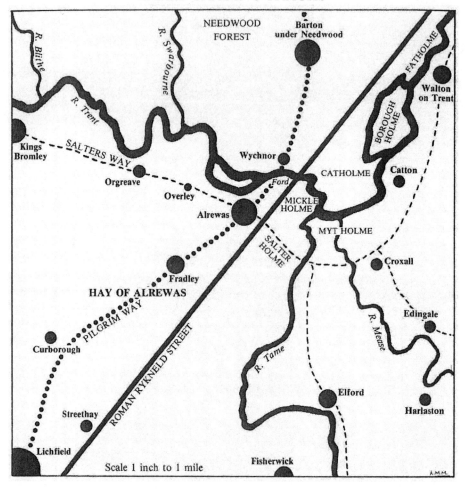

Scale 1 inch to 1 mile

A HISTORY OF ALREWAS

INDEX

A section of photographic reproductions with related captions is located between pages 80 and 81.

Preface

In the twenty-five years since the last edition was published, many alterations have taken place in Alrewas as the nature of the village has changed. There are fewer employment opportunities within the village; in consequence the majority of the employment is at some distance from the village and some of the residents commute daily to their place of work, some travelling quite considerable distances. The exodus by car starts before 7.00 a.m. so that a few can catch the train from Lichfield Trent Valley station for London. Others later on set off for Derby, Birmingham, or Manchester, with many other destinations between.

In recent years with the advent of the Internet and Broad Band, this trend for working away from the village has begun to diminish. More people are choosing to work from home, either setting up their own business or being an extension of their office, at the end of a telephone line.

The pressures of modern life and its expectations have also had an effect on the young people of the village, so that the once carefree groups of young people making their own entertainment around the countryside are a thing of the past. Computers and other associated electronic gadgetry have tended to isolate some in their homes, so that once well-subscribed organisations now have to work hard for their survival.

It is ten years since the death of Norman Stubbs, the author of the History of Alrewas; in that time there are parts of the village that he loved which he would find unrecognisable, especially where development has taken place. Fortunately there are other parts that have maintained a character with which he would be familiar.

The first edition of the History of Alrewas was eagerly read, and because of its scarcity is highly prized. The family of Norman Stubbs felt that this was an appropriate time to produce a second edition to make his work accessible to a wider public. They have also given me the opportunity to add a further chapter to cover the events and changes of the last quarter century. I am very conscious of the responsibility incumbent on me in trying to add to and maintain the quality of the undoubted previous scholarship of the work, and I hope that he would approve of what I have done, and forgive any errors that I may have committed.

Roger Hailwood.

Profits from this publication are
donated to the Alrewas, All Saints
Parish Church Fabric Fund.

CHAPTER 1

Early history of the area

It is difficult to consider the history of Alrewas Manor in isolation and it may be necessary at times to look beyond its boundaries and see how it was affected by outside events and influences. Alrewas had its beginnings several thousand years ago, when migrating races from Europe, following wave after wave over the centuries, penetrated the heartland up the river arteries from the North Sea. The land they settled on here was ideally suited to support them, with dense upland forests, rivers and streams, and wide river meadows, giving them a variety of food, with timber for their homes and fuel for their fires, rushes for bedding and thatch, clay for pottery and level areas of light land for grazing and growing their crops.

Along the main river banks of Trent and Tame, the last receding ice age had left river terraces of higher land, close to the river, yet safe from normal flooding, and it was on these terraces that the earliest settlers chose to live, and in many cases they are still the sites of modern villages. The primitive dwellings of these early people have long since vanished, leaving only faint burnt wood stains in the soil, but aerial survey is beginning to locate them from crop marks, filled in ditches and droveways which are undetected from the ground. It is certain that new scientific archaeology will bring to light more of these settlements, except for those which are buried beneath modern villages which occupy the original sites. Gravel workings have revealed very early sites at Hilton, Branston and Fisherwick, and we shall look later at the excavation of a typical Iron-age farm to see what it can reveal of life here 2,400 years ago.

How do we know of the presence of prehistoric men here, even before such excavations are made? Cinerary urns of rough clay, containing fragments of human bones, have been found in the past at Yoxall, Oakley and Orgreave, which have been dated back to 1200 B.C. and it is almost certain other such unmarked cemeteries lie undiscovered in the district. Over the years, a large

1

number of stone and flint tools and weapons have been found at Elford, Fisherwick, Yoxall, Barton, Fradley and Alrewas, while the writer has hand-axes, man's most primitive weapon and tool, found in the last few years at Orgreave, Wychnor, Tamworth, Croxall and a polished flint axe from Barton. It is significant to note that all these have been found very close to modern villages, which would indicate continuous occupation of the sites for several thousand years.

Most burial mounds, lows or barrows, have vanished with time, only two obvious ones remaining at Elford and Croxall. In 950 A.D., three barrows are mentioned as markers in the boundaries at Branston, large enough to be considered permanent features at that time, but all have vanished. Recent aerial and ground surveys have identified the sites of at least twelve barrows in Alrewas.

Some British or Celtic names have survived, mainly along the ancient tracks to be later taken over by the Romans, and renamed by them, as near as they could to the strange British pronunciation. Llwyd Coed of the Celts became Letocetum, the origins of Liccedfeldth or modern Lichfield, Penno cruca Penkridge while the British Rhydwaru (the dwellers by the ford) became the Ridwares of today. The names of permanent features like rivers and hills retained their ancient names from pre-historic times, Trent, Dove, Tame, Cannock and Needwood. Naturally many early names must have been lost, like the Parva Ridware of a thousand years ago, which was part of Alrewas Manor and was where the modern hamlets of Netherton and Pipe Ridware now stand. Wychnor gets its name from Hwicce, a British tribe who lived in Gloucestershire and Warwick, a group of whom must have migrated here and settled on the bank where the church is, and it is very probable that their Iron-age village was along the hill west of St. Leonard's Church.

Of all the commodities carried by traders' ponies along the early British tracks, salt was the most widely needed, and Salters' Ways threaded the country from the salt springs and mines of Cheshire and the Stafford area. One such track passed through Alrewas, coming from the north west via Kings Bromley, through Orgreave, along Overley Lane and through Alrewas to cross the ford of the Trent either at Mill End or the weir, and on to Wychnor and the north east, or forking south to cross the Tame Ford near the present Salters' Bridge, and continuing south-east. It is possible that the salt traders (and others) might at times be held up at the fords by flooding, and this could have been the reason why an Iron-age farm became a village, to supply the needs of the trading people. Aerial survey has shown traces of early settlements near to the ford over the Tame, on the large field called Stoney Furlong, and a possible connection along the north bank of the Tame with Fisherwick and beyond to the west.

Lastly up on the high lands of Cannock Chase, stand two ancient Iron-age fortresses at Castle Ring and Stonall, which point to a tribal structure in the area, where these defence positions could act as refuges in any inter-tribal conflict. There are archaeological mysteries too in Alrewas, in the shape of strange circles, once ditches cut into the earth. One is on the bank of the Tame opposite to Mytholm in the field called Rattlejack, farmed by Mr. G. Mallaber. Here in a dry season, the circle, fifty yards across, can be clearly seen, as the crops growing there like a fairy mushroom circle, are greener and taller than the rest. Near to the Sale, on the land farmed by Mr. D. Collingwood of the Bagnalls Farm, and only occasionally traceable on the ground, are three concentric circles encompassing about five acres, and these have been clearly shown by infra-red photographs taken from the air by a Birmingham archaeological team, which came, I understand from the University. The ground covered by these strange circles includes part of three fields, and their centre is roughly at the right angled bend leading to the Sale from Daisy Lane. Mr. Collingwood was informed that similar circles had been discovered at Handsacre. No one as yet, knows what these strange circles were for, but they may have been pens for drovers of cattle to rest their animals in, or for traders to confine their ponies. They do not appear to be either farms or defensive positions, and it must not be forgotten that at that time the area was mainly covered in forest, and such fenced and ditched pens would be very necessary during a halt.

The rapid opening up of sand and gravel workings along the Trent and Tame valleys, is bringing an urgency to the archaeologists to explore the threatened sites of early settlements before they are destroyed. To this end, regular aerial surveys are carried out using new scientific photography, which will reveal crop marks, drove ways, or signs of ancient soil disturbance showing signs of early farming or occupation. Such discoveries have been made at Fisherwick, Catholme, Barton Turns, Alrewas, and near the Tame south of Fradley, and four of these sites are either scheduled for sand and gravel workings, or have disappeared because of road development. The surface markings which can help

3

to find early sites are caused by variations in the crop growth, by variations in temperature, and by the effect of low sunlight on uneven ground. The continued deep ploughing of land can eradicate many of these traces, and, following the deepening of the rivers by the River Catchment Board, and the resultant lessening of flooding, many farmers are ploughing up the old permanent river meadows and pastures for arable crops, and this has constituted an added anxiety for the archaeologist.

Since the writing of the foregoing account, a further circular site has been located by aerial survey, and excavated by Nottingham University archaeologists at Barton Turns. The site has been identified as a burial ground, beneath which was found the remains of a building pre-dating it, and dating back to an estimated 2,000 B.C.

CHAPTER 2

A Local Iron-age Farm

From the excavations carried out at Fisherwick, it is possible to establish how some of the earliest farmers in the area lived and worked. New techniques in archaeology involving various branches of science, have brought to light information which would have been lost only a few years ago. Aerial survey first revealed crop marks and field patterns at a point where a brook joined the Tame, and where an ancient farm had been sited along a river terrace about five feet above the present flood plain. When excavations were carried out, most of the discoveries were made at depths of less than two feet, which would mean that on similar sites, disturbed by later continuous agricultural activity or by later village growth, no evidence would remain of such early occupation. Such sites at Alrewas, Orgreave, Elford, Croxall and Catton, where geographical conditions are similar to those at Fisherwick, would no longer be apparent, for Fisherwick was unique in being left undisturbed pasture for many centuries. The dig revealed a farm consisting of an enclosure about sixty metres square, with a gated entrance through the surrounding palisade, leading over the causeway to the river. A deep ditch or moat surrounded the fences, suggesting that defence was necessary against some danger, either human or animal predators. Inside the enclosure was the farm house, which had been rebuilt at various times, and out-huts and buildings for livestock and stores. The most recent habitation had been surrounded by a circular storm-water gully about fifteen yards in diameter, inside which was a ring of closely-spaced posts for the walls, with an inner of staging posts to support the roof. There was a central hearth, and the spaces in the wattle walls were filled with daubs of mud, clay and manure. From the door two log walls splayed out to form a courtyard with a hearth, probably used for cooking and domestic work which could be done in better light and air than could be done in the living hut.

Beyond the farm enclosure, narrow ditches divided the land around into fields, with droveways linking them to the farm, and at least twenty acres of such fields were indicated. It was in the ditch surrounding the farm, that most knowledge was preserved, for its lowest level was perpetually waterlogged, and this had preserved timber, leaves, pollen grains, grasses, seeds, insect remains, bones, and wooden artifacts. These included posts, pegs for jointing, a wooden blade and a wooden toggle for fastening clothing. Plants growing round the site, which radio carbon tests dated back to around 200 B.C., were knotgrass, henbane, ragged robin, water crowfoot, blackberry and elder, some of which would provide food. Tree pollen showed only limited woodland of birch and hazel, but the remains of forest animals like deer and boar indicated the presence of forest on the surrounding higher ground. Pollen also showed the presence of nearby arable fields where corn was grown, and the grain seed impressions of emmer and spelt wheat were found in fragments of daub from the farm house walls. Animal remains revealed that the stock was mainly horses and cattle, with pigs kept mainly in the farmyard, and the presence of the remains of dung beetles in the ditch, suggested that it was used by farm animals as a drinking place.

There were stone querns, which were used for grinding corn, metal slag indicating that the occupants had smelted and used iron, and shaped flints were also found, showing that there was a trade in flints from the south-east. There was variety too in the pottery fragments found, some of which were similar to pottery found in distant parts of the country. All these finds seem to indicate that the people who lived in this district over two thousand years ago must have had extensive and varied contacts with people in distant parts of England. The many remains of horses would indicate that these provided the transport for such trading and travel, rather than using boats on the river systems. The whole Midland area must have been threaded with tracks following the open secondary forests of the river valleys, along which the strings of pack ponies could carry various commodities for bartering. These would almost certainly include salt, iron, cloth, wool, dyes, pottery, honey, seeds, tools, weapons, ornaments, etc., and the tracks along which they were carried were along lines of the valley farms and settlements, where bartering could be easily carried out. Alrewas would, like other settlements lie on these tracks, and its origins as a village rather than an isolated farm, may have been its position near fordable passages of the Trent and Tame.

The site at Fisherwick was eventually abandoned, and not taken over by later settlers as were Elford, Croxall and Oakley on the opposite river bank. The pre-historic site of Alrewas was almost certainly around the site of the present church, and the terrace along Overley Lane to Orgreave, where stone axes and traces of ancient barrows have been found.

CHAPTER 3

The Romans

In 43 A.D., the Romans decided that England was valuable enough to be added to their empire, and its invasion and colonisation was begun. Within ten years of landing, Roman legions had fought their way into North Wales and secured the land over which they had marched. They passed through the midland forests along meandering British tracks, surveying and mapping as they went, and eventually, using local labour, they constructed two main military roads through the district, Watling Street which ran from London to North Wales, and Rykneld

Street which connected the south-west to the north-east. Recent excavation has shown how these roads in the area were constructed. They ran, where possible in a straight line from horizon to horizon, bridging rivers which had never been bridged by the Britons. The roads were about twenty-five feet wide, on a raised bank of sand and gravel, rammed and cambered to drain into ditches on either side. Their normal practice of paving the surface with stone could not be carried out here, because of the absence of local suitable stone. Along these roads military forts were built during the first century of the occupation, many of these changing in time to market towns, or barrack towns, with post houses situated at roughly ten mile intervals. Just as the roads followed the line of the ancient British tracks, so many of the Roman towns were sited at, or near, the positions of British settlements. Somewhere within the boundaries of the present Lichfield, was a British settlement called Caer Llwydcoed, which meant the place by the grey woods, where birch trees predominated, as they still do in Curborough and Cannock Chase areas. The site may have been a religious site for the Britons, as would be indicated by early records of standing stones, or the name of Weeford, which is a British name meaning ford to the heathen temple, and to the possible prehistoric implications of the traditional Bower ceremony, which could have had its origins in a Spring sacrificial rite.

The re-alignment of Watling Street and Rykneld Street, brought the junction of the two roads to a point two miles further west, and the Romans got as near to the original British name (roughly pronounced as Lydched) as they could by calling their town Letocetum. As time passed and the new town grew as a trading settlement, the original British settlement became neglected, especially as the old religion of the Druids died out, and it was not until five hundred years later that the site of the British centre at Liccidfeld would be revived by St. Chad as the centre of his Christian mission in Mercia.

Penkridge, too, was a British settlement called Penno cruca, which meant hill summit, the Romans taking over the site as Pennocrucium.

The forested midlands were not popular with the Romans, who preferred the south and south-west as centres of trade and agriculture, and other than a few towns and military stations like Menduessedum (Atherstone) and Rocester, there is little evidence locally of Roman occupation, except of course the station at Letocetum.

Rykneld Street was constructed half-a-mile south of Alrewas, and the fact that a line of ancient villages, Lichfield, Elmhurst, Curborough, Fradley, Alrewas, Wychnor, Barton, Tatenhill, Shobnall, and Anslow, are all in a line parallel to the Roman road, would suggest that this line represented the earlier track of the Britons. It can of course be argued, that the earliest Anglo-Saxons avoided building their villages too near the road along which their enemy might come, but this is a doubtful thesis. Most important to the Romans, was the bridge over the Trent at Wychnor, of wooden construction, where piles, still bearing the Roman lead stamps, were uncovered following a disastrous flood at the end of the eighteenth century. When the new bridge was being built to carry the dual carriageway in 1959, a perfect Roman vase was dredged from the river bed there. It was usual, as it was at Stretton, to station troops near to important bridges, to guard and maintain them, and it is almost certain that Roman foundations lie beneath the turf somewhere near to the bridge, and owing to the likelihood of flooding, they are possibly along the ridge from the bridge to Wychnor Church. In the 1930's, the writer was informed by the late Mr. Arthur Kent, who was sexton for many years, that there were parts of the churchyard at Wychnor where he found great difficulty in digging graves, on account of stone foundations under the ground, but it would only be conjecture to assume that the church had been built on much older Roman foundations. The archaeologists working at the site of the Anglo-Saxon village at Catholme in 1975, were of the opinion, from preliminary study, that there were indications of a Roman villa in the next field, which they hoped to investigate further in the future.

By 350 A.D. the Roman empire was beginning to crumble, and England began to suffer from bands of invaders from Wales, Scotland and Ireland. Mobile field armies were sent to Britain to counter this threat, and as the incursions grew in number and intensity, earthworks were thrown up across the Roman roads along which the barbarous Welsh Britons came to the settlements to loot and steal slaves and cattle. These earth forts were large enough to provide shelter for the local people, and hopefully, strong enough to hold back the invaders until mobile cavalry could be called up to drive them away. At Letocetum, a nine foot thick earth wall, backed by a turf bank, enclosed five acres across the Watling Street with three encircling defensive ditches in front to slow any attack. A similar defensive position has been found, again on Watling Street, at Atherstone. Despite these precautions, the raids grew in strength, and the end of Roman power was in sight. By 410 A.D., the last Roman legion had left Britain, and the country lay defenceless against the fierce tribes of Picts from Scotland, Scots from Ireland, and Britons from the Welsh borders, the only people with military training being army pensioners, settled mainly in the south, and east in the Colchester area. In addition to these local threats to civilised life, there came a greater one from ever-increasing numbers of pirates from Denmark and North Germany. These fierce bands were the forerunners of the mass migration of Angles, Saxons and Jutes, who were within the next hundred and fifty years, to emerge from the confusion and violent upheavals of the dark ages, as the dominant, settled inhabitants of England, the people who were to bring peace and progress to the torn land, who were to rebuild and rename most of our local villages, and give them names which have not changed much over more than a thousand years.

CHAPTER 4

The Anglo-Saxons

Some time around 600 A.D., many British farming and fishing communities in this area, including Alrewas, were taken over by the invading Angles, who set their capitals for the border country of Mercia successively at Repton, Stone and Tamworth. In 672 A.D., St. Chad died at what was to become Lichfield, after three years pacifying Mercia for King Wulfere, as his bishop. The conversion of these invaders by Chad and other Missionaries was accompanied by a profound faith in the efficacy of the shrines of the saints, whose burial places became the centres of pilgrimage. The fierce, violent fighters and conquerors became peaceful and settled farmers, each chief or head of a family group choosing a settlement site, the earliest being by the rivers, usually as tons or fortified places, but as time passed they moved into the tributory valleys or into the forest clearings. Three of the local saints were the cause of the later growth of towns, and cathedrals. Over the shrine of St. Chad grew Lichfield Cathedral, over the shrine of St. Modwen grew a great Benedictine Abbey around which Burton was to grow, while St. Wurburgh's bones were carried for safety from Hanbury to Chester, and over their burial place Chester Cathedral was built.

The Anglo-Saxons brought a new language, which was to take the place of the British or Celtic tongue, which slowly died out in England, but which remained basically the language of the Welsh people (named Wals or foreigners by the early English settlers).

Much of our present language is based on the Anglo-Saxon tongue, but altered by time and its mixture with Norman-French, and to a lesser degree by Scandinavian or Viking influence. Many of the modern names of things have changed little with the passing of the centuries, aldr alder, ac oak, aex ash, ael eel, beo bee, tripp trap, cald cold, brom broom, broc brook, suth south, etc. It was in this early language that names were given to villages, and areas, and a study of these names can often reveal what the site was like when its name was given, or what activities took place there.

Many of the rivers and hills, permanent in feature, kept their original British names, as indeed did a few villages. The name Trent for example is made up of two words, Tre and Santon, which means literally the trespasser or flooder of ways. The Tame means dark in Celtic, and Dove comes from the British word Dubo, which means black (Dhu in Gaelic). Ridware is made up of two British words, Rhyd and Waru, meaning the dwellers by the ford. The smaller river Mease was renamed by the English from Meos, meaning moss, a river with mossy banks, as was the Swarbourne, meaning a river with swar or heavy land. Cannock, the only really high ground locally, is again a British word, originally Cunucc or hill.

Places received their names originally because of some generally recognised feature or connection, and a name once given and accepted, stuck, even though the reason for the name might no longer be there, like Elmhurst, Oakley, Bromley, Byrkley, Hazelour, Hadley (Heather), etc., or where there was higher ground like Tatenhill, Stapenhill (meaning steep hill); or where tracks could cross rivers or streams like Elford, Weeford, Pyeford, etc. Most were named after the name of the man or his folk who settled there, like Fradley (Froda), Edingale (Edwin), Catton (Catti), Croxall (Crocca), Harlaston (Heorulf),

Branston (Branta), Wychnor (Hwicce), etc.

Looking at modern Alrewas, some of the new street names are after celebrated people with Alrewas connections. Turton Close is named after the first resident lords of the manor, who resided at the Manor House from 1670 to 1752, when they sold it to Admiral Lord George Anson, after whom Anson Road is named. Inge Drive is named after the Rev. W. Inge once vicar here, whose son was the celebrated theologian, the gloomy Dean of St. Paul's Cathedral. Some of our road names have altered during the last fifty years. Wellfield Road used to be Furlong Lane, and Furlong Lane was originally Back Lane. Exchange Lane is obviously recently named, and before that, was called Tunley's Lane from a basket maker named Tunley who lived there, and even earlier was called Malthouse Lane from the malthouse which stood opposite to the site of the surgery. Park Road is a name going back only seventy years, and then only to the part from Exchange Lane to the start of Mickleholme Drive. The Park Road of today, ending at Coronation Square, was until recently The Dock, or more fully The Puddledock, which at one time had a brook running along it, ending in a pool called Deepmore, near where the stream was crossed by a path leading from Essington Field to Deepmore Field (where Deepmore Close now stands). Before the arrival of the Post Office there, Post Office Lane was originally named Market Street, which long ago had its market on two days a week. Fifty years ago, Ridgetts Lane over the railway, was called Lidgett's Lane, and seven hundred years ago there was a gate there called Ludgate, which in early English was pronounced Ludyat, and the Turnpike Gate there in 1740 was called Lidyat Gate. Again, Dunmore Hay Lane at Fradley was originally called Dugmore Hay, what was years ago the Duckmore, while Cowhill was in 1260 called Caluhill, which could either have been a calu hill (bare hill) or Gallow Hill, where the Somerville Gallows were erected.

But to return to the Anglo-Saxon names in the district. In 771 A.D., this village was written as Allerwas, and the name consists of two words, Aldr and waesse, which meant Alder marsh. It is very likely that, before drainage ditches were dug, much of the area was indeed marshy, with brooks seeping through reed beds under large numbers of alder trees which thrive when their roots are in wet ground. There was an alder wood called the Alder scele (now the Sale), where stood in 1250, Aldersale Moor, which will be referred to later.

Fradley, founded probably later than Alrewas, was in the 12th Century, called

Frodeleye. The first element is an Angle name, Froda, and the ending ley comes from the word leah, which meant a clearing or open ground in a forested area, where ploughing and grazing could be undertaken with minimal kidding or clearing the ground. There are many such examples as Bromley (a clearing with broom bushes), Overley (a clearing on a bank), Hadley (clearing in the heather), Oakley (a clearing in Oaks).

Orgreave, while always being connected with Alrewas, has a very long story of occupation, and it was first recorded in 1195 as Ordgrave. The last element of the word is not a grave or pit, but early English greave, meaning a wood, and the first part is from orde, meaning the point or edge (as used to describe part of a sword), so that the name means the edge of a wood.

Wychnor again had a history before the Anglo-Saxons named it, but its early name has vanished. It was first written down as Hwiccenofre or Wichenovere in 1236, and this gives the meaning of the name. The ending 'over' was an Anglo-Saxon word meaning a bank, or slope, as is found in other local names like Hazelour, Overseal, Mickleover, Overley, etc. The Hwicce were members of a British tribe whose territory was around Gloucester, and some of these Britons had settled along the bank near to where the church now stands, and because their name was attached, it seems the Angles along the river let them remain and named their ancient site for them—the Hwicce people's bank!

In 733 A.D., Croxall was written as Crockashalle, and the name simply means the house or dwelling of Crocka, a name which would appear to be an early appearance of a Scandinavian in this area, as it is an old Swedish or Danish name. Near to Croxall, there used to be a settlement called Oakley, but it has vanished except for Oakley Farm along the Elford Road, for the railway cut the manor in half. It was, in 1002 A.D., willed to the daughter of a Mercian earl, Wulfric, who was killed fighting against the Danes. Its name means simply an open space in the oak woods.

Catton, first written as Cattiton in 1208, means the ton or village of Catti, as Catholme was Catti's meadow by the river. Edingale, once part of this manor, was early written as Edwinghalle in 1085, and has the long meaning of the hall of Edwin's people, -ing or -ung meaning folk, followers or people, as in Lullington, Essington, Willington, etc.

The original Barton, dating to around 600 A.D., was on the river terrace near to the branch of the Trent now cut off from the main river, down Catholme

Lane. The passing centuries saw the migration northwards across Rykneld Street, until the present village grew round the church in the 16th Century. There are many Bartons, and the words in the name, Bere and ton, mean corn or barley growing in the village.

Dunstall, like the same name in Alrewas manor, is Anglo-Saxon, and should be ton stealle, which means a village with a farmstead, i.e., an enclosed area of farmland, not cultivated in common like most other villages. Hamstall has the same ingredient, meaning "the homestead".

CHAPTER 5

The Danish invasion

By the year 800 A.D., Alrewas and its surrounding district had become a settled area, with most of the suitable farming sites having been taken over by the families of immigrant Angles, whose descendants were now the new English people.

Around the triangle of land formed by the confluence of the Trent and Tame, there had grown a number of small family settlements, many like Alrewas, Orgreave, Fradley, Croxall, Catton, Oakley, Edingale, Whitemoor Hay, Alrewas Sale, Mytholme, Rodige, etc., as well as some which have vanished like Bechesover, Heywigges, Alregate, and Aldecroft. At times, it was necessary to hold moots or meetings of these free people, at which local headmen could pass on information about the country's laws, commands, etc., where complaints and quarrels could be resolved, and where offenders could be tried and punished. Such Anglo-Saxon moots were often held at some widely and easily reçognisable high point, which they called a 'low', as was used for the County Hundreds which gathered originally at Offlow, Totmonslow, Pirehill, Cuttlestone or Seisdon. The minor meetings here at Alrewas had no obvious hill, so the local meetings took place in the centre of the water enclosed triangle at the Spellow.

The early English word spell means speech, talk, or discussion, and low had come to be the name of the meeting place. The name Spellow still exists in the name of arable fields along Croxall Road, areas of land which have for over a thousand years been called Wet Spellow, Dry Spellow, Wiggespellow, and in the 18th Century, The Spelsus. To this place then, on the day appointed, came all the men of the district to talk, to listen, to judge and to carry out the functions of local government.

The laws of these Anglo-Saxons applied to all, were practised in order to be understood by all, for every man's safety and security. They are of great interest, and give some insight on the ways the people related to their neighbours, and a look at one or two examples from the Laws of Ine, a West Saxon king, will illustrate how order was maintained in the 8th Century. "If a slave work on Sunday by his lord's command, he shall go free, and his lord shall pay 30 shillings fine. If a slave work without his lord's knowledge, he shall be flogged and pay the fine ordained. But if a free man work on the Sabbath without his master's command, he shall lose his freedom, or pay 60 shillings, and a priest twofold".

There were many slaves at that time, who could own possessions, and these laws were to maintain the Sabbath, which ran from mid-day on Saturday to dawn on Monday.

"If a thief be taken, he shall die the death or his life shall be redeemed by his weregild". This weregild was the value placed on a man's life, which must be paid to his dependents by the killer, a value which varied according to the victim's social status.

"If anyone steal, so that his wife nor his children know it not, he shall pay a fine of 60 shillings. But if his household know, they shall all go into slavery. A child of ten years can be an accomplice to theft". (A shilling at that time was the price of a sheep.)

To prevent raiding parties and feuding in a newly-settled land, the law said— "We call men thieves up to the number of seven. From seven to thirty-five, a gang, and above thirty-five, an army. He who is accused of belonging to a gang, shall clear himself with an oath of 120 hides, or pay the fine corresponding". These hides, which will be dealt with later, were areas of arable land of about 120 acres, which became a vague measure for tax and law purposes. Oaths like lives, varied in value, depending on the amount of land owned by the oath-giver. A very important thegn might have an oath valued at 60 hides. In other words, a gang member would have to find either two very important men as oath-givers for his surety, or a larger number of less important men to swear to his future good behaviour. To these people, their laws seemed to indicate that theft of other people's possessions was often worse than murder. Rich thieves were banished with their families, while poor thieves lost their freedom or their lives.

Their justice, cruel and primitive as it was, made England a safe and peaceful place, and made it possible for traders to travel great distances without fear of violence or robbery. It was claimed that along the trading tracks and roads, each drinking well or spring was equipped with a silver mug, none of which was ever stolen during these years of deep Christian faith, and even deeper respect for the law. It is easy to understand how St. Modwen of Burton, with only two nuns for company, was able to travel freely from Ireland to Northumbria and back, from Wales to Burton, on to Italy and back, as well as her continuous local missionary journeys, terminating in her last journey to Scotland, where she died, reputedly but doubtfully, at the age of 130, her body being brought back for burial at Burton.

Christianity became firmly established, and in 822 A.D., Bishop Aethelwald instituted prebends at Freeford, Weeford, Longdon, Colwich and Alrewas, which meant that the villages were capable of maintaining a priest or prebendary at the Cathedral, who would appoint a vicar to care for the religious needs of the communities. The first church would be built like all other local buildings, constructed from timber, with a thatched or shingle roof, for these early Angles were expert wood workers, and there was little local stone. There were possibly small chapels at Fradley and Edingale built later, for they were still there in the 13th Century.

By this time a new threat to Christianity and to England was beginning to be felt. Bands of Danish and Viking raiders began to plunder the coasts, and as time passed, they began to arrive in their longships in greater force, raiding far up the rivers, burning and pillaging town, villages and monasteries, slaughtering the priests and monks and abducting young people for slaves. In 874 A.D., a large Danish army reached Repton, the monastery was robbed of all its treasures, and the monks put to death with great cruelty. The Danes over-wintered there, and during these months, foraging parties would comb the surrounding district, especially along the rivers, to gather all available food from the villages. The local people would seek sanctuary in the depths of the surrounding forests, but it is likely that Alrewas, like other villages would be destroyed, the wooden huts and church being easy to burn. The nuns of Hanbury dug up the bones of St. Wurburgh, and carried them to the west for safety from the Danes, and they were eventually buried again at Chester, and over them was built a new shrine and finally St. Wurburgh's Cathedral. St. Modwen's shrine at Burton suffered too, but was later re-built with greater splendour. In 878, King Alfred, who was now welding England into one country, succeeded in defeating a huge Danish army, and made a treaty with the defeated King Guthrum. Under this, the Danes were to become Christian, they were to forsake their warring ways, and in return, they would settle in the eastern part of England. This was agreed, and the Danes settled down in what became an area called the Danelaw. In this area, the boundary between England and the Danelaw was the Trent and Tame and Watling Street, so that places like Walton, Catton, Croxall, and Edingale were under Danish rule. New Danish settlements at Derby, Ashby, Appleby, Bretby, Donisthorpe, were founded and for many years to come, this area was a troubled frontier region. To contain the Danes, and to control the rivers up which they would come, King Alfred had ordered the erection of forts or burhs on hills which overlooked the rivers. These could, in times of danger, be controlled by local English fighting bands called the fyrd, and would give protection to the local people, and provide a threat to Danish forces which might try to force a passage up the rivers. Burton got its name from Burh ton, a village with a fortress, which might have been at Stapenhill, and Borough Hill at Walton, still retaining its name after more than a thousand years, is a perfect example of the burh, with the remains of its defensive ramparts and ditches still to be seen rising above the river. Eight skeletons were unearthed near the farm at the top of it a few years ago, which the British Museum dated back to about 1000 A.D., and past records of the finding of human remains from the slopes, would seem to indicate that Borough Hill saw its share of the violent encounters between Danes and English, for the uneasy peace was soon broken.

In 918, shortly after leading her Mercian army to capture Leicester from the Danes, King Alfred's widowed sister, the Countess Ethelflaeda died at Tamworth, but Staffordshire was now freed from warring invaders. In 937, an English army under Athelstan defeated the Danes at Brunanburh, but after his death, his brother Edmund was unable to hold back the invaders, and in 943 they swept into Mercia and captured the capital at Tarnworth after great slaughter, carrying away booty and prisoners, among whom was the great lady named Wulfrune, who had a monastery built at Heanton (High village), which became known as Wulfrunes' Heanton, known to us today as Wolverhampton. Shortly after this event, when attempts were being made to defend Mercia, warriors were given areas by the King, so that they could provide men to defend the land, and in 942, King Edmund gave Alrewas and other local manors to a man named Maur Wolsye. This was at a royal gathering at Winchcombe in Gloucestershire, as a translation of the deed indicates — "Holy charter of King Edmund of Alrewas, Bromley and Barton, year of our Lord 942.

A perpetual inheritance, which in the theology of God, and the Holy Trinity, remains beyond all the workings of the human mind, shall be the reward for merit.

Wherefore, following truly the paternal footsteps of the ancient kings, Edmund, by the blessed protection of God, King and ruler of the Anglo-Saxons, among innumerable rewards with which he has bestowed upon the troops after every contest, is provoked by the old proverbs "A cheerful giver" etc., really enriches and honours in a praiseworthy manner, Wulsye, whose first name is Maur, granting to him and his heirs to be enjoyed forever, the lands at Alrewasse, and Bromleg and Barton and Tatenhill and Bronteston and Stretton and Rothulfeston and Clifton and Hagnetun. Now is this land forty hides. These lands in fine, King Edmund, in the year of our Lord DCCCCXLII, and in the third year of his sovereignty, has bestowed as gifts, with the agreement of the nobles whose names are noted below, to be held by Wulsye with a safe hand, not by reason of the love of wealth, but by the zeal of his most devoted loyalty. I, Edmund, King, willingly inscribe this gift with the sign of the Holy Cross, the ownership (in level or woodland places or in waters abounding with fish) for their enjoyment.

(Signed) — Wulfstan — Archbishop of York
Wulfgar — Bishop of Lichfoeld
Cenwald — Bishop of Worcester
Wulfhelm — Bishop of Wells
Cynsige — Bishop of Berkshire
Ethelmund, ealdorman, and five other ealdormen, with the rest of the

companions of the same military company, have inscribed this land charter with triumphal marks.

This royal gift has been made, to wit in the very celebrated place called Winchelcombe. Peace and eternal prosperity be to those who have determined to maintain the right of divine privelege, and the law of good human report, and those on the other hand who shall have denied it, resist the strict rule of God "Render unto Caesar the things that are Caesar's, and unto God the things that are God's".

For how long this Maur Wolsye survived in the wars is not known, but eventually, the manor of Alrewas passed into the hands of the Earls of Mercia. In 1002, King Ethelred, after failing in his weak policy of trying to buy off the Danes, ordered in secret, a general massacre of all Danish settlers. This treacherous slaughter was said to have begun at Houndhill near to Tutbury. Survivors spread the news, and Danish revenge followed swiftly. They came in increasing numbers, and in one of the many battles, Wulfric Spott, a Mercian, was killed, after having made a will leaving most of his great wealth to build a Benedictine monastery over the shrine of St. Modwen at Burton.

By 1017, a Danish king, Canute, was on the throne, and slowly, the old hatreds began to die. Mercia, the huge Midland earldom, was given to Leofric, and Alrewas became part of his personal estates in Staffordshire. His summer palace was at Kings Bromley, where he and his countess, the famous Lady Godiva, spent much of their time. It was here that he died in 1057, to be taken for burial to Coventry, but his widow, Godiva, retained some of his manors for herself, including Branston, and she spent many of her last years in this district. Her grand-daughter married Harold, the last of the English kings, who was to die at Hastings, and who kept Bromley as a royal manor, while Alrewas was held by Algar, the earl of Mercia.

So the Danish invasions came to an end, but we can still find traces of their presence here. Down the Trent valley from Burton to Alrewas, the river meadows and islands still retain the Danish name for island, which is holm, and we have Boroughholm, Catholm, Fatholm, Cherryholm, Mytholm, and Mickleholm, once known as Muckleholm (from the old Norse word Mikill, meaning large). The slang down Dark Lane has a Danish name, which means a narrow field, but it is over the Trent to the east where Danish names are most common.

CHAPTER 6

The Normans and the Domesday Book

In 1066 came the Norman invasion, and the defeat of the English at Hastings, when King Harold was killed. After this came the long and difficult task of subduing the country, re-distributing the land of the vanquished English amongst the victors from the continent, and maintaining an iron grip on the conquered nation. Mercia had taken no part in the battle with the Normans, for its army had been badly mauled by invading Norsemen at Fulford, near York, and they were unable to join King Harold. Because of this, the area round here was not at first brought under the iron grip of the Conqueror but slowly a system of Mott and Bailey castles spread over the land, until almost the whole of England was under the control of the Norman garrisons. Gradually these earth and timber structures were replaced by strong stone keeps and walls, and Tutbury, Tamworth, Chartley and Stafford became strong Norman military centres.

The curfew was introduced to prevent the native English from plotting rebellion at night, and the ringing of the curfew (couvre feu—French for damp the fire) signalled the extinguishing of lights, the damping of fires, the barring of doors and shutters, and the loosing of mastiffs to guard the villages. Rebellions however did take place, in Yorkshire and here in Staffordshire, led by Edwin the Earl of Mercia, and his brother Morcar, Earl of Northumberland, but they were put down by William with great savagery. The Vale of York and much of Staffordshire were laid waste, which meant that everything capable of supporting life was destroyed, houses, barns, mills, crops, livestock, fisheries, orchards, etc. The people who still lived after the onslaught, fled into the forests to die of starvation, though records show that some wandered as far as Evesham to find food and refuge, and it was to be many years before the devastated land was brought back to cultivation. In 1086, only little Rutland and Cornwall had smaller populations than Staffordshire, which had only five Hundreds (areas of local government) while Sussex had fify-eight, Kent had sixty-eight, and

19

Hampshire was split into forty-four.

Twenty years after the conquest, King William still knew little of the land he had taken, what was its population, how much tax could be collected, who were the landholders, etc. It was decided therefore, to carry out a survey of the whole country, and to record all the required information. It was a gigantic task, for thousands of manors and villages must send the information through a Priest and village headman or reeve, who would render the account under oath to commissioners and their clerks, centred in each hundred of each county. The same questions were asked of all villages, and the answers were to be recorded village by village, hundred by hundred and county by county, until the whole country had been surveyed. The records were to be bound into books and stored in a special store room in a building in London called Domus Dei (meaning the House of God), where sacred books were stored, and from this, the name Domesday Book was to come.

Each village had to supply the following information—

1. The name of the village.
2. Who held the village before the conquest, in the time of Edward the Confessor, and who is the present holder of the land.
3. The size of the arable plough land in Hides, the hide being a roughly estimated total of land strips held by the villagers, and being around 120 acres in area. This was an ancient measure of the status of a community and the power of its overlord.
4. The number of caracutes or plough teams, each team or oxgang ploughing 60 to 80 acres in a year. A man holding a bovate of land, i.e., half a virgate, or 15 acres, contributed one ox to the oxgang, so that most villagers, while sharing the use of the ploughs, contributed their proportion to the oxen which pulled them.
5. The number of ploughs on the demesne land, or land kept by the lord for his own use, and worked largely by the unpaid service of his tenants as day work or boon work, as part payment for their land granted by their lord.
6. The number of slaves, the number of poor peasants or bordars, and the number of villeins or farmers, supporting their families from their holdings on the vast open fields. Their holdings of half-acre strips of arable land varied up to about 30 acres. Priests must also be included in the census of the male population.

7. The size of the village hay meadow, which would indicate the number of animals which could be kept through the winter.

8. What extra taxable assets there were, like mills, quarries, salt mines, salt pans, fisheries, mines, etc.

9. The size of the wood. This was not forest, but cultivated woodland, to produce timber and fuel, and to provide food for swine in the autumn, called the pannage and mast.

10. What tax was payable before the conquest, and what was its present value to the King, and also to show whether a village was growing or shrinking.

We felt it necessary to give this explanation in order that the entry for Alrewas in the Domesday Book might be better understood.

Translated from the abbreviated Latin of 1086, the entry states:— "The King holds Alrewas. Algar held it. Here are three hides. Arable land is eight caracutes. One serf, twenty villeins six bordars with a priest, have six caracutes. Here are twenty four acres of meadow, a fishery yeilding one thousand five hundred eels. A wood one league by half a league. In the time of King Edward worth £10, now worth £11."

We consider it to be of local interest to tabulate the facts from Domesday Book as they relate to other local villages, as this would indicate their comparative sizes nine hundred years ago, and indicate any decline or increase. Those villages on the east bank of the Tame, Croxall and Catton, show their arable extent as caracutes, which was the Danish measure of 60-80 acres.

The two surprise entries are Croxall and Elford, both with larger populations than Alrewas, as the presence of two mills in each village would indicate. Earl Algar's manors, and King Harold's, were retained as royal estates, while the manors at Wychnor, Catton and Croxall, which had belonged to English knights, were given as reward to the Normans, Robert de Somerville, and Henry de Ferrers (whose family was later to become Earls of Derby). Robert de Somerville had, like many Norman knights, been given a number of scattered manors, a policy adopted by King William to prevent a combined challenge to his authority, yet from all the manors Wychnor was chosen as his central manor, and from it he took his title as Baron of Wychnor. It is interesting to speculate why, for it was an insignificant manor. It may have been a strategic siting, to have some Norman presence to guard and maintain the important bridge spanning the Trent. It was here then, that Robert de Somerville, the founder of the family which was to hold the future lordship of Alrewas, built his moated manor house on the level meadow below the site of the church of St. Leonard. It is interesting to speculate on the method of maintaining the water level in the surrounding moat. Did it come from the river by means of an early weir, which could also have served a corn mill near to the manor? Was it supplied from the stream, later dammed to form the fish pond for Wychnor Hall, which would have half a mile of flat meadow to cross? This would seem unlikely.

COMPARISON OF LOCAL VILLAGES
AS SHOWN IN THE
DOMESDAY BOOK

	Alrewas	Kings Bromley	Wychnor	Barton District	Branston	Burton	Catton	Croxall	Elford
Holder in 1066	Earl Algar	King Harold	4 Saxons Thegns	Earl Algar	Lady Godiva	The Abbey	Siward	Siward	Earl Algar
Holder in 1086	King William	King William	Robert de Somerville	King William	Burton Abbey	The Abbey	Henry de Ferrers	Henry de Ferrers	King William
No. of Hides	3	3	2	3	1½	1½	3 Car.	3 Car.	3
Plough Teams	8	5	5	18	5	2	7	8	11
Cottars or Bordars	20	11	4	17	5	9	14	35	24
Villeins	6	2	2	8	3	—	2	11	8
Slaves	1	2	—	2	—	—	—	—	—
Acres of Hay Meadow	24	25	20	20	24	16	24	22	24
Leagues of Woodland	1 League ½ League	1 x ½	½ Lea. 5 Furl.	2 Lea. x 1 Lea.	½ x ½	½ x ½	1 Furl. x 1 Furl.	2 Furl. x ½ Furl.	—
Extra Assets	Fishery	—	Mill	Mill	—	—	—	2 Mills	2 Mills
Worth 1066	£10	100s	£6	£6	60s	60s	60s	£3	£11
Worth 1086	£11	100s	£7	£7	40s	70s	60s	£4	£12

In 1086 then, Alrewas manor, a royal holding, which included Fradley and Orgreave, contained three hides of sub-divided common plough-land, roughly 360 acres, as well as some freehold land. The locations of the fields at Alrewas

was to change little during the next 700 years. They had already been worked for several centuries, gradually extending into the forest and waste land as the slow clearing or 'kidding' of trees and undergrowth had to keep pace with an increasing population and the greater dependance on corn rather than herds of swine.

One open field was Essington Field, which stretched along the length of what is now Main Street from Post Office Road to Rykneld Street, and north through Dark Lane, sloping down to the flat river meadow, and ending near Rykneld Street. (Its ending can still be clearly seen in the undulating strips half way across an enclosed meadow nearly opposite Willowbrook Farm.) The second, called Great Furlong, was a vast area extending from the canal through Walk Field, Oakfield Road estate, and across Wellfield Road to Rykneld Street, bounded on the north by what is now Furlong Lane, and ending in the south beyond Somerville Road and Daisy Lane. The third and perhaps newest field was across Rykneld Street and ran on either side of what is now Croxall Road. The western section, or flatt, was called the Dry Spellow, and the eastern part was the Wet Spellow. We shall see later how these fields were to shape the future Alrewas, which in 1086 was almost certainly clustered round the church.

The Common meadow of 24 acres, was called Essington Meadow, and occupied the right bank of the river from where the mill stream is now, extending as far as the river bridge and the Roman Road.

The wood, one league by half a league, consisting of a belt of tended timber, ran from Orgreave to what is now Fradley Junction. This is the likeliest place, as it fits the measurements, and from the later use of the remaining land in the manor, the only apparent area suitable for extensive woodland. A belt of timber here would also form a natural barrier between the forest of Cank to the west, and the cultivated manorial land here at Alrewas.

There was no mill recorded, and the people must either have used hand mills (or querns), or they took their corn to be ground at Wychnor.

There were only two fisheries in Staffordshire, and conditions must have been ideal for eel fishing, with the many streams and rivers, and there must have been a long tradition and skill in the use of basket traps, nets or strikes, or the special eel houses. The eels were taken mainly with trident spears, and the writer has such a spear which must be several hundred years old.

23

CHAPTER 7

Farming at Alrewas in the Middle Ages

The Open Fields

In considering life of the people of Alrewas in the past, it is necessary to look at their methods of farming the land, because for many centuries all the people were farmers, either wholly or in part. The land was life to them, landless men either died or were hunted down as masterless vagrants. Every house, every cottage, every hovel, was a farm, with its rickyards, its styes, byres, grainstores and barns, its orchard, its poultry or cock loft, and all occupants except the very old or very young, played a part in the wresting of a Living from their landholdings, and utilising the resources of their environment. The picture would have been so very different from today. Great expanses of open ground almost treeless, but divided up like gigantic allotments, with some hedges and hurdles round the long perimeters to protect the growing corn from the village herds and forest deer. Beyond that was the stretch of common grazing land, dotted with large trees, the remnants of the forest which had been cleared, and away beyond the manor boundaries were the forests, surrounding the village on all sides.

From Saxon times until the middle of the 18th Century, the pattern and methods of farming were to change little, only in its scale and location. By 1350, forests in this immediate vicinity had largely disappeared, as it was slowly cleared to provided more arable land and grazing areas. We have seen that Alrewas, like most villages, had its main plough land in three extensive ares, known as the Great Furlong, the Spellow, and Essington Field. There was a simple rotation of crops in these fields, which enabled the villeins to concentrate their work and the ploughs on one field at a time. One field was ploughed, harrowed and sown in the Spring, with what they called the etch grain, barley, oats or rye, etch meaning stubble, for it was on the turned-in wheat stubble that the seed was sown. The second field was left empty or fallow, to rest for a season and be manured either by cattle grazing the summer weeds, or by applying dressings of marl from the local marl pits. (The Lord's demesne land was often enriched by the manure from his dovecote, or from the grazing and droppings of the limited flock of sheep.) The third field grew the winter wheat (called tilth grain), when the fallow field was ploughed and sown in the Autumn. This practice of leaving a third of the arable land empty of crops, explains why so much land was needed for so few people, but it was the only and the traditional method they knew, for they had no fertilizers, and few stored animals to accumulate manure through the winter.

Each great field was divided into smaller areas called shotts or flatts, and these in turn were split into long narrow strips, each about a furlong or 220 yards long (a furrow long), but obviously varying in length according to the shape of the shott. In Alrewas strips were 11 yards wide (half a chain), each being divided from the next by an unploughed ridge or balk, the ends often being marked with stone pegs or posts. Few of these hundreds of strips were straight, for almost all followed a double curve like a shallow letter 'S'. This may have allowed the oxen and plough to turn easier on the wide headland, as they were already beginning to turn with the curved furrow. A curved strip would also give a greater area from the length than a straight strip. The villagers' holding of land varied from 60 strips, (this was a Virgate of 30 acres), to a Bovate of 30 strips (a Bovate was a contribution of one ox to the village plough teams), down to a six strip holding of the cottars or some village craftsmen or trades-men who were part-time farmers, such as bakers, millers, fishers, carters, smiths, wrights, foresters, etc. In 1244, the tenants of Alrewas brought an action against their lord after he had ejected them from their holdings and in the records of the court the list of tenants and their holdings of arable land is given. Three held virgates of 30 acres each, William of the Heath, William son of Amelot, and Richard Godrich. Seventeen held half a virgate—Richard Bishop, Richard the Palmer, Richard Pany, Richard son of Roger, Richard the Woodreeve, Robert son of Thomas Edwin, Walklinus, Walter son of Brun, William son of Geoffrey, Agnes the widow, Geoffrey son of Geoffrey, Gilbert Bernard, Gilbert son of Robert, Hawisia the widow, Matilda widow of John Tursteyn, and Phillip son of Geoffrey. Other tenants were Geoffrey the Smith with nine acres, Geoffrey the Southener with half an acre, Henry Sweetapple with half an acre, Hugh le Hoar with half an acre, Matilda widow of Robert Payn with a fishery, Margery the widow with a fishery, Richard the baker with two acres, Edward Duse with seven-and-a-half acres, William the Scot with a fishery, and William son of Oweyn half a rood of meadow. In addition to these there would be some freeholders on enclosed land, but it is interesting that the total acreage here is around 375, which is evidently the three hides of Domesday Book of 360 acres.

Since at least two men, and often three, were needed to work a plough and the ox team, it is likely that two adjacent strips would be ploughed together, the plough going up one strip and back down its neighbour, thus making turning easier, and the two strips would be an acre, which was a day's ploughing. All the ploughs would be working on the one field at the same time. This regular ploughing up and down the strips century after century, tended to contour the soil into long humps (lands or lants as local farmers call them), and these can still be found locally, though they are fast disappearing. Before levelling was carried out, these land waves on the cricket field caused problems for the fielders, as they did too for the footballers on the field off Furlong Lane, now the school playing field, both being at one time part of the Great Furlong. The numerous flatts on this field were separated by wide earth tracks or drift lanes leading to other parts, or by wide headlands for turning the ploughs, and these in time have become our modern roads, Fox Lane, Oakfield Road, Wellfield Road, Daisy Lane, Somerville Road and Furlong Lane. About 1740, when the open fields were surveyed, preparatory to dividing them into fields as we know them today, one part of the Great Furlong, where the open green is in Oakfield Road, was an area of Common Marshland. It is likely, that in Saxon or Norman times, when the village was clustered around the church, that the land on either side of what is now Main Street, Park Road and Furlong Lane were part of the arable land, and that the Spellow, away across Rykneld Street, did not come into cultivation until later, although it was an open field in 1259. It is interesting to note that both Exchange Road and William IV Road have the same shallow bends, and both would continue on to Dark Lane, then as part of Essington Field. Main Street itself, from the War Memorial to Rykneld Street, shows by its curves, that it too was once the track through an open field, following the curved strip line. Its importance as a thoroughfare did not come until the making of the new road to, and later past the Manor House, when the new Orgreave Road was made, and the Salters Track down Overley Lane was disused because of the building of Orgreave Hall. The old road, the Salter's Way, from Kings Bromley along Overley Lane to Mill End, followed the line of Church Lane, Dark Lane, and along Mickleholme Lane to Salters Bridge, the earlier position of which was near to Mytholme Cottage, once an inn.

Fradley's open fields were mainly to the south of the village, and over Rykneld Street towards Rodige, and Crown Farm (once called Catchem's Inn). Byker's Field adjacent to Dumore Hay Lane was one field, getting its name from an Adam le Byker, or Adam the Beekeeper, whose descendants lived at Fradley for many years. One virgate of land here belonged to the forest of Cank, and in 1287, a forest court or Swanimote was held there, and there were also a few scattered parcels of land belonging to the Prebendal Manor over whose tenants the Prebendal Court was owed suit.

The vestiges of Wychnor's open fields can easily be traced along Green Lane, and down on the meadows below the marl pits, where there are perfect examples still to be seen of the early strip system. Wychnor's open fields were the earliest to be enclosed, as the hedges and fences had been installed, and the land allocated by 1721. Orgreave's open fields were small, and few traces remain, for a study of early records would indicate that much of Orgreave was occupied by freemen, farming their own enclosed land in their own way, and not bound to the communal and controlled system under a steward, bailiff or reeve.

There were in the manor, certain enclosed holdings outside the boundaries of the open fields, some having been cleared from the waste with the lord's permission. Such closes were called assarts, and include such holdings as the Sitthills (now Sittles Farm), Baginhall Close (now Bagnalls Farm off Daisy Lane), Redditch (now Rodige Farm), Barn Close (part of Orgreave Farm near the Trent), and Overley Farm, and Whitemoor Hay. In the early records, men who held their independent holdings were recorded and named from them, as with Richard de Wytemay, William de la Heath, William de Bechesover, Hugo de Burway, Reginald de Orgrave, Roger de Orgrave, Reginald de Frodelay, Richard de Burhay, Hugo de Slanley, etc.

These then were the great open fields where men, women and children toiled to grow their corn on their long narrow strips, with only the severest of weather and Holy Days to halt their labours, for in those distant days, it was a case of 'grow you food, or starve'.

CHAPTER 8

The meadows and commons

The animals raised by the people in this district were mainly pigs, which supplied most of their meat, cattle for meat and a little milk for cheese, with bullocks as the chief working animals, and an apparent abundance of poultry, ducks and geese. The early Alrewas records make no mention of sheep, for they were not encouraged near hunting forests, because their close grazing would deny food for the royal deer. In Branston about 1130, there were "two plough teams of oxen, one horse, one bull, fourteen calves, twenty four sheep and seven idle animals". Small flocks of sheep may have been kept by the lord under strict control, as they were needed to provide wool for their cloth, though much of this would be brought to the local fairs by the traders. Horses were mostly used by the Knights, though there are occasional references in the early records of horses being owned by the villeins. For example, in 1250, an Alrewas man named Roger Twoyenhold (nickname for two year old), had offended the lord in some way, and he had run away, but he returned before he was outlawed (after a year and a day) and saved the forfeiture of his land. His goods and chattels however, had been impounded for a year and a day, and these included a foal. At his trial at court, he produced two sureties for his future conduct, Robert son of Walter, and Robert Haliday, who would keep the foal for a year and a day, and after paying his fine, the foal was surrendered by the lord to his friends. Soon afterwards, his goods, and his hus and ham (house and croft) were returned to him. Again in 1273, Julian of Brauntestun was pledged at our manor court to find a draught horse for Sir John de Somerville or pay a fine of three shillings.

One of the greatest problems facing people in early days, was feeding themselves and their animals in the winter, for there was no silage, no mangolds, no kale, no meal or cattle cake which farmers have today. What grain they had, they needed for their own food, and stored hay had to provide most of the winter fodder. Acorns and mast were gathered for the swine, but the coming of the Spring saw many beasts so weak that they had to be helped from the byres to reach the grass which was starting to grow. The bullocks provided the energy that pulled the ploughs, and this power could be lost if there was insufficient hay to feed them through the winter. Failure of the hay crop could have tragic and lasting consequences for a community, and this made the protection of the meadow a vital responsibility for the Hayward until the hay was safely gathered in. Because of this, the meadows were enclosed by hedges and fences, to prevent village animals or stray animals, from grazing the growing grass. In addition to being a barrier, the long hedge was a useful economic asset, in addition to quick thorn, holly, briars and blackthorn, it also contained useful trees giving fodder for animals from oaks, beech, ash, hazel, chestnut, crab, quince, etc., and gave fuel and necessary wood for buildings, wattle, baskets, hurdles, pegs, handles, etc. The hedge round Essington meadow here, even counting the river as the boundary to the north, must have been over a thousand yards long.

There were two sorts of meadows, firstly the large common meadow, from which all tenants of the land had the right to gather hay in proportion to their holding of arable land. The cutting and carrying were under the supervision of the Hayward and Provost (Reeve). There were also smaller common meadows at Fradley and Orgreave, but in addition there were also a number of freehold meadows which were not subject to village control, and by 1300 there were a number of such 'closes', some along the river banks and others above flood level, though the river meadows were more lush. Men would go to great lengths to increase their amount of hay, even as late as 1601, as the following entry in the Parish Register shows:—

"The 8th day of January 1601 was one Richard Chard drowned at Salters Bridge, out of a boot (boat), having a great bottle of fodder in the boote with him, which after he was in the water, tooke holde of the same bottell of fodder, and was carried by the same until he came almost to the nether end of Mytham, and there peryshed, divers people beholding the same, bothe men and women. But could not save his life," (This was the year when the bridge was widened.) "And the firste of February next, after he was founde and taken up and brought into the churchyard and layed in the grave and covered with a borde. And by the commandment of the coroner, was buried after a viewe of his bodye being taken by honest neighbours the 3rd day of February 1601."

The holdings of meadowland was strictly and legally guarded. In 1208, amongst claims for other arable land at Croxall, Alice de Somerville, widow of Robert de Curzon of Croxall, who had later married Roger de Somerville, claimed on Roger's death before King John at Nottingham, as part of her dower, one acre of meadow. Throughout all early records, there are many references to small meadows of a half or one acre, important because they provided Autumn grazing as well as hay. On the 17th May, 1260, Richard the Palmer granted seven crops of hay from half an acre in Orgreave meadow to Sir Alan of Lichfield (he was a Somerville and a canon at the Cathedral) for 5s 8d, and gave him two wax candles. This would tend to show that they divided the meadow into half acre strips like the arable fields. In 1261 Geoffrey Swan paid 4d to Sir John Somerville for leave to have five crops from half an acre of meadow belonging to Robert Alwyn, which lay on the side of the Trent, between the Mill Pond and Darneford, and for which he had to pay 30 pence. (Some of these river meadows still show the half acre divisions.) On 26th July, 1259, Robert son of Alice of Fradley was fined 12 pence for carrying hay from his meadow which had been put under distraint as punishment for some offence. The fine of 12 pence was a heavy one because of the value of the hay crop.

As late as 1423, when the rent of arable land was three pence an acre per year, the rent for meadow at Catton was 12 pence an acre, and at Walton, it was 14 pence an acre, which gives an idea of the relative importance of meadow land.

When all the scything and drying were over, and the hay carried back to the homesteads, probably on sledges, and every vestige of the hay had been gleaned, then the village herd was taken in through the gaps or intakes in the hedges, where the fences or 'planks' had been taken down. Now there was good grazing until November. The 'Spring Planks' as the fences were called, were stacked after being taken down, ready to be put up again in early Spring to let the new grass grow. Even as late as 1794, they were still used as the following entry in the Parish Register shows:—

"A very severe winter. A great frost began 22nd December 1794 which continued till February 9th 1795, seven weeks and one day. The rivers Trent and Tame were frozen over, and the corn mills unable to grind. A great flood succeeded the thaw, Tuesday February 10th great damage was done by ice and water to several bridges, Kings Bridge and the bridge next the Swan Inn at Wychnor on the Turnpike Road to Burton. Great part of the Spring Planks washed away."

In November then, the store of hay, acorns, etc., were assessed, and any animals which were surplus to the fodder supply, were slaughtered, and the meat smoked or salted down in barrels for the lean winter months. Every village needed its cooper to provide the barrels for storing the meat and in 1260, Alrewas had one, Bibun the Cooper. Lard and tallow were rendered during this very busy time, but for a while there was a time of plenty, feasting on the parts of the carcasses that must be consumed quickly, as they could not be saved. The remaining bones, after the dogs had had their fill, were burned on the bone-fire (we still call outside fires bonfires). There must have been many columns of smoke over the dark forest in these November days, for at this time too, parts of the surrounding wastes were burnt off, to rid them of gorse, broom, bracken, brambles, etc., and to provide more grazing for the herds. The pigs were fat from rooting in the woods from Michaelmas to Martinmas, for the tenants could pay the lord for this privilege of 'mast and pannage'. In 1260, Henry Averil was fined 3s 4d for putting more pigs into the lord's wood at Orgreave than was permitted, and had to find two sureties and pledge his whole land, his hus and ham, and two sows worth 40 pence. In 1272, Thomas, son of Robert Angnes of Hedenighale was fined sixpence because he did not pay the full pannage money for his swine in Alrewas wood. In January 1271, Richard Mogge was fined for concealing of his pannage against his lord for one sow, and two hogs priced at 3s 4d, and was judged by the whole court to pay 3s 4d. In December 1273, the same Richard Mogge was fined 3s. because he brought back the pigs of Richard at the Church, to his home without paying the pannage money, namely six hogs (valued at 6s.). In the same court, Matilda the maiden was fined two shillings for keeping back pannage money for four pigs and four hogs valued at eleven shillings.

In great forests, the swine belonging to great lords ran wild, and were rounded up in early Autumn to be slaughtered for stocking up the larders and stores of their castles and manor houses. Around 1350, Sir Philip Somerville, the greatest of all the barons of Wychnor, was given Tatenhill and part of Draycott by the Duke of Lancaster, on the following conditions:—

"That he or his attorney should go to the castle of Tutbury on St. Peter's

Day, and show the steward that he is come to hunt and take his lord's grese, (wild swine) at the cost of his lord. On this the steward shall cause to be delivered to Sir Philip an horse and saddle worth 50 shillings, or that sum to provide one, and one hound, and shall likewise pay to the said Sir Philip for every day to Holyrood Day (14th September) 2s 6d for himself and 1 shilling for his servant and hound. And all the woodmasters of the Forest of Needwood and Duffield, with all parkers and foresters, are to attend upon Sir Philip, while his lord's wild swine are being gathered in the said forests, as they would upon their lord. And the said Sir Philip shall deliver with the parkers or foresters, that which shall belong to their lord's lardyner at Tutbury, and with the remnant, the said Sir Philip shall do as he please. And at the expiration therof, Sir Philip shall deliver up the horse and barcelet (hound) to the steward, with whom, when he has dined on Holyrood Day, at the castle of Tutbury, he shall kiss the porter and depart."

Perhaps this could have had some bearing on the institution of the Flitch of Bacon custom at Wychnor, which will be dealt with later.

In early days, villages near the hunting forests were not allowed to tan the skins of the slaughtered beasts, they had to be taken to distant towns like Stafford, where the tanning pits could be supervised. This was to prevent local forest villagers from destroying oak trees for the bark, and to remove the temptation to conceal, by turning into leather, the skins of poached deer from the royal forest.

From Saxon times until the early 19th Century, the land holders in Alrewas had inalienable rights on the extensive countryside which lay between the arable and meadow land, and the surrounding forest. This land was the common. It had no defined boundary, and on it, the villagers would graze their animals at all times of the year, where fuel could be gathered, and where they had the right of 'shack and turvage', that is the right to construct shelters and cut turf for burning and building. The village flocks and herds were collectively tended by elderly herdsmen and boys, and girls, who usually tended the geese or sheep. The village greens were originally assembly points for animals to be driven away to the commons in the morning, and dispersed to their byres or cotes from there, on their evening return.

Since there were no barred limits to the commons, except where a river or wood formed a natural boundary, it was very possible for animals to escape the vigilance of the herdsman, and wander into the surrounding forest or waste, from which they could eventually join the animals on the commons of a neighbouring village. This eventuality was catered for by each village having a small fenced enclosure called the Pinfold, Pound, or Pinder, where stray animals could be held until claimed by their owners. A fine would have to be paid, its amount depending on the length of time of the penning, usually determined by the Pinner, the local official in charge of the Pinfold. Local animals which were found wandering, or grazing in the wrong places, were penned, even though their owners were known, for stray animals could do great damage on the open fields. In Alrewas, the last pinfold was sited between Gaskell's Wharf and Moat Bank House, and its sale for a housing plot brought complaints from old villagers, who mistakenly thought it was common land. The official in charge of the common was the Shepherd and this was the case here even with few sheep, for in July 1273, William Wymer was brought before the Manor Court on the orders of Nicholas the Shepherd for "not caring properly for a beast found on a field called Holme". William was probably the Pinner. At the same court, Robert of Burway was fined two shillings for digging a pit for trapping animals on the common "to the injury of the whole manor".

In 1261, Biburn the Cooper had to pay the lord 12 pence to have his two cows freed from the Pinfold, and in 1272, Ricard Mogge, Richard son of Alice, Gilbert at the Churchyard, and William at the town end, each had to pay the large fine of four shillings to recover their beasts which had been found grazing in Sir John Somerville's park at Wychnor, and had been impounded.

Alrewas commons stretched beyond the Spellow and Rodige over to the Tame, and from Overley Lane south to Fradley and the Sale, while Fradley commons were very extensive, across Hay End Lane and Heath Gap, and as late as 1797, the heathland there stretched from Kings Bromley, through Curborough to the Sittles, an area of well over 2,000 acres. In 1797, it was stated that everyone in Alrewas having a messuage, yard land (virgate of 30 acres), half yard land, or a quarter yard land, is entitled to and has immemorably been entitled to right of common for all premises of the Chase, Commons, or Waste Lands called Alrewas Hayes, and at other waste and commonable places within the said Manor of Alrewas at all times of the year. In 1613, the following interesting entry in the Parish Register illustrates the commons in use:—

"Robert Neville the father, and Robert Neville the sonne being in Salteholme field the 26th day of June 1613, tending of the town beastes in the herdsman's walk there beyond Stony Furlonge side, about three of the cloke in the afternoone of the same daye, there was a mighty tempest of Rayne, lyghtning and thunder. And the father and sonne, standing under an oke tree to save themselves from the rayne, weare both of them stricken to death, the barke of the tree rent in great length, the leaves of the tree smitten and blowen away the most part of them. One other younge youth of tenne yeares age, Thomas Francis, being there to feare or helpe the herdsman, being within a compasse of tenne yeardes of the same place, was saved and nothing hurte as the others, the heares of their heads singed with lyghtning and in some part of the body and face blackned". (Original spelling kept.)

In the fields on the Alrewas side of the Sale, which was once part of the commons, are the vestiges of three concentric circles, on the perimeters of'which, at times of the seasons, the crops grow greener and taller. They occupy an area of five or six acres, and have been noticed by Mr. Dennis Collingwood, who farms at the Bagnalls, for some time, but in 1981 they were observed by an archaeological survey team on an aerial survey. A similar circle was discovered on the same survey at Handsacre, and the writer has inspected, at the invitation of Mr. G. Mallaber, the farmer, a further large fifty metre diameter circle on the banks of the Tame almost opposite Mytholme Cottage in a field called Rattlejack, formerly called Senseley. The purpose of the circles is unknown. They would not appear to be defensive forts, and the absence of any evidence of field workings cancels the idea of farms. They may have been pens for holding cattle when drovers were resting for the night, for ditches and staked banks could hold cattle like a more modern ha ha does. Recently we came upon a strange coincidence, for in 1272, the manor court in Alrewas made a bye-law, which said that Aldersale Moor (the original name of the Sale) should no longer be used for horses or cattle which were to be sold, even though the lord was supposed to receive six pence as a tax for each animal sold. It would appear that Aldersale Moor was a traditional cattle market, and the order was obviously resented, for in the following court, Robert son of Ralph was fined the large sum of three shillings for having his animals in the forbidden place, Adam the Provost or reeve was reported for the same offence, but pardoned, William son of Thomas of Stanley was fined 12 pence and Nicholas, son of Avice, was fined two shillings. At the same time, it was ordered that an enquiry be made about those who were said to sell oxen in the prohibited place.

These commons, free to all for a thousand years and more, were finally lost in 1810, when they were enclosed to make the farms and fields we know today, and the poorer tenants lost their grazing rights and their independence to become the landless labourers, with pitiful gifts of small allotments as compensation.

CHAPTER 9

The forest

For many centuries, Alrewas was within the boundary of Cank or Cannock Forest, a vast, wild area of 250 square miles, stretching from Stafford to Erdington, and from Wolverhampton to Alrewas. From Saxon times, its natural boundaries had been rivers, the Trent, Tame, Sow and Penk, and the early Mercian kings and later Earls hunted in it from their capitals at Stone or Tamworth. From early records and from the names of places in the area, we know that oak, elm, beech, ash, lime, birch, hazel, alder, elder, holly, pear, apple, broom, gorse, and heather all thrived, with open heath land and moor, often interspersed with dangerous marsh and fen, wild boar, wolves, wild cats, martens, wild cattle, and deer roamed as well as the small mammals still found in our woodlands. Golden eagles, buzzards, falcons, bittern, ravens, grouse and woodcock nested hereabouts, as they did only a few centuries ago. Much of this extensive area must have been trackless waste, and the sound of church or monastery bell, or the sight of a tall steeple or column of smoke above the trees must have been welcome to unguided wayfarers. Royal parties and travelling courts were guided across the forest by local barons who held their land as long as they fulfilled this role of guides and protectors. The early English settlers were free to use forest at will, for timber, fuel or food, ranging it from their settlements by the rivers, or from the 'leys' or natural clearings within the forest itself. Some groups of settlers enclosed their farms or steads with fences, which they called a 'gehaeg' (pronounced yehay), which in time became hay, as in Streethay, Bears Hay (Burhay), Brookhay or even Highlands (originally hay lindes, a clearing in lime trees). This is quite different from later hunting hayes.

It is difficult for us to conceive the extent of these early forests surrounding Cank, with Sherwood, Charnwood, Needwood, Hopwas, Bentley, Arden, providing several hundred miles of continuous forest land, and it must have been no idle boast that a squirrel could travel from York to Stratford without leaving the trees. One influence they had throughout England's early story, they tended to isolate and insulate the forest folk from the stirring events that made up the country's early history. There were few battles in the area, rebellions and insurrections are notable by their absence, and armies tended to move through the dangerous forest cover quickly, in fear of ambush.

The coming of the Normans brought to an end the freedom enjoyed in the forests by the English, who lived within or on the fringes of the forests, for the conquerors claimed them as exclusive hunting grounds. All the land within the forest bounds came under the control of the Chief Forester, who had an army of verderers, woodmen, äxemen, and agistors to preserve and protect the game, to create clear passage for the hunters, to provide the royal castles and manors with fresh or salted meat, to collect the dues from villages whose cattle and swine fed in the forest, and to see that the many forest laws were kept and the offenders against them tried and punished. In 1269, there were two under foresters in Alrewas, one written as Henry le Berne, and the other as Walter le Beryn, berne or bernard the local name for an under forester or ranger.

The game laws forbade the killing of deer, boars and hares, and in the early Norman times, men caught killing game were either hanged, blinded, outlawed, or mutilated by having a hand cut off. In 1195, the County Sheriff's accounts show three men, Alluredas, Ade, and Coiling, had had all their possessions sold, which meant they had almost certainly been sentenced to be hanged, though the record states that Coiling escaped by claiming sanctuary in a church. The laws not only forbade hunting, but prohibited the carrying of weapons, especially the bow and arrows. Men were not allowed to take dogs into the forest, and the guard dogs in the forest villages had to be lamed by pulling out the claws of one front paw to prevent them from harassing the deer. Fuel could be collected by hook and by crook, in other words, branches could be pulled down with a crook and slashed off with a hook, and verte or greenwood could be gathered at some period of the year. The felling of trees was carefully controlled, but in any case, this could only be done by chief tenants. If a forester could stand on the stump of a felled tree and could see five other stumps or stubs, then the wood was considered wasted, and the tenant would be fined by the forest justices, a fine which could be repeated on subsequent circuits of the justices if the signs of tree felling were still there. When offenders against forest laws were discovered, the local foresters held summary courts, often beneath the forest trees, to ensure that the offender would be brought to trial at the periodic Swanimote or Woodmote, the forest court where a court trial would take place. In Needwood Forest, the woodmote was held in the various lodges, Tutbury, Byrkley, Chapel House, Barton, Marchington or Eland. The offences recorded at these motes were the taking of verde or greenwood which could be food for the deer, beating down acorns and beech mast, stealing the hoar-lint (the inner bark of the lime trees), the bast was used for mats and cordage and the word still survives as has ket, or bass broom. The actual hoar lint was the white (hoar) wood left after the bast was stripped off. Other offences were the breaking of the palings or fences round the forest, or damaging the many gates through them, hunting deer with dogs or catching them with nets, engines, traps or buck stalls, and lastly, trespass by horses, cattle or sheep during the fence month or fawning season in mid-summer. At one court, Burton monks were accused of poaching deer before Lent, and several local Lords of the Manors also appeared, including Sir Phillip Somerville, Rys ap Griffith, his son-in-law, Gresley of Drakelow, Horton of Catton, and others.

At all courts, representatives of local villages had to present themselves, or the defaulting village would be heavily fined. This made sure that all men knew the laws and the consequences of breaking them.

By 1200, punishments were less cruel, and fines replaced mutilation, for the kings realised that the forests could be a major source of income. In early Norman days, Chief Foresters were rewarded for their services by grants of lands and manors, but this was changed, and they paid the king highly for the privileges and opportunities which the office provided.

Each village within the forest area was visited annually by the agistors, who made an estimate of the price to be paid for feeding the village cattle and swine within the forest limits, an estimate which varied according to the mast and acorn crops and the number of animals being fed. With so many petty forest officials, there was a great deal of corruption and abuse of authority, and early records illustrate this. In 1230, two foresters, James de Puties and Adam Hangdogge, caught a group of Alrewas men who were said to have caught a roebuck. The foresters agreed to say nothing about it, if the men paid them three shillings and surrendered the dead deer. In the same period, some local villeins who were driving swine along the highway, were stopped by foresters who took money from them after accusing them of unlawfully feeding their animals in the forest. Trees were cut down and sold by the two foresters, William de Cardon and Benedict the forester, twenty being felled and sold from Alrewas. In 1280, Alrewas people were wrongfully charged for cutting fuel from the roadside, even though a law of Edward the First had ordered the cutting back of all undergrowth at the side of the roads 'to prevent the lurking therein of evil-doers who had been committing deprevations, murders and other offences'.

One forest official used to visit the villages to inspect the dogs to see if the claws had been removed from one front paw, and he extracted fines by always claiming that the claws had been drawn from the wrong paw. In 1326, Sir Robert Mavysin was steward of Cannock Forest or what was left of it, and he issued an order that all foresters were to appear before him at Penkridge and Wednesfield, with four men from each village with their dogs, and all other owners of dogs in the forest boundaries were to bring their animals too, presumably to inspect them to see that the claw law was being obeyed, and to check breeds, for the common folk could only keep mastiffs and not hunting dogs. So great was the resentment felt against these many oppressions, that on one occasion, a mob of 200 men, led by three priests, attacked the forester's men at Lichfield, and then came to Alrewas, where a swanimote court was being held. Here the mob broke up the court, chased away the court officials and destroyed many of the forest and court records. This outburst appeared to have a salutary effect, for no punishments appear to have been meted out following the riot.

The King held Alrewas until 1204, and it was sometimes necessary for the Sheriff to restock the royal manor for him. In 1199, Alrewas was provided with eight oxen, one cow, one bull and a horse, at a cost of £1 13s 0d, and the Sheriff also had to find £1s 0d to buy ten sows, ten young pigs and a boar. Privileges were sometimes granted in the forest by the Crown. The church was allowed to quarry sandstone from Hopwas for building Lichfield Cathedral, and to site monasteries in the quiet seclusion of the forest, though in 1166, the monks of Radmore moved to Stoneleigh in Warwickshire because of the annoyance and disturbance of their devotions by the boisterous activities of the foresters and hunters. Timber was given on occasions for buildings and bridges, and in 1237, King Henry III sent the following instruction to the chief forester: —

"Mad Hugh of Rodbaston, with three huntsmen and deerhounds, shall take 50 hinds from the forest, and must supply the keeper of Wychnor Bridge with 3 oaks for repair work, and 30 oaks from the forests of Alrewas, Hopwas, and Bentley must be given to the Friars Minor at Lichfield for the building of their house and chapel there".

The hinds were to be salted down and sent to the King's house at Woodstock, near Oxford. Some of the nobles were allowed limited hunting, like Phillip Marmion of Tamworth Castle, who in 1271, was allowed to take one stag and one buck, but his castle was well provisioned with poached venison, for he was too powerful a favourite of the King's for the foresters to interfere with his hunting. On Christmas Eve, 1263, Ralph Bassett of Drayton Bassett, who was collecting forces to join Simon de Montfort's rebellion, took a party of his men into the forest and killed 16 deer. In 1271, long after the end of the rebellion at the battle of Evesham, when most of the men involved in the poaching were killed, the trespass was reported to the forest justices, and the sole survivor of the poaching foray of eight years before was arrested, tried and found guilty. He was fortunately found to have been reduced to the status of a poor minstrel, and was pardoned. Hugh de Nonant, Bishop of Lichfield, frequently poached deer, and even threatened to excommunicate any forester who tried to stop him. In 1190, large areas of the Cank forest were sold by Richard the Lionheart to raise money for his crusade. One around Sutton, between Tame and Bourne, went to the Earl of Warwick, and became Sutton Chase, and the other, which was to become Cannock Chase, was acquired by the Bishop of Lichfield, and both became private chases. By the middle of the 13th Century, the forest was losing its importance to the kings and nobles, and 1300 saw the beginnings of the clearance of Sutton Chase, whose trees were to vanish in the hearths of the charcoal burners. The greater use of iron for military, agricultural and domestic purposes made charcoal a very valuable commodity. This particular area became known as the Colefield, hence the present name of Sutton Coldfield. Eventually, by 1350, Edward III agreed to the disafforestation of the whole area, with the exception of certain hunting preserves called hays, which were to be connected by corridors of cover to allow for the movement of deer, and the hunters, from one hay to another. The hays were Hopwas Hay, Gailey Hay, Ogley Hay, Bentley Hay, Cheslyn Hay, Teddesley Hay, and the largest of them, Alrewas Hay, which included Alrewas, Orgreave, Kings Bromley, Curborough, Handsacre and Fradley, where a hunting lodge was built. Records reveal that: "In the hay of Alrewas, there were two foresters on foot, appointed by the justices, who paid to the King two marks (1 6s 8d.) for their bayliffs at the Hundred Court. They collected their tithes for the baileywick, and received twenty hens per annum. Also that this hay, then answered for herbage for the kings use, 50s 6d., which was entirely at his option".

Although the original forest had lost its density, and assarts (grubbed out land) and manors continued to grow, the area was still forest in character, for even as late as Elizabeth I, a terrible storm blew down 15,000 oak trees in this area. It was not until 1725 that the hay of Alrewas vanished as such, and Alrewas Hayes, with extra parochial rights, was created as a barrier across the old hunting ground, and the deer, rabbits and hares which threatened the growing crops, were destroyed by John Turton, Lord of the Manor, acting under the authority of a Bill of Parliament.

CHAPTER 10

Land holding

During the Middle Ages, wealth and status were mostly measured by the land a man held. From the crown, the lands of England were divided down in layers, each layer with more divisions and a corresponding decrease in the size of the parcels of land, finishing ultimately with the few acres of the peasants. Each group of landholders had to pay in various degrees with military service and money to the higher layer who had granted them the land. The dukes and earls and other chief tenants paid the King by providing knights and men for the war, and large sums of money for the privy purse, all of which they extracted from their tenants. And so the extraction of men and money ran through the whole feudal system from the bottom to the top.

The humble villeins and cottars in the manors held their land from their lord, in return for which they paid him rent, in some cases rendered military service, and gave their work in the running of the manor and the cultivation of the demesne land. They were, in effect, as tied to the manor as the woods, the hills and the streams, they were born in it, they worked in it, and died in it, owning little without the lord's permission. In 1414, a Ralph Leysing of Barton, had his duties to his lord recorded. He had to mow the meadow of the demesne for one day, carry the lord's hay in his own cart for one day, mow the corn for three days, cart the lord's wheat, plough one strip for Winter sowing and one for Spring sowing, carry victuals and other necessities for the lord when required, to act as reeve or provost when elected, to be taxed with his neighbours every Martinmas; he may not allow his son to become a priest or his daughter to marry without the lord's consent and payment of a merchet fine. "And when he dies, his lord shall have his best beast, all his copper vessels, his cart and iron bound wagon, all his beehives, all his uncut woollen cloth, all his colts, oxen, porkers male and female, all his sides of bacon, and his treasure, if any. His land to be returned to his lord until a blood relation shall satisfy as to his inheritance".

Inventories were made of a dead person's possessions and a valuation made, the lord taking one third after all debts had been paid.

In 1378, a Richard Holland died and his inventory was as follows: Wheat and Hay 30s, 2 steers and 1 mare 14s 4d, 12 sheep 15s, 1 sow 2s 6d, 1 pair of wheels 5s, 2 counterpanes 3s, 1 chest 3s, 1 dish 3s, 8 lb of dyed wool 2s, 1 pair of new sheets 2s, 3 old buckles 7d, 1 cock and 3 hens 6d, 1 skellet 6d, 1 down 2s, 1 border cloth 2s, thread for sacks 3d, 1 cloak 12d, 1 bedding 4s, 5 silver spoons 4s, 1 winnowing fan 12s, 1 purse 6d, 1 pair colanders 12d, in cash 6d, 1 bow and 1 baselard (dagger) 12d.

These were the possessions of a fairly prosperous villein, and give some idea of the comparative austerity of living in those days, and the little need for money when there was only 6d in cash, and the lord of the manor took one third of this. There were times in history, when national or even local disasters, like plague or the effects of wars, reduced the number of workers, leaving land untilled, and lords in their manors or tenants in chief were often prepared to give tenants possession of land under curious, yet still legally binding, conditions, and some strange local rents and customs are recorded.

In 1244, Isabelle de Somerville, wife of the third Roger, Baron of Wychnor, gave 13 marks (£8 13s 4d) to John Perdrich (Partridge) for land in Marston Sukeburg (Shugborough) to be held for a pair of white gloves yearly.

Roger de Rydware held Callingwood in 1246, with pannage for 30 hogs in Needwood Forest, paying annually a pair of gold spurs at Easter for all services.

In 1290, Geoffrey de Gresley gave land at Edingale to Roger the Smith of Edingale for an annual payment of four barbed arrows. Philip de Somerville granted use of some of his land for common at Wychnor in 1345, to all tenants. Each free tenant holding a virgate of land, was to give in return one penny to the poor, with the bacon, and each native (born servant) to give two pence, and all were to give 24 sufficient hens on Christmas Day for all services.

In 1350, Sir Philip granted to Hugh, son of Walter of Newbold, (just after the Black Death), a messuage and two crofts at Dunstall, a piece of land called Scaicliffe, with six acres of arable land and two-and-a-half acres of meadow. In return, Hugh had to give four loaves of bread, corn and bacon to the poor, and agreed to give Sir Philip and his heirs eight hens on Christmas Day, and one bunch of red and white roses, for all except foreign services, to the Flitch of Bacon on the Feast of St. John the Baptist. In 1414, the Mynors held Blakenhall still, by service of a pair of gilt spurs, and held five acres of Catholme for a rose, and other holdings for a half-pound of pepper, and a pound of cummin (seeds of an aromatic plant).

At the same time, Thomas Griffith, baron of Wychnor, held houses at Tatenhill for one sparrow hawk each year, and held Brideshall for setting the first dish before the King at Tutbury on Christmas Day, and Dunstall and Newbold for a quarter Knights Fee. In 1521, in the free tenants roll, Lady Margaret Veir and others held the Hooked Pool near the bridge at Wychnor at an annual rent of 12 pence and 1 lb of pepper. The Abbess of Polesworth held one cottage and a virgate of land for an obiit (prayer for a soul) celebrated annually on the Crucifixion for the soul of Sir Philip de Somerville (died 1355).

Walter Scheperd held a meadow for the rent of 11 catapults with heads (crossbows and bolts).

Sir Philip de Somerville extended the authority of the manor, and during his lordship, notwithstanding the estimated hundred who died of the plague in the Black Death, Alrewas became a borough, and probably took in the survivors of surrounding stricken villages, like Croxall. He was a great favourite of John of Gaunt, the Duke of Lancaster, and from him, held many villages beyond Wychnor and Alrewas, on the curious condition of the Flitch of Bacon. How the custom began is a mystery. It may have been a jest concerning Sir Philip's annual duty of rounding up the forest swine, it may have been a sarcasm against the common folk and their near worship of pork meat, it may just have been a drunken joke, almost like the Dunmow Flitch begun at about the same time. We have written the deed in full and original form:

"Nevertheless, the said Sir Philip shall fynd, meynteigne and sustain one bacon flyke hanging in his halle at Wychnor, redy arrayede at all times of the yeare bott at Lent, to be given to everyche mane or womane married, after the day and the yeare of their marriage be passed, and to be given to everyche mane of religion, archbishop, bishop, priest or other religious mane, and to everyche priest after the yeare and the day of their profession finished, or of their dignity received, in forme following.

Whensoever that any such byfore named will come for to enquire for the baconne, in their own persone, or by any other for them, they shall come to the bayllyfe or to the porter of the Lordship of Wychnor, and shall say to them in the manner as ensheweth. Bayllyfe or porter, I do you to know that I come for myself (or, if he come to for any other, showing for whom he demandeth) to demand on flyke of baconne hanging in the hall of the Lord of Wychnor, after the forme thereunto belonging. After which relation, the bayliffe or porter shall assign a day to him upon promise by his faith to return, and with him to bring twain of his neighbours. And in the meantime, the said bayliffe shall take with him twain of the freeholders of the lordship of Wychnor, and they three shall go to the manor of Rodlow belonging to Robert Knightley, and there shall summon him, or his bayliffe, commanding him to be ready at Wychnor the day appoynted at prime of the day, with his carriage, that is to say a horse and saddell, a sack and a pryke, for to carry and convey the said baconne and come a journey out of the county of Stafford at his costage. And the said bayliffe shall, with the said freeholders, summon all the tenants of the said manor, to be ready at the day appoynted at Wychnor, for to do and perform the services which they owe to the baconne. And at the day assigned all such as owe service to the baconne shall be ready at the gate of the manor of Wychnor from the sun rising to noon, attending and awaiting for the coming of him that fetcheth the baconne. And when he comyn, there shall be delyvered to him and his fellows, chapeletts, and to all those which shall be there to do service to the baconne. And they shall lead the said demandant wyth trompes and tabors and other manner of minstrelsy, to the hall door, where he shall fynde the Lord of Wychnor or his steward, redy, to deliver the baconne, in this manner. He shall enquire of hym which demandeth the baconne, yf he hath brought twain of hys neighbours wyth hym, which must answer "They be reddy". And then the steward shall cause these two neighbours to swere yf the demandant be a weddyt man, or have been a man weddyt, and yf sith marriage one yere and one daye be passed, and yf he be a freeman or a villein.

And yf his said neighbours make othe, that he hath for hym all thies three points rehersed, then shall the baconne be take down and brought to the halle door, and shall be laid upon a half a quarter of wheat, and upon half a quarter of rye. And he that demandeth the baconne shall kneel upon his knee, and shall holde hys right hand upon a boke, which boke shall be layed above the baconne and the come, and shall make othe in this manner. "Hear ye Sir Philip de Somerville, Lord of Wychnor, maintainer and giver of this baconne, that I—A, since I wedyt—B my wyfe, and since I had her in my keeping and at my will by a yeare and a daye after our marriage, I would not have changed her for none other, farer ne fowler, richer ne poorer, ne for non other desended of greater lynage, slepying ne wakyng at noo tyme, and if the said—B were sole, and I sole, I wolde take her to be my wyfe before all the womyn in the worlde, of whatsoever condition they be, good or evylle so help me God and His seyntes and this flesh and all fleshes".

"And hys neighbours shalle make othe that he hath sayd truly, and if it be found by his neighbours that he be a free man, there shall be delyvered hym, half a quarter of wheat and a cheese, and yf he is a villein he shall have half a quarter of rye without the cheese.

And then shall Knightley, Lord of Rodlow be called for, to carry all these things before rehearsed, and the come shall be layed upon the horse and the baconne above ytt and he to whom the baconne apperteigneth shall ascend upon hys horse, and shall take the cheese before him, if he have a horse, and yf he have none, the lord of Wychnor shall cause hym to have one horse and a sadyll to such tyme as he be passed his lordship, and so shall they depart the manor of Wychnor with the corn and the baconne, before hym that hath wonne it with trumpets, tabourets and other manner of minstrelsy. And all the free tenants of Wychnor shall conduct hym to be passed the lordship of Wychnor, and then shall all return except hym to whom apperteigneth to make the carriage and journey without the County of Stafford at the costys of the lord of Wychnor.

And yf the said Robert Knightley do not cause the baconne and come to be conveyed as rehearsed, the lord of Wychnor shall do it to be carryed, and shall distrain the said Robert Knightley for his default for a hundred shillings in his manor of Rodlow, and shall keep the distress so taken, irretrievable".

There are no authentic records of any claimants for the Flitch, but a flitch of bacon hung over the great fireplace in the hall of the manor for centuries, and later, the custom was continued by a carved and painted wooden model of a side of bacon which still hangs there. The coaching Inn there, was at one time called the Flitch of Bacon, but a later Flitch of Bacon Inn stood within living memory at the junction of Catholme Lane and Rykneld Street, but it was demolished during the building of the dual carriageway.

It is interesting to note how the almost sacred fitch of Bacon was to be treated, for Hugh, son of Walter of Newbold, and Agnes his wife were granted land at Dunstall by Sir Philip de Somerville on the following conditions or services:—
"That when the flowers shall be heaped together in hys halle at Wychnor by hys servants there, and the said flowers be prepared by them to dress the baconne as usual, Hugh and Agnes, or their deputys shall dresse the aforesaid baconne with those flowers already there for them, ten times a yeare from Easter Eve and each month until the feast of St. Michael. On All Saints and Christmas Eve, they shall decorate it with boughs of ivy. On the daye of the dressing of the baconne, Hugh or hys servants shall be feasted at the table of the steward of Wychnor. On the death of Hugh and Agnes, the service must be performed by their sons, Thomas and William, either to Sir Philip de Somerville, or to Sir Rees ap Griffith. Witness of the deed 16th Edward III (1314), Rees ap Griffith, John Myners, John le Rous, Richard de Callingwoode, Richard de Holland, John de Somerville".

From this it would appear to be a similar custom to the well-dressing ceremonies still maintained in Derbyshire, as at Tissington.

The greater land holders like the Somervilles, held land from the king and chief tenants like the Duke of Lancaster, and for this they paid a cash rent, and then a responsibility for military service. The Knights' Fee as this was called, bound a baron to attend his lord to the wars for 40 days in every year if called upon, or to find an equally able substitute. Knights fees were proportionate to this, half Knights fee being a military liability of 20 days, and so on. In time, Kings found it better to permit cash payments in lieu of service, when mercenaries could be hired with the money, to give more reliable and continuous service. This was called Scutage, and the value of a Knights fee was at first two marks, but between 1275 and 1375 it varied from £10 to £20 per year according to the military needs of the time.

CHAPTER 11

Self-government in Alrewas in the 13th Century

Seven hundred years ago, the people of this village, bound to the manor and to each other by the bonds of common work and interests, resolved most of their problems and difficulties in their own way, with little aid or interference from beyond the manor boundaries. The spiritual centre, meeting place and refuge, was the church, standing like a rock in the centre of the huddle of thatched cottages, byres and store huts. Its bell from the squat tower marked the passing of the day, signalling Vespers or curfew to call in the herds and labourers from the distant fields and pastures. Saints' days and festivals marked for them the passing of the year, and fixed the days of meetings instead of our modern custom of a month and date. The Sabbath was the one different and significant day which brought relief from long toiling in the fields. It was almost certainly in the nave of the church, the only structure capable of accommodating the large body of men, where they met regularly to resolve the affairs of Alrewas, Fradley, Orgreave and Edingale. During the records of the manor court rolls covering twelve years, the names of at least 180 people are recorded, so that the number of suitors at the court was so large as to need a building like the church.

The control and organisation of all the secular affairs of the community, was mainly in their own hands, through the Manor Court, which met every three weeks. Its highest authority was, of course, vested in the Somervilles, the Barons of Wychnor, but it was delegated to the Steward, who in his turn, left the control of the court to the Bailiff, who guarded the interests of the lord in the everyday running of the village. The clerk, who was a priest, kept for the lord the records of the court, so that the lord would know the amount and the sources of revenue from his tenants.

There were at that time, various types of tenants owing service or suit to the court. The freemen and Socmen of the manor, and holders of land here who came from Curborough, Croxall, Wigginton, Sutton, Streethay and Ridware, were only obliged to attend the Great Court (Curia Magna) which was held once or twice a year, or to the ordinary court, if summoned to defend themselves in any complaint, or to be witnesses in cases before the court. The lower tenants, the copyhold villeins, were obliged to attend all meetings of the court, though any man could excuse, or as they called it, essoin himself from attending, through another person present, but only for three consecutive meetings, and his third excuse must be by two sureties, who themselves would be fined if he failed to appear at the subsequent court.

The socmen of the manor, the descendants of former royal retainers when the manor was held by the King, enjoyed privileges similar to freemen, but were subject to ordinary villein services, like work on the lord's demesne land and boon work during ploughing or harvesting, and the usual dues and customs such as heriots, which were either death duties to the lord, fines on admission to or transfer of land, or the sale of livestock or possessions or even the privilege of brewing ale. There was also the merchet due, a fine payable to the lord by any tenant whose daughter married, the fine being heavy if the bride left the manor, and it also included merchet for a son who joined the priesthood. No tenant could leave the manor without paying for a licence to do so. Notwithstanding these penalties and restrictions, there was no servitude in their tenure, and they could even sue their lord in his own court over customary dues, injustice or wrongful ejection from their holdings. For this they had to obtain the grant of a "lesser writ of right" addressed to the Sheriff, or even to the president of their own Great Court. Even the humblest cottars or bordars, who were descendants of tenants who possessed their land at the time of its grant from the Crown, yet were not retainers, had similar privileges to the Socmen. There were also servile tenants whose holdings had been granted by the lord since the royal ownership, who paid full villein service for their land. In Alrewas, as in some other manors, there was the ancient custom of Borough English, where the copyhold land was inherited, with the lord's approval after the appropriate heriot was paid, not by the eldest son, but by the youngest, and in Alrewas the age of responsibility for taking over was fifteen years.

There was great variety in the business of the court, offences against neighbours, like stealing, slander, neglect of hedges or ditches, failure to pay debts, damage to property, failure to keep agreements, allowing animals to stray, etc., and offences against the lord, like failure to attend the court, non-payment of rent, dues or fines, breaking the assize of ale, mead or bread, taking wood or verte from the wood, failure to pay the pannage money for feeding their swine in the lord's wood, etc. All these types of offences were tried and judged by the whole assembly of the court, which also awarded the appropriate fines. It also re-affirmed, or originated, customs involving the whole manor. In all these affairs, the lord or his steward had no part to play, except that fines could be reduced, but not increased, or offences could be pardoned by the lord or the steward. Thus the body of suitors attending the Manor Court acted as prosecutors, jury and judges.

In a community such as this, it was essential for certain men to be responsible for overseeing the different farming activities, and others to supervise the arranging and organisation of the court, and to ascertain that its judgements and decisions were carried out. The chief officer or village manager was the Reeve, or as he was called in Alrewas, the Provost. Three were elected by the court, one each for Alrewas, Fradley and Orgreave and they supervised the activities on the common fields, particularly the arable land, during the ploughing, sowing and harvesting, with responsibility for the care and maintenance of the ploughs and plough teams. The village ploughs were often hung around the walls in church for safe keeping and brought out and blessed on Plough Sunday. The provost was usually an elderly, experienced and respected person, whose decisions and advice could be trusted by his neighbours. A villein could not refuse the office if elected, the penalty for doing so being a heavy fine or loss of his land. The Hayward was chosen to supervise the hay meadows, to maintain the hedges and fences, to control the gathering of the hay harvest, and the following grazing of the cut meadows by the village herds and flock. Next came the Shepherd, who was not in this area responsible for great flocks of sheep, his main duty being the supervision of the commons and the herds grazing there, and, with the Pinner, to care for strays from other villages and confine them in the pinfold or pound until claimed. He also supervised the clearing of unwanted gorse, broom, bracken, brambles and heather, by burning them off in November on part of the common, or by grubbing them out, to increase the grazing potential of the common. The Woodreeve's responsibility, in caring for the growing timber in the wood, was solely to the lord and not the villagers.

As well as these officials, men were appointed by the court to watch over production and sale of two main commodities, bread and ale, the principal food and drink of the villagers at that time. One was the Breadweigher, whose functions were to ascertain that the village baker did not cheat the women out of the dough they brought for baking, to check the quantity and quality of bread for sale in the market, where he also dealt with complaints of bad meat or fish being sold. There was the Ale Taster, who guarded the quality of ale brewed for purchase by others under licence from the lord, and saw that the villeins did not break the Assizes of Ale and Mead, which controlled all the conditions relative to the brewing, licencing, quality, malting and even the production of the barley malt itself, which must be grown on the land of the lord, if the ale was brewed in his manor.

In addition to these elected officials, there were the officers of the Court, the Beadle, the Summoner, and later, the Constable. The Beadle was, for centuries, to be the law officer responsible for maintaining the authority of the court, and seeing that the orders and decisions of the court were carried out. The Summoner or Sumner as he was called here, was responsible for assembling the court and ensuring the notification of defendants, claimants or witnesses. During the years to be reviewed, it appears that one man carried out both functions, and there is no mention of any constable during that period 1259-1273.

Since all men were concerned in the business of the court, everyone became familiar with the laws and customs governing their community and it was an effective deterrent to the breaking of those rules especially when men could, at times, find themselves responsible for the future conduct of their neighbours, or having to guarantee that their fines would be paid. The only delay in the working of the court seems to have been when freemen were being tried for an offence, for they could only be tried by other freemen, who could each essoin themselves three times and thus delay any final judgement for many months. In 1341, there were twenty freemen in the manor, eleven of whom were free by royal charter, and nine who "of ancient time have been and are accounted free socmen".

Finally, there was authority given to the Somervilles by the Crown, on payment of the appropriate fee, to hold in the manor of Alrewas, the View of Frankpledge. The Frankpledge was an association of ten good men, bound by a mutual guarantee, to maintain justice together, a collective liability, each individual standing security for any of the other nine, a group of men responsible for the good behaviour of each member. The Frankpledgers also brought to the notice of the court the misdemeanours of others, and this may have been the reason for the constable being an irrelevance. The View of Frankpledge was an inquiry into the affairs of the manor as they concerned the functions of the Frankpledgers, and the review was held once or sometimes twice a year at the Great Court. Such an arrangement of policing had been in operation in large villages since Anglo-Saxon times in the 10th Century, when each free man had to belong to a Tithing or group of ten, who were collectively responsible for his good behaviour and his appearance at court, if charged. Records at the time of Edward the Confessor state: "When they saw that some foolish persons willingly transgressed against their neighbours, the wiser men took counsel among themselves how they might restrain them, and so placed justices of each ten frithburgs, whom they called headmen, in English tyenth-head, that is head often. These men dealt with suits between townships, and between neighbours, and according as transgressions occurred, they made ordnances and amends, namely as to pasture, meadows, crops, quarrels among neighbours and many things of this nature which often arise".

As recently as 1825, the heading of a property title deed in Alrewas was headed, "Manor of Alrewas", to wit the Court Leet, View of Frankpledge and

Court Baron of his Right Honorable Thomas William, Lord Viscount Anson, Lord of the Manor of Alrewas, etc., held at Catchem's Inn . . .". This was what is now Crown Farm on Rykneld Street at Fradley. The new occupier of the property had to pay a heriot of 6s 8d to the lord for the transfer.

CHAPTER 12

Early Alrewas names

A study of the names by which people were known and thus recorded in the Court Rolls, is interesting and revealing, providing information about their occupations and the manor in which they lived. Their names fall into four categories, though everyone had a Christian name with which they were baptised, but these were insufficient to indicate which Robert, or which Geoffrey or John was being referred to, so an additional identification was needed. We today, carry the name of our sire, our surname, which, with Christian names added, can usually identify us. A few of the men of Alrewas 700 years ago had surnames such as we do, like Gilbert Alwyn, Henry Averil, Richard Mogge or Adam Falin, etc., but they were only a small minority. The first of the old ways of naming was to couple the person's Christian name with the Christian name of their father or their widowed mother, like Henry son of Gunhilda, Robert son of Reginald, William son of Walter, Margery daughter of Robert, or Geoffrey son of Gilbert the Beadle, etc. The second group is far more informative because the additional name added to the Christian name, was the person's special occupation, and we have included all those found, because they indicate the variety of work done at that time. Henry the Fisher, Robert the Smith, Richard the Clerk, Robert the Cook, Robert the Baker, Thomas the Forester, Richard the Palmer, Robert the Carpenter, Henry the Miller, Adam the Beadle, Geoffrey the Sumner, John the Boatman, Nicholas the Wheelwright, Alan the Bridgeman, William the Carter, Isolda the Laundress, William the Shepherd, William the Gardener, John the Plumber, Thomas the Bullier, William the Reaper, Adam the Beekeeper, William the Woodreeve, William the Provost and Simon the Cellarer (storeman of Wychnor). It is interesting to note that most of these were eventually to become surnames.

The third group are identified by the place where they live locally, as we have not included the many names associated with neighbouring or even distant villages like Elmhurst, Curborough, Lichfield, Sutton, Hartshorne, Coven or Blackfordby, etc. Local names include Roger of the Gorse, Ralph of the Heath, Thomas at the Stile, Sibella of Fradley, Robert of Burway, Richard of the Churchyard, William at the Townend, Richard of Burhay, John of Oakley, Richard of the Chapel, Robert at the Spring, Ralph of the Brook, Robert of the Weir, Richard of the Cross, Geoffrey of the Bridge, Henry at the Mill, Bateman of Boreway, and John at the Water.

Again a number of these have been passed down after becoming surnames.

The last group of names are nicknames, some perhaps given in childhood, or descriptive of appearance or personality. Henry Sweetapple, William Halfpenny, Henry the Southerner, Margery Sparrer, Robert Wolley, Nicholas the Serious, Edith the Blonde, Roger Twoyearold, Nicholas the Brown, Geoffrey Goodlad, Henry the Mouse, Robert the Bird, Henry the Brown, John Breakdish, Owen the Wolf, John the Piper, John Atelard, and William the Scot.

When we study the Court Rolls and see what appear to us today to be insignificant fines, we must remember that the 13th Century was not like ours, a consumer society, it was for most people a "struggle-for-survival" society. Our way of living today is based on a wages economy, where men and women sell their labour, skill and time, on a more or less regular and permanent system. In those far-off days, most men worked for themselves, to grow their own food to maintain themselves and their families, and the opportunities for accumulating what little money was in circulation, were few. The principal way was to sell on the regular weekly markets, any surplus produce or livestock, or the commodities like baskets, thread, cloth, etc., which were produced in the home by the housewives and children. Some of the villagers, holding only a few acres were able to spend time in developing and extending their particular skills with wool, iron or providing necessary services like milling, baking, brewing, etc., and were paid for their products or service. A great asset to any man was to have several sons to work with him, enabling him to increase his land holding, and thereby produce greater surplus and increased wealth.

The currency in use at that time was the pound silver, divided into twenty shillings, and the shilling into twelve pence, and the penny into half pence. Larger sums of money were often reckoned in marks, the mark being worth 13 shillings and 4 pence. Wants in those days were comparatively simple, the luxuries of today being undreamt of, so when we quote a fine of 12 pence, it was a heavy loss to the offender, and 3 pence or 4 pence was punishment enough for most villeins, when that sum could be the rent for several strips of land for a year.

CHAPTER 13

The Alrewas Manor Court Rolls 1259-1273

The priest pushed the filled and closely-written roll of parchment across the trestle table for later reference, and smoothed the long, creamy skin before him. Dipping his quill in the ink horn, he looked round at the motley groups of peasants, standing or squatting on the rushes in the cool gloom of the low, arched nave, and carefully wrote at the top of the skin in close Latin script: —

"Curia apud Alrewas die Sancti Barnabe Apostoli, anno Regni H. filii Regis J. XLIII".

And this, if the reader will pardon the flight of imagination, began the first of those preserved rolls of the Manorial Court of Alrewas, which were to lie safely in the Church Chest for over 700 years, for the priest had written:

"Court held at Alrewas on the day of St. Barnabas the Apostle in the 43rd year of the reign of King Henry, son of King John".

And this was 11th June 1259, and this cleric and many who succeeded him, were to leave for posterity, their records of the proceedings of many of the court meetings during the next hundred years or so. The particular rolls dealt with here are from 11th June 1259 to 6th May 1261, from 13th December 1268 to 24th August 1269, and from April 1273 up to 18th December 1273.

These manor court rolls are the oldest in Staffordshire, and may owe their unique preservation to the fact that they were stored in the ancient, strong, triple-locked oak chest in the church, the churchwardens from Alrewas, Fradley and Orgreave holding the keys. This would strengthen the theory that the Court met in the nave of the church, which, with no pews and with a rush-covered floor, would be the only building capable of accommodating such a large gathering.

The court met every three weeks, and all the holders of land in the Manor, as well as outsiders from Curborough, Croxall, Wiggington, Sutton, Streethay and Ridware who had acquired land here from the lord had to attend the court. Freemen on their own land (there were over a dozen of them), were only obliged to attend ordinary court meetings when summoned by the Summoner, either as witnesses, or to answer complaints against them, though they were obliged to attend the Curia Magna (Great Court), or as it later became called, the View of Frankpledge, which was usually held annually. Any man could excuse himself from the court through another person present in court, but only for three consecutive meetings, and his third essoin or excuse must be by two sureties, who would be fined if he failed to attend the next court.

The majority of men were tenant farmers (or villeins) holding few acres, yet still having their rights upheld by the court. In 1243, Sir Roger Somerville ejected many of his tenants from their holdings and they brought an action against him in the King's Court which resulted in their reinstatement to their land holdings. There were 33 of them concerned, who held between them 375 acres, three with a virgate (30 acres) each, 19 with half a virgate, two with a quarter virgate, and the rest with holdings of from two acres to half an acre, while three claimed to hold fisheries on the rivers, each rented at nine shillings a year. Presiding at the court was the Bailiff, and on rare occasions, the Steward of the Manor, with the priest or clerk as he was called, keeping a record of fines, dues, agreements, land transfers or grants, election of officials, offences against the lord or neighbours, restatement of old, or passing of new rules or customs, etc. Also in attendance were the reeves or headmen for Alrewas, Fradley and Orgreave, who were known locally as provosts. Then there was the Beadle (who seemed at that time to be Constable as well), who carried out the judgements of the court, and the Summoner or Sumner, who was responsible for assembling the court, and ensuring the attendance of complainants, defendants and witnesses. There was no judge or jury, it was the whole court which decided issues, and the whole court which determined the fines or confiscations, when guilt had been proved. Everyone was involved in some way in the working of the court. Offenders had to find sureties for the payment of their fines, or for their future conduct, in other words, the responsibility for the conduct of individuals was placed squarely on the shoulders of their neighbours who would themselves face punishment for any future repetition of the offence by the offender.

Perhaps the most important purpose of the court rolls, was that they were a legal and permanent record of the tenancy, or ownership, or obligations of the individuals to the lord of the manor and to their neighbours.

There are hundreds of items in the rolls, many of them repetitions of excuses from court, of breaking the assizes of bread or ale, or transfers of bits of land, so it may be best to take the account of one typical court, then select the most interesting entries, and finally to list the parts of the manor which still carry the same names today. The account chosen is that of the court which met on Friday, 3rd June, 1272.

Geoffrey, son of Nicholas, excused by Robert son of Nodi	First time
Henry the Woodreeve, excused by Reginald Gamel	First
William son of Reginald, excused by Henry the Miller	First
Robert the Boatman, excused by William Badde	First
Henry the Smith, excused by Peter son of Dike	Second time
Reginald of Fradley, excused by Henry son of Reginald	First
Gilbert Owen, excused by Robert son of Walter	First
Simon son of the Reeve, excused by John Piper	First
Robert Gadelying by Robert his son	First
Henry the Smith of Edingale by Thomas son of Henry	First
William Adam, excused by Richard at the Church	First
Henry the Provost, excused by Henry the Clerk	First

Geoffrey son of Alice of Fradley is fined 6 pence, because he did not have his corn ground at the Mill of Alrewas to which he was tied. His security given by Henry, son of Gunnild.

Richard of Fradley Heath is fined 12 pence for trespass.

Robert son of Ralph, was fined 3 shillings for his animals which were found

in Aldersale Moor, a prohibited place. Forgiven by the lord, but fined 12 pence.
Adam the Provost is accused of the same. Forgiven by the lord.

William, son of Thomas of Slanley, fined 12 pence for the same, which the
lord had.

Nicholas, son of Avice, fined 2 shillings for the same.

An enquiry is to be made by order of the court about all those who are said
to sell oxen that had been placed on Aldersale Moor (Anglo-Saxon Alder
Sealh—meaning Alderwood).

William, son of Reginald of Fradley, is fined 6 pence because he had brewed
ale contrary to the assize, and had sold bad ale.

Nicholas is amerced for breaking the assize of ale. Forgiven by the lord.

Henry the Provost 6 pence, William Adam 6 pence, Simon the son of the Provost
6 pence, Roger the Cook (Forgiven), William at the Sieving Mill 6 pence,
Nicholas son of Robert the Bondman 6 pence, Adam Falyn 6 pence, all fined
for breaking the assize.

Geoffrey Kute fined 12 pence for a small loaf.

Ralph, son of Walter, fined 12 pence for breaking the assize and Robert of
the Weir twice broke the assize but was forgiven.

Adam Hedemon is fined 2 shillings for swearing and assault to William Bernard.
William Bernard fined 6 pence for abusing the said Adam.

Richard Mogge (5 shillings), Henry son of Gunnild of Fradley (6 shillings),
Robert the Baker (4 shillings), William Messor (8 pence), Robert Owne (2
shillings), Richard the Cook (Twelve pence), were all fined for not reporting
the circumstances of the affray between Adam Hedemon and William Bernard
(These men were Frank Pledgers).

Ralph of the Brook distrained in his suit against Simon the Clerk of Lichfield
at the request of the said Simon.

Avice the widow of Geoffrey Swan paid the lord 3 shillings to have and to hold
the land of the said Geoffrey to the end of two years.

Simon Huberd fined 6 pence for felling four small oaks in the lord's wood.
Surety was Adam the Beadle.

Roger the Cook was fined 6 pence for receiving some malefactors in his house,
who had committed offences in the Hay of Alrewas (Pardoned by the lord).
Henry the Baker was fined 6 pence for the same.

Reginald Herring was fined 12 pence for selling hurdles made from the lord's wood.

Henry the Baker fined 6 pence for the same offence.

William of Streethay had been summoned to wage his law against the lord and did not come. He was therefore distrained.

Robert of Brewood from the whole court, to have full seison of land that Henry Averil held in the village of Orgreave, and he was to pay the lord four silver marks, two marks on the Feast of St. John the Baptist, and two marks on the day of the feast of St. Michael. Sureties or guarantors for the silver were William Edrian, Robert son of Ralph, Richard Mogge and Robert the Baker.

This then was an account of a typical court, the fines paid bringing valuable income to the lord of the manor, and following this are some of the more interesting entries selected from the Rolls beginning at 1259.

Henry Averil is fined 6 pullets for a complaint that he altered a footpath at Orgreave.

Robert Aylmer of Alrewas freed into the lord's hand in the presence of all men in full court, all his land of one virgate to Thomas son of Robert the Palmer of Bromley, for which he will receive 22 shillings from the said Thomas, and pay to the lord John de Somerville 5 shillings for his permission to hold the land under the previous rent, and Robert Aylmer and his wife Avice are to be kept in food and clothing etc at their messuage by Thomas for the rest of their lives (Thomas had married their daughter).

Reginald, son of Alice, paid the lord 6 pence so that he could take over one acre of land formerly held by Henry the Provost of Alrewas, the rent for which was half penny a year paid on the feast of St. Michael.

Richard Mogge is fined 6 pence for obstructing a path at Orgreave. His surety is his hus and ham.

John the Tinker fined six chickens—paid and was quit.

Roger Twoyenhold found sureties who would have his foal for a year and a day, or else pay 10 shillings for the price of it. His sureties were Robert, son of Walter, Robert Haliday, and others. Note: Roger paid 6 pence for the keep of the said foal.

(Roger had run away with the foal, but had returned before being outlawed, and saved the forfeiting of his lands. Goods as well as land, were forfeited to the King in cases like this, the sheriff holding them on the King's behalf, but transferring them to the lord of the manor, on payment of a small fine.)

Hugh, son of Osbert, fined 6 pence because he took his horse from the lord's park without permission.

Robert Alwyn is fined 6 pence for breaking the assize of Mead.

John the Tinker complained that Robert the Forester had basely insulted him by his words, and had wrongly accused him before other foresters. John said he was unwilling to suffer the damage done to him for 20 shillings, or the shame for half a mark. Robert denied the accusation word by word, and called the said foresters to vouch that he had not accused him.

Robert Alwyn is fined 6 pence for breaking the assize of Bread, while Avice wife of Richard is fined 6 pence for breaking the assize of Mead.

All the men of Edingale are fined 2 shillings for hiding Geoffrey White.

Henry Lupum fined 3 pence for taking away the oak of Roger Monte Alto without permission (Roger was lord of Manor at Elford).

Note: Simon Hubert, Richard son of Avice, Henry son of William, Alexander son of Thomas, Richard le Mey of Fradley and Nicholas became sureties for the child Avice, daughter of Margery from Fradley, and shall individually be responsible for her and her future behaviour.

Geoffrey son of Alice is fined 6 pence because he struck Avice daughter of Margery. Sureties for the said Geoffrey are Robert son of Alice and William of the town end and William son of Alice. Two freemen will look into the matter to find out more of this offence.

Edith the Blonde is fined for falsely raising an outcry. Sureties William the Provost and Gilbert son of Geoffrey. The steward will consult with the lord before awarding punishment.

Richard Bishop paid the lord 2 shillings to take over the land which Thomas Bishop formerly held in Alrewas, for himself and his heirs, at the old rent. Sureties for Matilda, wife of Nicholas the Cooper, who promised to live with her neighbours in Alrewas without making trouble or trespass, were Adam the Beekeeper, Robert Gamel, Robert son of Ralph, Robert Alwyn, William Rufus and John the Bond. (It needed six sureties for a woman's future conduct.)

Gilbert son of Geoffrey of Fradley is at the lord's mercy and fined 6 pence because he pulled a grave to pieces in the graveyard at Fradley.

Robert the Beekeeper is fined 12 pence for the misdeeds of his wife.

William the Provost is fined 20 shillings for his offence. Sureties Richard son of Avice and Adam Biker. (He had probably failed to collect the money from other tenants.)

William, son of Reginald, is fined 12 pence for breaking down his father's straw. Note: that John Breakdish of Oakley, gave up to his daughter Agnes, half a virgate of land which had been freed by John de Somerville in Alrewas, with the whole messuage and half a meadow, and also half of all his remaining property, and should John die before her, then the said Agnes shall inherit the whole virgate of land and then to her heirs, and if Agnes should die without heirs of her marriage, all the land with messuage, meadow and all other belongings shall revert solely to John de Somerville.

On this day 7th June 1260, Adam le Biker is presented to the court, and sworn in as Provost of Fradley.

All the land of Thomas of Curborough was taken from him into the lord's hand, because of his offences, and his many absences from court.

William the Provost is fined 6 pence for the misdeeds of his son, who had killed Ellis Aylmer's cow.

William le Fow should be further distrained, because the distraint (or confiscation) of his overcoat had not been sufficient to make him come to court. Hugh son of Osbert, is punished and pledges hus and ham (house and holding) for defaming the Steward, to whom he must make amends. Sureties Gilbert Owen, Edrian the Beadle, Henry son of Gunnild, and Ralph son of Amelot. Gilbert son of Geoffrey is fined 25 shillings for taking down a fence before the proper time, and for unjustly and secretly destroying the corn of Reginald, son of Alice. He must also make amends to Reginald, the amount to be decided by trustworthy men.

Robert Bird and Henry Fader defended themselves against Robert Count and William the Beadle because a horse of the said Robert Count which they had impounded at the Beadle's orders, had died, and they must prove that it died by accident and not through any fault of theirs. Sureties for Robert Bird are Walter the Fisher and Gilbert son of Thomas, and for Henry Fader, Richard Wytemay and Robert Gamel.

Reginald the Fisher is fined 4 pence, because he had wrongly accused Richard the Fisher of robbery. Sureties to make amends to the said Richard are to be considered by the reliable men, Ralph the Fisher and Henry at the Mill. Henry the Mouse is fined 6 pence for cheating his mother in law of her dower.

All the sureties of Richard Wytemay are to be punished because the original debt of his rent was not paid at the proper time, and Richard is to be distrained for not attending court.

Edith at the Mill and her son Walter, and Hugh the Provost of Croxall are to be punished for settling their dispute without bringing it to the lord's court.

Henry, son of Richard the Baker produced his sureties: Reginald of Fradley, Gilbert son of Robert, Robert Pertrich, Robert son of Alwyn, Robert son of Ralph, Richard Bishop, and William Scot, in order that the said Henry shall in every way keep the peace, and if he commits any offence, then the former pledged jurors shall be fully responsible for him.

Henry son of Gunnild paid 2 shillings, merchet for his daughter's marriage.

Henry Averil is punished because he hid his pigs against the lord's pannage. Sureties for payment are Richard Hawis and William at the town end, and at the same time, all his land, and two cows worth 11 pence, and 6 hogs if they can be found. Fined 3 shillings and 4 pence.

Bibun the Cooper paid the lord 12 pence to have his two cows freed from the pound.

Emma, wife of Geoffrey the Mouse, paid the lord 12 pence for giving her daughter in marriage (Geoffrey was Emma's second husband).

Luke of the Prebendary land paid 15 shillings to Sir John Somerville for 4 years rent for a stretch of water between the Bridge of Wychnor and . . . . . . (entry illegible).

Henry Cute and Robert Perdrich were presented and sworn in to serve the offices of Ale Tasters in Alrewas.

Twelve men each paid the lord 12 pence for licence to brew ale from December 1268 until Easter.

Richard Bishop grants to his son Richard all the land which he formerly held, half a virgate, and he paid 6 shillings to Sir John de Somerville for permission to make the grant. Richard the father, is to have his bed in the house for as long as he lives, and also the third sheaf, but he must still pay his son the third part of the rent.

Thomas Bernard will pay the lord one dozen fowls in lieu of his fine.

Gilbert Cribal tried for trespass in the lord's wood at Wychnor. Fined 6 pence.

Geoffrey, son of Henry Goderich was fined 12 pence because he had not only brewed bad ale, but sold it contrary to the assize.

Consideration is given in full court that Aldersale Moor shall not be used for horses or oxen which are to be sold. The lord of the manor shall receive 6 pence if the order is not obeyed.

Roger Wytemay complained that Richard of the Cross had broken his agreement and sold him defective goods by which he suffered to the extent of 2 shillings. Richard fined 6 pence.

Roger Wytemay fined 6 pence for abuse and swearing at William Martin.

William Martin fined 6 pence for trespass against Roger Wytemay.

William son of William Fox paid the lord 8 shillings to have full occupation of all his father's land, and Simon son of the Provost is to have the said land for eight years if William should unfortunately die while still a minor. (Simon was the elder brother and this illustrates the custom of Borough English, that is, inheritance of copyhold land by the youngest son.)

Robert at the Weir is fined for breaking the assize of bread along with seven others, but was forgiven by the Bailiff.

Gilbert Partridge is fined 6 pence, because he kept 4 shillings and 6 pence which he owed to William Fox and Henry the Woodreeve.

William Macurnays was fined 6 pence because he had sued Robert by means of the King's writ before the itinerant judges at Lichfield instead of before Sir John Somerville at his free court at Alrewas, who wished, and was able, to give him full justice.

Henry the Baker is fined 12 pence because he sold putrid and bad meat in the Vill of Alrewas.

William Martin fined 12 pence for the same offence.

It was presented by the Frankpledgers, that Robert, son of Ralph placed a basket trap in the waters of the lord without permission, to trap the lord's fish. He is therefore fined 11 pence by the decision of the whole court.

Decision of the court is that the lord, Sir John Somerville should be summoned to the next court against Alice the Fair, to plead in accordance with the King's writ.

Geoffrey the clerk of Edingale is accused that he struck John Burdon and drew blood. Sureties Thomas at the Stile and Walter Beryn.

Gilbert Kidd accused of taking greenwood in the lord's wood. Pardoned by the Bailiff.

Hugh Burdon distrained for taking greenwood.

A local law passed by the Court in December 1273 stated:

"It is decreed that no one in this manor may enter upon any land
after the death of his ancestor, except by the will of the lord, and
after paying a fine to him, but this does not apply to the six socmen."

In January 1273, Eliot Aylmer, Nicholas Kenworth, Geoffrey son of Alice, William of Slantley, Robert son of Avice, Gilbert Alwyn and Geoffrey son of Geoffrey, were all fined 6 pence for taking greenwood, as was Edith of Fradley. In February, Isolda the laundress, Adam Falin, Richard the Smith, Robert son of Hawis, Thomas Edeman, Alan the Bridger, Nicholas the wheelwright, Richard the fisher, William son of Reginald and Thomas of Botolph, were all fined for breaking the assize of ale or brewing bad ale.

Henry of Streethay complained of Alan the fisher, and said that he swore at him in the King's highway in Streethay and struck him there. Surety for the prosecution, William of Streethay, and Alan excused himself against the said Henry, nevertheless the court ordered that he should be distrained.

Geoffrey Goodlad was fined 4 pullets for taking greenwood, and Hugo of Elmhurst fined 4 pence for the same offence.

(It must have been a severe winter as there were numerous other cases of trespass and taking greenwood (or growing branches) from the lord's wood—January 1273.)

Roger son of William Edrian, paid the lord 4 shillings for leave to marry Ede the widow, and to have the said Ede's land.

For heriot for Nicholas the Brown, 6d.

Heriot for Gilbert, son of Geoffrey the Southerner, 2 shillings and 6 pence. (These were death duties paid to the lord.)

Julian of Branston found pledges, viz Robert son of Walter, William Ceblone, William of Winshull, William Honfrey, to find a draught horse at the bidding of the lord, or to pay 3 shillings.

Isolde at the churchyard is fined 6 pence for brewing bad ale.

Margery Sparrer fined 3 pence for the same.

John Hayine who was summoned and did not come to court, was distrained (lost his land holding).

Roger son of Nolbe and Margery Sparrer were distrained and were to appear at the next court to answer the charge of raising a false hue and cry (August 1273).

Roger son of Nolbe is at the lord's mercy because he had annoyed Margery Sparrer against the peace of God and his lord. He was fined 4 chickens (September 1273).

Geoffrey Goky is fined 6 pence because he broke an agreement made between himself and his father that he had failed to provide one pair of shoes on the Feast of St. Michael, which he had agreed to give, and had not done so. Sureties Robert the Smith and William Hodam.

Eliot Aylmer is fined 6 pence, his pigs having been found in the lord's park at Wychnor. Surety Thomas the Forester.

Let an enquiry be made before the next court (December 1273) as to who stole two lots of brushwood at Fradley.

Millicent Potter was fined 12 pence because she carried her malt from the lord's manor to brew ale on the prebendal manor. (Part of Fradley was in the jurisdiction of the Prebend of Alrewas—the ecclesiastical manor.)

The boys of Robert Wolley gave 13 shillings and 4 pence to the lord for leave to sell their land at Fradley, and a final agreement was made for the sale and purchase. Sureties Robert son of Heyne and Henry the Woodreeve.

Thomas Edemon is fined 12 pence for raising the hue and cry at the home of Henry the Provost.

Robert of Burway was distrained and must come to the next court to answer the charge of keeping a certain field enclosed at a time when it should be open for common pasture.

Adam Falyn distrained for failure to pay the pannage money for his four pigs.

These then are some of the entries in the Court Rolls over 700 years ago.

Some of the names of the areas of Pasture and arable land in use then, are still in use today, as the following extracts show.

1268—Richard Bishop transferred to William the Forester, one acre of arable land situated beyond the water which is called Trent, and one acre situated in a field called Redditch. (This was the Reed ditch, and is now called Rodige—the farm and the lane to it.)

Roger Wytemay transfers to William Adam one acre of Arable land in a field called Spellow.

1273—Roger Wytemay sells to Robert the Smith one half acre of arable land in a field called Baginhall.

1259—Robert Partridge paid 6 pence to the lord to take over from Alice of the Water, in a meadow called Muckleholm, rent to be half penny for all services, paid on the feast of St. Michael. (Name slowly changed to Mickleholm.)

1261—Geoffrey Swan agreed with Robert Alwyn to have 4 crops from one acre of arable land in a field called Essington.

1260—Lord John de Somerville gave permission for Henry the Clerk to take over 3 half-acres of arable land freed by Richard Hubard, one in Essington, another in Wet Spellow and the third in Aldercroft, at an annual rent of half penny each.

CHAPTER 14

The Church

In 672 A.D., after three short years as bishop of the extensive middle Kingdom of Mercia, St. Chad died, having been largely responsible for the uniting and pacifying the warring tribes of Britons and Anglo-Saxons, and establishing a centre for Christianity at Lichfield. For the next 150 years, the influence of the Church spread through the wild forests and fertile valleys of central England, and in 822 A.D., Bishop Aethelwald decided to make this influence stronger by increasing the cathedral establishment. Prebends were instituted at surrounding settlements, each one the centre of a group of small villages. Alrewas, as an old established community was one of those chosen, the others being Freeford, Weeford, Longdon and Colwich. It is possible that the first church built to replace the open air meeting place around a cross, was a wooden structure, thatched like the cottages which surrounded it. Simple and crude it may have been, but its effect and influence on the fishing and farming folk around it must have been great indeed, for from that time onwards, the church became the controlling and guiding force in the area. In its early history the village was never controlled and dominated by the will of a resident feudal lord; it did not rely on the shelter and protection of a castle or fortified manor. It survived, unlike many local communities, as a quiet backwater in the violent currents of national life, because of the sturdy independence of its people and the quiet influence of its church.

The church was sited above flood level, at the crossing of two ancient tracks. The first of these was the Salter's Way, along which pack horses carried the salt from Stafford and Cheshire, via Kings Bromley and Orgreave, to the south-east, crossing the Tame by a ford from the line of Dark Lane, Salterholme fields, and on to Croxall and Elford. The second track from Lichfield to the north-east, had replaced the Roman Rykneld Street, which had probably sunk into the marshes in places. This newer track for the higher ground, fording the Trent at Alrewas or Wychnor shallows. It may have been an ancient British trading track to the north-east, for along it lies a line of very old villages; Curborough, Fradley, Alrewas, Wychnor, Barton and Tatenhill, most of which are prehistoric in origin. There still exists a line of footpaths following this track. At the crossing of these two tracks then, the first church stood eleven hundred years ago, commanding the river and its wide valley, and around it clustered the primitive dwellings of the Anglo-Saxon farmers and fishermen. This first structure was probably destroyed in the Danish invasion of 874 A.D., when an invading army wintered at Repton.

In 1143, Pope Celestine II confirmed "the donation of the churches of Alrewas and Kings Bromley, together with their churches and appurtenances in the diocese, to the Bishop of Coventry and Lichfield, and that no one shall dare to impede or contradict the same, under danger of incurring the indignation of the Almighty and His blessed Apostles St. Peter and St. Paul. Dated the first year of the Papacy".

1195 saw the confirmation of the church by the Archbishop, and it is probable that the lower fabric of the church and possibly the tower, were constructed by then. In the tenure rolls, is a document stating: "King John gave the church of Alrewas to Henry, son of the Justice, who held it till the Pope plundered it of all it's revenues, after which the King gave it to a certain Roman, at whose death, Roger de Weseham, then Bishop of Chester, gave it to Thomas de Ferrers, but by what warrant it was not known".

In 1259, a document issued by Archbishop Boniface confirmed that: "the Church of Alrewas with its chapels (Kings Bromley, Fradley, Edingale and Parva Ridware) constitutes the Chancellorship of Lichfield Cathedral". Another interesting parchment gives the quaint picture of the dignity and respect to be given to a visiting prebend, and lays down his rights and privileges.

"To all sons of the Holy Mother Church whom this letter concerns. The representative of the Lord Bishop of the Church of Lichfield, (the Bishop being absent in remote parts of the Diocese) sends greetings in the salvation of all Since the prebended church of Alrewas was instituted, certain matters have been settled, namely, that the Vicars living at Alrewas should work in harmony with their chaplains in the Churches of Alrewas and Kings Bromley, and should administer in harmony the churches of Parva Ridware and Edingale. That with the agreement of the said prebend, they should have a house at Alrewas, with one entrance for themselves, and a separate one for the prebend, and there should be an exit leading towards the tithe barn of the prebend. They should also make the same suitably secure. And should the prebend, through misfortune, need a period of convalescence, they should see to it that nothing disturbs his peace and quiet. Next, the said vicars should have from the houses of their chaplains at Edingale and Parva Ridware, rent to pay for their expenses on the same. Next the said vicars should have for their sustenance, and for their chaplains, all gifts and offerings brought to the altar, including animals that have been killed, and every third swan, and the tithes of wool and of lambs, tithes of hay from Parva Ridware and Edingale, with the grass from the churchyard, and tithes brought by the "skilled" craftsmen. Moreover, there shall be saved for the prebend, a tenth of all tithes received.

To which agreement we have fixed our seal on the 15th day of May, 1224. This is to be kept in a casket, to be placed on the right hand side of the high altar, and also a book of sermons given by Master Lucas of Ely. And whoever shall remove either of them shall be accursed. The present vicar is the fifth, and is John de Horsborough, the first being Richard Blene, the second Richard Blene, his son, the third Henry Blene, and the fourth Richard de Harewood". Around 1276, another deed states that: "Robert, the son of Walter de Alrewas, grants to Adam de Walton, Chancellor of Lichfield, and to the Prebendary of the Prebend of Alrewas, lying near the churchyard on the east side thereof, land to be held of the same Adam and his successors forever, for

66

which grant he paid twenty shillings of silver.

Sealed and witnessed by Henry, Clerk of Alrewas, Willielmo, Gilbert Eliot, Henry Eliot, William the brother of Walter, Gilbert Kyde, and Richard, Chaplain of Alrewas". This would be the land now occupied by the new cemetery, and the vicarages old and new.

The church, as it stands today, though altered, heightened and enlarged, still retains in its character, the rugged qualities of the sturdy people who created it, worshipped in it, and now lie buried in its shadow. It is no architectural gem-like cathedral, but is an accumulation of the efforts of succeeding generations of humble folk to maintain and improve the focal point of their worship.

Its tower, squat, thick and strong, and the nave with its massive walls, were built in the 12th Century. The west doorway of the tower is extremely old, and is in the undecorated Norman style. The chancel was built probably at the same time, with a similar steeply pitched roof and small low windows, and on the north wall, the curious low-side window. It has been described as a leper window, through which the unfortunate outcasts could receive food and alms as they hobbled on their lonely journeys to the leper hospital at Freeford, or from which the priest could examine them if they became cleansed. It is most likely however, that from the window, which faced the clustered huts of the main village at Mill End, a small bell, hanging in the window, was rung to summon the peasants, and to exhibit the Host of the High Mass. At a later period, the roof of the chancel, like the nave and south aisle, was raised, and more windows added. The angle and height of the original roofs of chancel and nave can easily be seen, and the raising of the roof must have necessitated a new set of stone pillars. It must have been a major work of reconstruction, carried out probably in the 14th or 15th Century.

In the days before the Reformation of the English church from 1547, the churches and especially the chancels, were ornately decorated, and the plastered walls were painted with murals depicting ecclesiastic and biblical subjects. About 1550, during the reign of Edward VI, when Roman Catholicism was being ruthlessly replaced by the reformed Church of England, commissioners, or 'visitors' as they were called, were sent round with royal authority, to see that the new reforms of Church doctrines were carried out, and to supervise the removal or destruction of any outward signs of popery or 'idolatry' in the churches, which might suggest sympathy with the old Faith. Many of the richest and most artistic furnishings were removed, and the mural paintings were obliterated with thick layers of lime wash. A holy water stoup, removed to prevent its destruction, was found hidden up a chimney of an old cottage, now part of Coates' Butcher's premises, and can be seen at the rear of the church. In the 1870's, when repairs and alterations were in progress, most of the thick plaster in the chancel had been removed, before traces of these mediaeval paintings were noticed by the workmen, who reported it to the vicar, the Rev. W. R. Inge. He stopped any further work, but the paintings were destroyed except for one small piece. This surviving fragment, in its protecting frame on the north wall of the chancel, depicts a bishop carrying out a confirmation, with a clerical musician blowing a long trumpet.

The Vicars of Alrewas from 1547

1547	Robert Alsop	1818	Hugo Bailye
1569	John Faulkner	1830	John Hinckley
1619	William Bockinge	1832	John Moore
1637	Richard Martin	1857	R. K. Hazlehurst
1646	John Bould	1868	George Frazer
1657	Thomas Bladon	1869	G. H. Walsh
1669	Isaac Sympson	1869	William Inge
1676	John Jenner	1881	William J. Webb
1696	John Bradley	1890	William A. Webb
1708	Matthias Langley	1923	Edgar Burford
1720	John Piper	1929	Thomas H. Brookes
1739	John Fletcher	1931	Jasper S. Caiger
—	Danvel Remington	1937	W. Dennis Boone
1789	Charles Baldwin	1941	Hugh F. Hodge
1797	John Edmunds	1947	John Griffiths
1801	John Wainright	1964	David R. N. Wells
1814	William Oster	1974	John E. Colston

The roofs of the nave and the south aisle are of the 15th Century and provide an interesting example of the craftsmanship of the early woodcarvers, for the bosses on the rafters are deeply carved, some into crude, fantastic faces, and others into writhing animals and floral designs. Both roofs have been raised above the steep pitch of the originals, which gives some idea of the great age of the lower walls.

The exterior of the church is continually being weathered, the soft sandstone crumbling in wet and frosty winters, as well as the summer heat, and there have been, over the years, many expensive efforts to reface the stonework. However, along the south wall, near the porch, there can still be found many old and deep grooves, worn vertically in the stone. They have obviously been made by rubbing with steel. It is impossible to sharpen a blade or a scythe on a flat wall, only points can be sharpened on such a plane. The ground running from the Church Lane and the new vicarage, eastwards across the canal to Main Street, was called Butt Croft, and it is very likely that the grooves were made by the men and youths of Alrewas, who were compelled by law until the early 17th Century, to practice archery on the archery butts, the nearby church walls providing a convenient surface for sharpening arrow heads.

The later years of the 19th Century saw great changes in the appearance of the church. In 1891, the north wall was taken down and the new aisle added. The chancel roof was raised, and the chimneys were removed from the fires which had warmed the private chapel of the Turtons, which is now the Vicar's vestry. The floor was re-covered and new seating installed. In 1866 the porch was added in memory of Hannah Stephen Hazelhurst, over the grave of Matthias Langley, who had died in 1728 after being Vicar here for twenty years. In 1886, the tower was restored and altered, and the ringing floor was lowered by two feet, and the present choir vestry made beneath it. About 1700, this space had been called "the little chancel", and was occupied during service by the girls who were safely separated from the boys who occupied the gallery above their heads, watched by the attendant beadle with his long and ready staff of office. The constable, too, added his authority to maintain proper conduct in church, as an entry in his accounts for 1776 states: "To the expense of shirshing the public in church time". In 1887, the clock on the east face of the tower was added to commemorate Queen Victoria's jubilee, catering for the eastward spread of the village. The original time-keeper had been the sundial on the south wall, whose arm still marks the shadow on the dial, though the numbers to which it pointed have long been obliterated, by the time they were designed to indicate.

The old clock, still working perfectly, was installed in 1704 as the following extract from the Parish Accounts show:

1704—Spent when we bargained for ye clock	—	1s	4d
For ye hire of a mare and gig to Linton and other expenses when I went about the new clock	—	2s	0d
Spent when ye clock was set up	—	2s	0d
To Mr. Adams for boards for Clock House	—	8s	0d
To John Noflby for a new clock and a new hand for ye said clock, and a new lock for ye clock house door.	— £5.	14s	0d
For nails for ye clock house	—	11s	0d
To Edward Smith for a new clock house and for wood and boards which he found about ye said clock house	— £1.	1s	1d
Total cost of new clock	£8.	0s	3d

On 17th June 1767, an agreement was made between the churchwardens and Mr. John Follit, for the repair and maintenance of the clock, as follows:—

"We, the churchwardens of the parish of Alrewas, in the County of Stafford, do hereby covenant and agree with Mr. John Follit, clock maker, in the City of Lichfield, to repair the church clock of Alrewas, within the space of six weeks from the day of the date hereof, and to make the same in good condition, and that he shall make the said clock to go forty eight hours and upwards at one winding up, and that the said clock continue to go well, and fail in no part of the workmanship thereof after it is repaired by the said John Follit before Easter next ensuing, then we, the churchwardens do promise to pay to the above named John Follit, the sum of four guineas for his trouble, to be then paid by us, the Churchwardens, or our successors, whom we shall appoint Churchwardens for the said parish.

But if the said clock should not continue to go well or should fail in any part of the work thereof before the expiration of the time aforementioned, then I, the said John Follit, do hereby promise and agree, to have nothing for my trouble, and the above agreement is void.

70

Also by these presents I do agree and covenant with the above parties, to keep the aforesaid clock in good repair for the sum of five shillings per annum after Easter next ensuing".

Witness our hands

(signed) John Follit   (signed) William Smith   Church Wardens
John Smith

This John Smith was a cordwainer or leather worker in the village.

The cavities in the wall and rear pillar, where the sockets for the supports of the gallery were filled with new stone blocks, can easily be seen, as can the remains of the stair sockets in the walls near to the Charities Board.

This board gives details of gifts and charities to be given to the poor of the Parish, and was originally fixed to the south wall. In 1699, the accounts record:—

"Paid to ye painter for setting up a writing in the church of ye gifts to ye poore—10s 0d."

The Poor Box at the rear of the church, is rather unique, being cut from solid timber, and bears the words—"Remember the Poor 1710". The Parish Records reveal the following about it:—

1710—Paid to Joseph Morely for timber to make ye poore box—		6s	0d
Paid to James Fisher 5 daywork working same	—	5s	0d
Paid to Thomas Fisher for going to Lichfield to by a lock for said box	—		6d
Paid for a new box lid	—		6d
For putting on a plate and lock on box	—	1s	0d
		13s	0d

At the back of the church near the font, are two interesting pieces of obsolete fittings, which may at one time have been part of the gallery or ringing chamber. The first is an oak rail, but the other is the more interesting, being a long dark oak board, on which is carved "F.H. R.W. R.B. Churchwardens 1633 W.R. R.R. Young Men". There are four pieces of lettered wood-carving in the church,

71

all done between 1627 and 1639, during the reign of Charles I, and just before the Civil War, and from the style and shape of the lettering, appear to have a common craftsman. In the example above, the names can be identified as:—

"Francis Harris, Richard Wildblood, Richard Beal,

Churchwardens. Walter Rose, Robert Reynolds Young Men."

At the time of writing, the vicar's vestry contained a sideboard on which is carved: "R.M Vic 1638. W.T., T.G., J.C. Chur", and carved into the door panel are the large letters "J.P. 1626". The first group of initials refer to Richard Martin Vicar 1638, William Turton, Thomas Gilbert and Joseph Cooper, Churchwardens. The identity of J.P. has not so far been found.

The pulpit appears to have been constructed and adapted from some timber reclaimed after the demolition of some other church feature, perhaps the rood screen. This too received the woodcarver's enthusiastic work, being ornately decorated, and bearing the legend: "Jesus Christ and Him crucified. 1639". The exterior of the West door also received the woodcarver's attention. An intricate pattern of parallel lines forms lozenges which contain the initials "T.W., R.M., J.B. 1627" being the initials of Thomas Worley, Richard Marshall and John Browne, who were wardens at that time, and whose memory has been perpetuated over the centuries of weathering.

Several of the above-named men were members of noted local families—the Gilberts of Fradley (in those days there was a warden for Fradley), the Reynolds, yeomen farmers of Orgreave (at one time at the now-vanished Barn Close), the Turtons, who were bailiffs of the manor and later its owners, and the Wildbloods, one of whom, living up to his name of Robert Wildblood, was "wounded by a soldier and was carried to Lichfield to ye surgeon, and died, and was buried the 16th April 1644". He probably expressed his royalist or religious opinions too strongly to a Roundhead trooper.

The Turtons, lords of the manor in the 17th and 18th Centuries, furnished their private chapel, now the vicar's vestry, with a fireplace and chimney, and with pews in the Chancel, and their memorials and achievements can easily be read around the wall. Outside, on the south wall, is the memorial to John Kirkland, who served the Turtons from 1662 to 1729.

The installation of the present organ in 1882, at a cost of £383 effectively closed the arch from the Chapel, which was now cut off from the chancel, and in any case there were no Turtons left here to use it.

At Fradley, the Gilberts and Gorings (one member of the family was a famous officer in the Civil War) were succeeding lords of the manor, yet though they were residents of what is now the Old Hall Farm, occupied for many years by the Shaw family, no stones mark their resting places. It is remarkable that for over a thousand years, folk have died and been buried here, yet few graves date back for more than two hundred years. Many lie of course, under the church floor, and in the past, the poor had no memorial except perhaps a small wooden cross, and even the soft local sandstone of the richer memorials soon weathered, or sank into the ground to be moved later for new burials.

The tower, though a massive buttressed structure, and held firm with steel tie-bars, shakes at the swinging of the eight bells, which, with their fittings, weight upwards of ten tons. All the bells carry their original inscriptions:

1. Treble Bell — W. A. Webb, Vicar, H. A. Kent, Clerk 1922.
2. 2nd Bell — H. W. Brierley, G. H. Lord, Churchwardens 1922.
3. 3rd Bell — God save this Church 1711. Recast 1922.
4. 4th Bell — John Yeld, Clarke 1711. Recast 1922.
5. 5th Bell — Joseph Smith in Edgbaston made me in 1711. Recast 1922.
6. 6th Bell — Matthias Langley Vicar. John Kirkland, William Staley and Henry Kent, Churchwardens 1711. Recast 1922.
7. 7th Bell — My mournful sound doth warning give That heave me cannot always live. 1711. Recast 1922.
8. Tenor Bell — J. Taylor and Co., Loughborough, Bellfounders. W. Inge, Vicar, Edwin Sellick, Jos Reynolds, Churchwardens. I was given by William Thomas in his 45th year of being Parish clerk. Tenor bell recast by consent of next of kin A. Byrne, his niece.

The Parish records contain some interesting references to the bells:

1585— This yeare, the 6th July 1585, the seconde bell, and the greatest bell weare cast at Nottingham by Henry Oldfield, Bellfounder.
In 1586, William Oldfield, son of the bellfounder, married Emma Thorniworke, an Alrewas girl.
1596— John Daniell was killed by a piece of borde that laye over the hoole in

the steeple, and with the fall of the clapper of the great bell, brake the borde and the ende of the same borde hitte him on the heade, and after that he lived about the space of eight houres, and then died, never speaking any wordes, only these "Lord have mercy upon me".

1618— The littel bell in the stepell of Alrewas being new cast, weyed before it was cast 3½ cwts and 12 lbs. The same bell now newly cast, wayeth 3 cwts 2 qtrs 7 lbs. The casting of the bell is £2 and 12 pence. The mettel cometh to £2. 11. 0d. The carriage to Leicester and backe againe, and our expenses firste the carrying of the bell with an other of Whittington, 20 shillings for oure parte.

1711— John Kirkland by ye Church for Alrewas, William Staley for Ffradley, and Henry Kent for Orgreave, serving Churchwardens for ye second yeare, ye 4th bell being cracked, and ye rest being ill bells and not tunable, were recast by Joseph Smith of Edgbaston in ye County of Stafford, he being in ye charge of taking down, carriage etc., finding or making everything good, except ye frame, wheels and ropes, for £25, according to Articles of Agreement, and a £300 Bond for performance.

The church was given new seating arrangements in 1854, when it was re-pewed by Mr. Beckett of Lichfield, and by 1890, the central heating had been installed. At that time the church was lit by about twenty brass lamps, hanging from the roof, which could be raised or lowered, using a pole which could be hooked into the lamp. By 1930, electricity was brought to Alrewas, and its installation in church brought to an end the arduous task of lighting, cleaning and filling the old oil lamps throughout the winter months. The many memorials in the church need not be included here, as they carry their own messages, as indeed do most of the fittings and furniture which have been presented as memorials. At the rear of the church are two ancient oak chests, whose ages it is impossible to assess, but I have heard an authority on old church chests of this description express the opinion on examining them that they are of rare antiquity, and may be almost as old as the church itself. The oldest rolls which one of the chests contained are now safely deposited at the County Records Office at Stafford. The Parish Registers date back to 1547, and are not merely a list of births, marriages and deaths, but contain many comments by the clergy on local and national events and conditions, and we shall include many of these, some translated from Latin. The original spellings are maintained:

1547— Thomas Morris, Cicily Motte, Nicholas Sylvester, Thomas Baggaley, baptised. From 1549-1568, the Vicar, Robert Alsop neglected to keep the register. (A family of Alsop lived in the Parish for a number of generations.)

1577— This yeare, the 11th November, appeared a biassing starre, which was seene forty days after.

1581— This 21st day of December 1581, was the water of Trent dryed up and sodenly fallen so ebbe, that I, John Falkner went over into the halls meddow in a lowe peare of showes about three of the cloke in the afternowne, and so it was never in the remembrance of any man, and the same water in the morning before was banckc full, which was very strange.

(The Hall meadow was round the site of the old Wychnor Manor House beyond the river weir.)

1584— Anna Kent, daughter of Edward baptised 2nd April 1584.

1584— This yeare 1584, the fyfth day of August was the house at the Trent yeat buylded, or as we saye begonne to be reared, which house was buylded by Henry Griffith Esq.

(This was the beginning of Wychnor Hall. Trent yeat was, in our modern language, Trent gate—perhaps a gate into the Park, or a narrowing of the river below the hill—c. Simons yeat, Lydyat or its modern name Lidgetts Lane.)

1586— The 10th day of October, William Tunall of Orgreave, being suspected of felony, and haveing not God in minde, did cutte his owne throte with a knyfe and died 13th daye of October. And the Crowner (coroner) gave orders that he should be buried neare to the church pale without ringing or service.

1592— Johes Warde de Loupin buried 9th June 1592.

1593— This year in the summertime, their was a great plague in England in divers Cities and Townes as in London, their died to the number of 2000, and in Lichfield their died to the number of eleven hundred and odde, and as at this time deane ceased.

1593— This yeare the 21st of Marche, was an exceeding great Tempest of Winde, which continewed all the daye longe, and did great hurte in many places in Blowing downe of Steeples, dwelling housses, Barnes, Trees inumerable in every place. Within this pishe (parish) their weare seven barnes overthrown, in Lichfield the toppes of steeples of St. Michaels, and St. Marys by the market place were blowen downe.

1595 — This yeare was the Free Schole at Barton under Needwood buyled, founded by one Thomas Russell, a Londoner.

1596 — The mills at Wichnor weare burned the 25th day of Marche, being good fryday that yeare, at nighte about nine of the cloke in the nighte, which fyre consumed and burned all things in the Mille, the milners bread, come, hennes, the fyre burste the millstones.

1600 — This yeare 1600, in January, I began to sett Grasse and plant stocks, pippins and other trees in this orchard, and I sette them very thycke that they might be removed.

1601 — This yeare, the first of July, the bridge upon Tame, called Salters' Bridge, being greatly in decaye and broken down, was of new begonne and made broder by two foote, which cost the workmanship tow hundred poundes, whereof this Hundred of Offeley payed one hundred poundes, the other four Hundreds payed the reft; the 17th July the foundations began to be layed.

1601 — The eight day of January 1601 was one Richard Chare drowned at Salters Bridge out of a boote, haveing a great bottell of fodder in the boote with him, which after he was in the water tooke holde of the same bottell of fodder, and was carried by the same until he came to the nether end of Mytholm and there peryshed, divers people beholding the same, bothe men and women, but could not helpe to save his lyfe and the first day of February next after, he was founde and taken up and brought into the churchyard, and layed in the grave and covered with a bourde, and by the commandment of the coroner, was buried, after a view of his body being taken by honest neighbours, the 4th day of February 1601.

1604 — On the 3rd of May, Thomas Ball alias Smith, was slayne by John Saunders.

1605 — The fyfte daye of November the Parlament should have begonne, on which day there was a great treason should have been wrought against the kings magestie, and all the whole house assembled together by the devise of a number of papistes who had conspired by one Thomas Persey, a pentioner, with others, to have blown up the parlament house with gunne powder, which was placed in a Vaute under the house, to the number of 36 barrells, with faggottes, colles, and billets, but the same was prevented, by God almightie, by a letter sent the lorde Mountegle.

1607— Nicholas Fouden, one of the sonnes of John Fouden, deceased, hanged himself the 15th daye of September 1607, his mother being gonne to Lichfield to the market, and with a corde upon the poote hangle over the fyre place lyke unto a gybbett, so he peryshed being the age of 14 years.

1607— This yeare, 1607, their was a great froste and snowe, the which begane the fyfte day of December, and so continued until the fouretenth daye of February, being Valentine daye, all which time all our rivers weare frozen, and in moste partes, they would beare horse and man loaded, and cartes loaden; the moste parte of mules weare so frozen up that they could not grynde any come, but with much adoe, and did much hurte to many things, as wheate, gresse, and herbs.

1608— The 29th daye of November 1608, William Hanson of Fradley, being very olde, and a man in cutting and falling downe of an oke tree for fyrewood, and he himself takeing hould of a boughe of the tree, pulled the same upon himself, and overwhelmed and stroke his head into the ground and killed him, and was buried 3rd of December.

1609— A serten poore woman, name not knowen, came to Fradley beging, and suddenly fell down and thar died.

1609— Thomas Mee (May), the 31st day of August 1609, intending to wade over the water betwixt Belocks Bridge and Salters Bridge, the water being great, he purposing to goo to Catton to sheare peas, was overcome with the watter, was drowned, and the 6th day of September was founde, and the crowner appoynted him to be buried the 7th day of September.

1611— Margery Reynolds wife of John Reynolds was buried 20th day of August 1611. She hath given 20 shillings in money to the heires of the said John Reynolds and to pay 2 shillings yearly to 4 poore people dwelling in Alrewas towne, the same 2 shillings that as 6 pence apeece, three dayes before Christmas, whylest the world endureth.

1611— John Selvester of Shenstone, a laboring man, being hyred to drive the teame of one Thomas Smythe of Shenstone, to fetch two grindle stones from Branston. And by great mischance sitting upon one of the stones, over waited the weane upon the heath, in the highwaye, and the stone, the which he satte upon, fell upon him and killed him, the 11th day of September 1611, and was buried at Alrewas 13th day of September 1611.

1611 — There was a young man named Towne, born at Calengewood, within the parish of Tatenhill, who was drowned at Choter bridge, the 26th of December 1612, his parents desiring to have him buried at Tatenhill.

1613 — Robert Nevell the father, and Robert Nevell the son, being in Salterholme field the 26th of June 1613, tending of the towne beasts in the herdmans walk there, after Stony Furlonge side about 4 o'clock in the afternoon of the same day, there was a mightie great tempest of rayne, lyghtning and thunder, and the father and sonne standeing under an oke tree to save themselves from the rayne, weare both of them stricken to death, the barke of the oke tree rent a great length, the leaves of the tree smitten and blowen away the most parte of them. One other younge youth of ten yeares age, Thomas Frauncis, being their to fetch or helpe the herdman, being within the compasse of tenne yeardes of the same place, was saved and nothing hurte as the others, the heares of their head singed with the lightning and in some parte of the body and face, blackened.

1614 — The mill in Alrewas hay was reared and sette up the 20th day of November 1614, but it did not grind until the 21st of December after, being the feast of St. Thomas the Apostle.

1616 — The 12th of December 1616 was drowned at Chiter bridge, one William Turner the sonne of William Turner of Dunstall, servant to William Barnes, of the wood mill in this parishe, rydding towardes Burton market, his mare slipping on the bridge, fell into the water, the water being out, could not be saved, he being of the age of 20 yeares, and many neighbours in the company.

1617 — Poor unknown woman died April 15th. This poore woman was not knowen, from whence she came nor her name, and as it was enformed by some that sawe her overnight was druncken, and layd in the Common Field called Estington in the highway, and died that night.

1617 — James our King returned to Whore Cross on the 30th of August, and remained there on Saturday and Sunday.

1621— This yeare the fallow fields of Alrewas were first sowed with pease.

1621— August ye 21, King James at Whichnour and ye court dyned at ye hall there.

1623— Richard Webster, blind many yeares before his death, was buried May 31st 1623. This summer, Brook Hay was kidded. (Cleared of trees and undergrowth.)

1624— The King at Whichnor August 19th.

1624— Wm. Foden, Wm. Lovat and John Dorrington were buried July 19th 1624, the said three men were drowned in the river Tame near a place called Stockford green, on Sunday 18th of July.

1625— Rudolf Bailey, three years old or thereabouts, fell from the little bridge into a muddy pool on this side of the place known as Depmore on the 24th August as night was nearly fallen, was snatched out by his parents still alive, but died the same night.

1624— Anna Collier, wife of John Collier, met her death in the Mill Pond which is near the embankment of the well-used path, at dawn on the morning of Wednesday. She had left her husband a short time before in bed.

1638— Henry Westcott, Armiger of Handsacre, journeying late at night between Yoxall and King's Bromley, after having dined and wined with others at Yoxall, was riding on horseback, having left his servant behind, when he was suddenly thrown into the River Trent, and losing his horse, died a pitiful death in the deep water, on the 5th of September. His body was recovered in the Mill waters at Alrewas on 24th December.

1639— It is recorded that on the 17th day of April 1639, in the middle of the night, John Durham, suffering a punishment at the hands of the devil, foully and horribly murdered his wife Joy in cold blood as she lay asleep in bed.

1642— 16th October, on which day was a great battle fought by the King and Parliamint, at or near Kinton in Warwickshire when was slain on the king's side, Lord John, brother of the Duke of Lennox, Lord Conway, and divers others of note, and taken prisoners, the Earl of Lindsay etc etc.

1643— On the 21st day of April (being Friday) the Close at Lichfield, after three weeks siege and the loss of some men, was yielded up to Prince Rupert, together with the ordnance and ammunition, all sorts of arms (except the horsemens arms and a certain number of muskets, and all such treasure which had been formerly conveyed in thither and did not belong to the soldiers there. These soldiers were part of those forces under the command of the late Lord Brook, who was killed (by Dumb Byott) in his assaulting this cathedral, by a shot in the eye.

1643 — Upon the 13th August, being the Lord's day, there happened in this towne of Alrewas a suddaine and fearful fire in the house of George Thorniworke, an alehouse neare the church, occasioned by the shooting off a home-gun, which in one hower's tyme consumed the said house and most of his goods, and the barne and hay of John Fitcher, and the house and all the goodes of John Francis, and burnt up the trees about them, and had like to endangered the whole towne. God give us grace hereby to amend our lives Battle, murder, theft and blood, overflows this kingdom like a flood; Our sins the cause, Almighty God forgive us, and take off Thy rod, And give us grace our lives to mend, for fear we perysh in the end.

1644 — Upon Wednesday and Thursday, May 15th and 16th, in divers places in Staffordshire and Warwickshire, their fell great stormes of haile, with haile stones of divers formes, some round as big as walnuts, and some flat as big as half crown pieces, with thunder and lightning in three or four several places at one instant, the like seldom seene.

1644 — Robert Wildblood was wounded by a soldier, was carried to Lichfield and died there.

1644 — May 11. John Hall of Orgreave had a cow brought forth a monstrous calf alive, with four eyes and two noses and mouthes, having teeth and tongues in both the mouthes, which lived one day and then died.

1645 — Humphrey Swayne was buried 26th of July 1645. He was bitten with a mad doge in the hand upon the third day of the same month or thereabout, and that was the cause of his death.

1678 — Buried in woollen. At the end of the 17th Century, there was a decline in the wool trade, and in 1678, an Act of Parliament was passed, entitled—"An Act for the lessening of the importation of linen from beyond the seas, and for the encouragement of the Woollen and Paper manufacturers of the Kingdom". By this Act, all bodies, with or without coffins, must be buried in woollen. Every priest must enter such burial in the Parish Register, testifying that the body had been buried in woollen,

Main Street with White Hart Inn, early 1900's

The Green, Alrewas.

Post office Road, 1910.

The School and Canal, early 1900's.

Kents Bridge, c.1920.

Dedication of the War Memorial, 1920.

Gallows Bridge and Church from Butt Croft, c.1910.

Laying the foundation stone of the Chapel, 10th March, 1897.

Gaskell's Bridge and Statfold Bridge, early 1900's.

under penalty of £5, half to go to the informer, and half to the poor. All burials in the register after this, are for many years followed by the note "Certified buried in woollen".

1680 — Collected from hous to hous for the release of captives in Algiers, the summe of one pound six shillings and nine pence halfpenny.

1682 — Jonathan Jenner (Vicar), Thomas Smith (for Alrewas), William Baggaley (for Fradley), Isaac Charles (for Orgreave), Churchwardens.

1683 — About ye beginning of December, it began to ffreeze very vehemently, but with some intermission, till about the Twentieth day of ye said Month, when it did ffreeze with such vehemency and severity, that not only the rivers were so ffrozen over that ffoot men and horsemen, yea, carts and waggons laden with coals, with iron, and with timber, did ordinarily pass over the ice; but all things were generally ffrozen within doors, insomuch that many suffered great loss in their drink, and not only small drink, but March beer and ale. Yea, hoggsheads full of either sort, were burst with ye ffrost. And milk sett in ye very Oven did ffreeze.

The Thames was so ffrozen over at Gravesend and Sheerness, that men passed over on the ice; yea, that ye salt water about Deal was ffrozen from ye shore into ye sea about two miles, and that persons had gone a great way into ye sea up ye ice.

But what seems strange as being a thing I never heard of, was the Riving and Cleaving of great trees, both fallen and growing, many growing oaks in Fisherwick Park, in Wychnor, in Bear Hay, etc., were cleft in, and I suppose, by this ffrost some from almost the Top to the bottom, others many yards till some knott stopped ye cleft, and this cleft went usually to the heart of the tree.

And I saw at my own Vicaridge door viz: The best of my Ashes that grow by Trent side, cloven allmost from ye Topp to ye Bottom, insomuch, that standing on ye ground, I could thrust a knife into ye cleft to ye haft, and did do so.

Many poor tradesmen, as shoemakers, maltsters, weavers, dyers, tanners and skinners, etc, were put to hard shifts. Any many of ye richer sort were forced to drink water for sometime. It was reported and is so, that Robert Wright, who keeps a Lyker House in Lichfield, lost Tenn pounds worth of bottles not reckoning the drink in them, broken with ye ffrost.

Several who left water in Brass Pots, had by next morning, the bottoms of their Brass Pots broken with ye ffrost. Lambs born in ye night, ye Shepherd found next morning, ffrozen to ye ground. Rosemary, Bayes and Laurell generally killed, and sage and lavender.

Ye severest ffrosts, were in ye brightest Sun shining days, and clearest star-light nights and no wind. Insomuch that windmills were useless for some time, and water mills could not stirr, and others with great labour were made to move, but very heavily and unevenly.

And ye it was said, that Ffisherwick Mill was never stopped, ffor its waters come from Quick Springs near the Mill, which never ffreeze.

And in Trent, I observed that at the Corner of ye Hall meadow, ye Mouth, there was a place about ffour yards over, which never did ffreeze.

On Thursday evening, Jan. before Hilary Term, it began to thaw, but on Monday Morning after, it ffroze again most vehemently, and so continued till February the ffifth, when, at ye change of ye moon, the air changed and grew warm and high.

It is said that ye ffrost has gotten three quarters of a yard into ye ground, or more, and that if this thaw should continue, yet all the ffrost and ice would not be wasted till Lady Day.

John Jenner—Vicar.

1687— Marjory Kent, aged 7 years, daughter of John Kent, deceased, and Ann his widow, was suffocated and drowned in a pit or well, as she was drawing water, by falling into the well, Jully 11th 1687.

1692— Mary Wilcox, aged 40, was drowned in the River Tame, at a place called Wildblood's Holm, Nov. 19th.

1711— Thomas Browne of Fradley, aged 102 years and four months, was buried at Alrewas, March 4th.

1717— Quakers at Fradley. (These were the Oneleys and Sylvesters.)

1719— Daniel Woodcock, who lived near Fisherwick, to avoide being taken by a warrant that was out against him, upon the 8th September, did run from the house of widow Wilcox of Orgreave towards Trent, and the next day was found drowned in the river. Upon the 10th, the coroner's inquest found it an accident, and upon the 11th he was buried at Alrewas.

1726— This yeare, an Act of Parliament was obtained for discharging and disfranchising the Chace of Alrewas Hay in the County of Stafford.

1740— George, son of George and Elizabeth Lucas, was unfortunately drowned in the River Trent. He went from the Swan at Wychnor Bridge, in order to return home betwixt nine and ten of the clock on Sunday night, Dec 21st, it being a very tempestuous and snowy night, and was not found till February 6th. Was buried Feb. 7th, 1740.

1743— George Lucas, who was unfortunately killed by a fall from his horse, was buried July 22nd.

1752— Thomas Dagley junior, who was accidentally drowned in the River Trent as he was returning from Wychnor Lodge in the night, was buried Jan 7th.

1756— Samuel Newey, a poor boy, servant to Humfrey Hadley the Miller, slipt through one of the trap doors at the flood-gates as he and another lad were laying the leaps to catch eels, and was washed into the flood-gate hole and drowned.

1763— John Kirkland, supposed to be frozen to death, was buried January 6th.

1767— Edward Hall who was touched and cured by His Majesty King Charles II for the Kings Evil, was buried Jan 19th, aged 110 years.

1772— Orgreave Hall was occupied by George Adams Esq., who afterwards took the name and estates of the Ansons of Shugborough.

1777— William Stoddart of Alrewas who was drowned in the Navigation (canal) was buried 1st July.

1778— James Dagley of Alrewas, who was drowned in the Navigation near Stafford was buried Dec. 9th.

1780— Thomas Hunt of Fradley, a lunatic who drowned himself in the Navigation was buried Jan 31st.

1783— A great frost and snow for three months.

1783— James, son of Catherine Dagley, widow of Alrewas, who was accidentally drowned in the Navigation, was buried Sept. 25th.

1 784— Thomas Wheat, who was killed by a fall from a load of gravel, was buried Nov. 5th.

1785— Joseph Barrisford, who was drowned in the navigation, was buried July 5th.

1786— Jane, daughter of Joseph and Sarah Cartmail, who was drowned in the Navigation, was buried May 2nd.

1787— Arthur, son of Joseph and Eleanor Woodward of Alrewas Mill, who was drowned in the River Trent, was buried April 23rd.

1789— Samuel Bakewell of Fradley Hall, farmer, who was found hanging in the dove-cote with his throat cut, all of which he did himself, was buried June 14th. The coroner's inquest, sate upon the body, and brought in their verdict—lunacy.

1789— Mrs. Margaret Fieldhouse of Alrewas Hall, aged 100 years, was buried Dec 31st.

1791— Thomas Farmer of Fradley, who was found hanged in his coal-house was buried Jan 3rd. A verdict of lunacy was given.

1793— Mr. James Gildart, butcher of Alrewas, aged 52 years, a very corpulent man, who weighed when living 26 stone and five pounds, was buried May 20th. His coffin, was six feet in length, two feet nine inches over the shoulders, and 21 inches in depth.

1793— This year a general survey was made of old enclosed and likewise the common land within the Parish of Alrewas by Robt. Wyatt of Burton-on-Trent, surveyor.

1793— There has been erected within a few years past, a cotton manufactory at Alrewas, belonging to which there are 300 persons daily employed; the present proprietors of the said manufactory are Messrs Dickins and Finloe, of Burton-on-Trent.

1794— A hot summer, and a great drought, very little rain from April until the latter part of July.

1794— The annals of agriculture for the last century have not exhibited an instance of so heavy a harvest having been housed in this Kingdom within so short a period as that of this present year. The corn and grain of every kind were housed and completed in the parish of Alrewas by 16th August.

1794— This year six troops of yeomanry cavalry were raised for the use of the County of Stafford, and they were trained and disciplined on Fradley heath.

1795— A great frost and snow began on Monday 22nd December 1794, which, with some intermissions, continued until Monday February 9th. 1795, which was exactly seven weeks, a very severe winter. The rivers Trent and Tame were frozen over, on which rivers there were mountains of ice. The corn mills were unable to grind, wheat sold at 9 shillings a stroke. A great flood succeeded a sudden thaw, on Tuesday Feb 10th, great damage was done by the amazing quantity of ice and waters to several bridges, viz. Kings Bridge and the bridge next the Swan at Whichnor, both of them over the river Trent and the Turnpike road from Lichfield towards Burton-on-Trent, were washed down. The spring planks on the side of the canal, leading from Alrewas to Whichnor church, were washed down. It is very remarkable amongst the variety of damage done to many bridges, that Salters Bridge over the river Tame, sustained very little damage, which is supposed to be preserved by the extensive breadth of the centre arch.

1795— On Wednesday, March 11th as the Birmingham and Sheffield coach was going from Burton to Lichfield, four of the horses were drowned, by attempting to pass the ford in Essington meadow (by reason of two of the bridges being washed away and swept down by the violence of the great flood of February last). The two fore horses with the postilion, plunged suddenly into the deep, and drew the other four horses and the coach after them. The two leading horses disengaged themselves from the others, and they, with the postillion and the coachman, were with difficulty preserved, the other four horses being drowned. The passengers had just before alighted from the coach, and were afterwards conveyed forward in chaises from the Swan Inn at Whichnor bridges.

1795— On Friday, April 24th, a young woman passenger in Allen's stage waggon, from Birmingham to Burton-on-Trent, was killed by the waggon being overturned at the temporary bridge in Essington meadow (the original bridge being washed down by the late flood). She was buried at Stapenhill, that being her native place.

1795— On Monday July 27th, a tumult or riot was nearly affected at Alrewas mill, owing to the great scarcity of corn, flour and bread. The Staffordshire Cavalry were sent for, and by their timely arrival, tranquility was restored. Riots in Birmingham, Coventry, Nuneaton, Hinkley and Atherstone etc. (due to the bearness of provisions) were dispersed by the military.

1795— The three new brick bridges or arches, each in Saltram (Salterholm) were built, and the turnpike there was raised. (These arches remained until the dual carriageway was built about 1959, and allowed the flood water to pass under, without being funnelled to the river bridge.)

1796— The oldest man living cannot remember such a January. Warm and dry. Vegetables everywhere very forward, hardly to be credited, in August bacon sold at 11 pence a Ib, in September, cheese was 52 shillings a cwt of 120 lbs, a sixpenny loaf was 2 lbs 12 ozs, Mutton and lamb 6 pence a Ib, a good bullock 4s 6d a Ib, Pork 9 shillings a score, Bacon 8½ a lb by the fitch.

Few other entries are noted other than births, marriages and deaths.

CHAPTER 15

The Church and tithes

The word "tithe" is the old English word meaning tenth, and priests of the early Church relied upon the generosity of the Christian community to support them by donating in kind, a tenth of their produce which they obtained by farming, fishing or hunting. The tithe system was a fair one, those with much, giving more than those with little. However, as time passed, and settled agricultural communities were established, and the Church grew in authority and power, the tithes, instead of being basically a voluntary assistance to the priests, became obligatory, failure to produce the tithes demanded being punished by Law.

We have found little evidence of early tithe records in Alrewas, and the alleged tithe barn near the Lych gate would appear very small for so large a parish. It is very possible, that an early arrangement was made between priests and villagers to abandon the complicated and contentious payments in kind, of their harvests, livestock, fruits, etc., and replace it by agreed cash payments. An early account of Wychnor states that the tithe barn was on the Great Lawn, west of the church, and search there revealed extensive brick foundations forming a large platform covered with turf, but easily traced near the centre of the large pasture, still called Potter's Lawn, or the Great Lawn.

Some extracts from neighbouring parishes are of interest in indicating how the tithe system could have operated three or four hundred years ago in Alrewas. The first extract is from the Croxall records of 1717, and illustrates the difficult and embarrassing task of the vicar to extract his tithe due from the Manor Household.

A Memorandum—17th June, 1717

On the 28th of the same month, I went to the several tenants of Catton Lordship, and before witnesses, made a demand of all their tythes in Catton, come only excepted. And presently upon this Midsummer 1717, Mr. Clement Kynersley and Mr. Smithson of Uttoxeter came to my house and most earnestly importuned me to let things rest till ye young heir of Catton came of age, and offered me a gynea to hand, as an earnest of Madame Horton's kindness and said that she, by her kindness for the future, should make it out yt I should be no loser by my forbearance, but I refused it, and so we parted. On the 10th of October following, being frequently invited, I went down to Catton, and Madame Horton earnestly importuned me that I should not shue (sue) for the tythes, but that their might be a friendly end made in that matter, and said that tho she could not make an agreement for her son's estate, he being under age, yet she would engage that as soon as he came to age, he should make a friendly agreement for them, and in the mean time, she would by her kindnesse make it out that I should be no considerable loser for my forbearance, and praid me to accept a gynea at present as an earnest of her future kindnesse for the four years to come.

Then I told her it was but an underhand way of dealing which I did not like, and I told her more over, that tho for peace sake upon so many promises from her, I would yield to her maine request to forbear shueing her out of ye same, yet she must not except I should give any more receipts for the Tythes in the forme that ye former receipts had been in, because of the ill uses that they would make of them. And that whatsoever she gave to prevent suits at present, should be entered in the receipts as a part of his rent for tythes used, that I would no longer give a receipt for a forehand rent of Tythes for the year current, and so after many importunitys and promises of kindnesse, and complaints of my unkindnesse to the widow and fatherlesse if I should shue her, how I should undoe her and her children, and drive her from her house, with many like complaints and wars.

(Here part of the Memorandum is missing.)

An amiable end made of that busyness, either before, or at least as soon as young Mr. Horton came to his age, which earnest importunity of his I at length yielded to, and so he went up to Madame Horton's Chamber to tell her what he had done, and she promised immediately to come down to the parlour to us, and accordingly did doe, and then I told her that at Mr. Smithsons importunity, and upon his fair promises, I would not shue for the tythes till that time. I at last took the gynea as an earnest of her promise of kindnesses to make up the price of tythes till her son came of age, and so we parted very good friends.

This memorandum illustrates the authority the vicar had, even over the family of the lord of the manor, and the fear generated by the threat of the Law.

An interesting follow-up to the last entry on Catton.

This Madame Horton was Elizabeth, daughter of Thos Kynnesley of Loxley, whose husband Walter had died in 1716. She had six children, the eldest being Christopher, who was born in 1700. Later, his son, also named Christopher, married Anne Luttrell, daughter of Simon Luttrell, later made Earl of Carhampton. Three years after Christopher's death, in 1769, Anne Horton married the Duke of Cumberland, brother of King George III. This royal marriage to a commoner, led to great uproar in the Establishment and it was followed by the passing of the Royal Marriage Act by the Parliament, which was to forbid royal marriages without Parliament's approval.

The second extracts illustrate-the way that tithes were calculated and the variety of tithes that had to be paid, and are taken from the "Custom of the Manor of Barton in the Parish of Tatenhill for the year 1587"

"The Custom of the manor of Barton-under-Needwood for and concerning the payment of all manner of tithes by the inhabitants there to the Parson of Tatenhill payable on and by the Easter Book or Roll for Barton at the Chapel there yearly".

Corn   Every inhabitant is to pay his tithe of corn in kind whatsoever grain it be, by carting out or setting forth the same in sheaf, coyle, nick or reape as hath been overmore used, and the same to be taken away by the Tithe gatherer.

Item— It hath not been known that the parson hath heretofore required tithe of rakings of rye, barley or oats if the same have been gathered by the owner in a cleanly and husbandly manner, without overmuch scattering and shedding of loose corn, whereby to deceive and defraud the parson of his due tithe, for which practice, some inhabitants have of late years been questioned about.

Item— In all meadows, grounds and pastures that be mowed, the tithe is set forth in kind, every 10th cock or coyle of hay.

Garden Every inhabitant having a garden to his home, by the custom ought to pay a penny.

Bees Every inhabitant keeping any hives or stalls of bees, shall yield no tithe for the same, until he shall sell or kill any of the same. Then at Easter next following, he is to pay 3 pence in the name of his tithe of bees, wax and honey.

Sheep For the manner of payment of the tithe of wool and lambs, it is thus. The owner, out of every 10 fleeces, shall make his choice of the first two, and then the parson shall make choice of the third for his ithe fleece, and if after the tithering, there shall remain 7, 8 or 9 fleeces, the parson shall take the last fleece thereof, and give the owner allowance of a halfpenny for every fleece short of ten, but if there be but six or fewer fleeces to be tithed, the owner is to pay the parson a half penny for every fleece being six or under.

Offerings Every occupier of a messuage or yard land, freehold or copyhold, doth pay for his offering yearly, at or before Easter, the sum of four pence, for which he, his wife, and two of his children or family not earning wages, are to receive communion freely without any further charges to be paid to the parson, and likewise the clerk for his wages. Every person dwelling upon a cottage payeth also for his offerings 2 pence, and 2

	pence more yearly for the clerk's wages.
Kine & Calves	Every owner of kine shall pay at Easter yearly for his tithe, one penny for every cow that gave milk the summer or winter last, as well as for his new milch kine as for his barren kine, except the cow or kine which calved the tithe calf. (Then follows a long and complicated account of various circumstances and times of calving and the tithing procedures to be followed.)
Doales of Meadows	(These were half acre strips of meadow.) The occupier is to pay the parson one penny for the tithe, and not pay hay in kind.
Handycraft Trades	Every man of handycraft trade which is the last tithe in the Easter Book or Roll, is to make agreement with the parson for the tithe of his trade, mystery or craft, one, two, or three pennies as he can conclude on, and besides this, his offering a penny to be paid as above said.
Young Folk	For young folks, whether they be men or women, every one of them taking no wages and receiving Communion at Easter, book a penny in their name for his or her offering.
Poultry	Every inhabitant is to pay against Easter yearly, for the tithe of his House Cock, old hens, ducks and turkeys as followeth. For every cock and drake 3 eggs, for every hen, duck, or other, 2 eggs and the 7th, 8th, 9th or 10th gosling or young goose. If the owner have no more than those several numbers without giving or taking any allowance for that behalfe for the number under ten, or the number above ten so that they exceed not 17 goslings, pay two for the tithe and so pay but two. (That illustrates the complexity of the tithing!)
Swine	No inhabitant is to pay tithe for any swine other than young pigs, and thereof the parson shall have a tithe pig at seven, eight, nine or ten, and take his choice after the owner hath taken two of the best. (Another complicated calculation follows on the arrangement for tithing various numbers and littering of pigs.)
Pears	For the tithe of pears and apples, the owner is to yield the 10th part by estimation, and the same to be fetched at his house,

and for cherries, plums, and nuts, the parson is to have the tithe if he shall come or send to get him a dish of the same, otherwise not.

Hemp, Flax Lastly the 10th parte of hemp and flax is to be yielded to the parson after the same hath been washed and dried, one or more bundles when the tithe man cometh or sendeth for such tithe of hemp or flax, and if the owner send the tithe to the parson, then the bringer is to be requited for his or her pains with fitting victuals as hath evermore been accustomed to do in former parsons' times.

(Note—That Barton is a Chapel of Ease within the Parish of Tatenhill and the inhabitants and others pre-deceased have always paid their tithes according to the custom herein expressed and consequently so the whole manor.)

The long process of changing the tithing system, from payment in kind to commutation for cash, was completed by the Tithe Commutation Act of 1836. Since the end of the second world war, legislation for the full redeeming of tithes was passed, all tithe payers giving a small lump sum to terminate the annual tithe payment, and all tithes must be redeemed by the year 2000.

CHAPTER 16

The century of changes

Great changes were sweeping over England during the 18th Century, in industry, transport, and agriculture, with new towns growing around the centres of industry, and for the first time in its long history, Alrewas was changed by national events. It was in agriculture that the greatest transformation occurred, which was to affect most of the people. In parts of England for a long time, the traditional strip system on open hedgeless fields, was being slowly eroded, by fields enclosed with hedges and fences, a group of such fields adjacent to one another, and with the dwelling of the family which worked on them, quite independently from the rest of the community. The impetus to these changes was often given by enthusiastic lords of the manor, for interest in agriculture became a new fashion, following the royal example, and for the first time in history, it was realised that the holding of land was not just a traditional and inherited responsibility, but could be a source of wealth and interest.

It was impossible to implement all the innovations in farming methods with huge fields divided into narrow strips, with a farmer's land widely scattered across them, and with his cattle mixed with the whole village herd on the commons, with no chance of improvement anywhere. Where the old system satisfied the needs of the village community, it now failed to satisfy the hungry thousands in the growing towns, and new and drastic measures were necessary to supply the hungry needs of the urban populations. It soon became clear, that the only way of meeting this demand, was by completing by law, the start that had been made on enclosing the open fields, commons, waste land and forest. Small manors with few land holders could easily be enclosed by mutual agreement, and Wychnor was enclosed in 1724, and the land divided into blocks of enclosed arable and meadow lands between fourteen holders, Edmund Antrobus, John Cooper, Crue Offley, Walter Hollyer, Richard Miles, Thomas Moor, Robert Rope, John Shipton, John Slater, Henry Smith, William Smith, John Turton Esq., William Warwick and Thomas Webb. The maps of enclosure, painted on parchment by Harry Walker in 1724, reveals the presence of the weir and a mill stream from it, both of which were later utilised, after modification, by James Brindley in his construction of the Grand Trunk canal. He strengthened the weir and deepened the mill stream to enable it to take laden barges. The map reveals some interesting old names, which were either old open fields, or newly enclosed land, such as Oxe Home, the Great Lawn, Cliff Close, The Three Graves, Coney Gay, Goose Acres, Wild Orchard, Flax Piece, Butt Flatt, Faggress Close, The Twitch, etc.

Alrewas enclosures were carried out much later, and were not completed until 1810. Between 1771 and 1780, 642 such Enclosure Acts were passed by Parliament, and between 1801 and 1810, 906 went through, giving some idea of the scale of the changes taking place. The holders of four-fifths of the land had first to agree on the enclosures, and a notice was put in the church porch for three Sundays, so that villagers had the chance to object in writing. Commissioners visited the village, and maps were drawn, showing all the Villagers' holdings on the open fields. After this, following receipt in writing of claims to the land, their Award was made, dividing the land into large fields allocated to the new owners. Many villagers were unable to write, and many failed to make their claims. Within a year, the awarded blocks of land had to be surrounded by a double fence, protecting a newly-planted hedge. Many of the villagers found this a difficult task, as a fence round a four acre field would be over 600 yards long; a lot of fencing. In these first years of enclosures, many poorer villagers gave up their land, selling it to new wealthier farmers, and during this early period, Lord Lichfield's estate took in most of the manor land, and the bulk of the waste and common. The loss of rights on the Commons was compensated by the gift of allotments of land, where food could be grown, in addition to the cottage gardens. One such allotment field was at the bottom of Wellfield Road, next to Ryknield Street, and a larger one was on the west side of Fox Lane, and the lane which served the allotment holders, still exists there, but there are no longer any allotments.

Among the long list of persons who in 1810 received allotments, the following may be of interest:—

Joseph Bean, John Byker, Thomas Butler, Daniel Dolman, Nathaniel Edwards, Elizabeth Fisher, John Fox, William Gill, Thomas Goring, Daniel Heath, Walter Hickson, Eleanor Kent, Joseph Kent, Thomas Kent, John Lakin, Samuel Lakin (Malster), Samuel Lakin (Victualler), Thomas Lakin, William Lakin, Daniel Leeson, Ann Shemmonds, Mary Shemmonds, Thomas Shemmonds, William Simpson, John Smith, John Smith (Cordwainer), John Smith (Yeoman).

These from a list of 105 people.

For the first time, the village was to see landless labourers, and among the less fortunate, hunger and poverty abounded, but the large farmhouses springing up supplied homes and employment for farmworkers, dairy maids and domestic servants, and some of the deprived villagers migrated to find work in the growing industrial towns.

A few fortunates probably found work in the servicing of the canal, and in the several wharves and warehouses, for by 1771, the canal was in operation here. The digging of drainage ditches and the making of new roads and access lanes, with the gravel from the local gravel pits at Fradley near Pit Crossing, also provided work under the Surveyor of the Roads. Some employment too was found by the construction and establishment of the cotton mill in the early 1780's, but the story of the mill will be dealt with later.

The first real step in the agricultural changes, was the termination of the ancient hunting Chase at Alrewas Hay to put an end to the deprivation of arable crops on the open fields, by deer and rabbits. To carry this out, it was necessary for Parliament to pass an Act empowering John Turton to enclose part of the Chase, and this was passed in 1725. It will be interesting to quote passages from the original Act, to understand what was proposed, and to appreciate the problems of the local farmers, which it was intended to alleviate.

"Whereas John Turton of Orgreave, proprietor of the Chase of Alrewas-Hay (which extends over a large Tract of Waste and Common, as well as over most of the improved lands with the manors, lordships and parishes of Alrewas and Kings Bromley) keeps great numbers of Deer and Conies, which make vast havock and destruction in the several Cornfields, Meadows and Pastures belonging to the Lords and Tenants of the said Manors of Alrewas and Kings Bromley, who have Right of Commoning in and upon the said Chase of Alrewas-Hay.

The said John Turton hath (upon the desire and application of the several owners of the said lands, and persons who have Right of Commoning and Depasturing Cattle in and upon the said Chase), agreed to destroy his said deer and conies, and in compensation therefore, to accept a part of the said Chase, to be secured for him, his heirs and assigns, which will encourage improvements and good husbandry and tend to the publick good.

We beseech your most excellent Majesty, that it may be lawful for said John Turton to take in and enclose that parcel of waste land lying in the said Chase of Alrewas Hay, which includes both the Lodges there, all the Dark Alders, with some ground between the Dark Alders and the Woodmill pool, part of the Heath, part of the Shrub's Copy, and that part called Old Copy; all which parcel of the said Chase, together with some ancient Enclosures and Lands, is now staked out, meered and bounded, and amounts to Three Hundred and Forty Six Acres of Land.

It is further enacted, that the said John Turton and his heirs, shall or may lawfully convert the inclosed piece into a Park for the keeping of Deer, and other Beasts and Fowls of Park and Warren, or may convert the same to such other use or uses as he shall judge convenient. And that it shall not be lawful to keep, plant or preserve within any part of the said Hay or Chace, any Deer or Conies. That if the said John Turton shall neglect to remove or destroy the said deer and conies, it shall be lawful for all and every Person having Right of Commoning in the said Chace or Hay, to take, kill and destroy, either with Dogs or Guns, any Deer or Conies of the said John Turton that may be found within any Part of the said Chace or Hay, without being liable to any Penalty.

It is found by experience, to be highly inconvenient to the several commoners of both the Manors of Alrewas and Kings Bromley, to intercommon on so large a Tract of Ground as Alrewas Hay, which may be prevented. For the remedying whereof, it is hereby enacted that all the residue of the Chase or Hay, shall within twelve months be parted, separated and divided by divisionary fences, one from the North side across the North part of the said Chace, near to the Rails at the corner of the Close occupied by Edward Mott, Gent, and where several Stakes are set for that purpose. And the other of the said fences to be erected on the South side of the new inclosure, beginning at a place above Dark Alders, and to be continued along the South side of the said Chace, to the Woodmill Pool, till it join the fences of the ground occupied by Widow Startin, where stakes and meers have been fixed and placed for that purpose. (Widow Startin kept an Ale House at Curborough.)

The said divisionary fences, shall be erected within the time limited; and from time to time, be repaired with necessary Gates, Stoops, Rails, Quickset, at the Costs and Charges of the said John Turton. The commoners of each Manor shall only have rights of grazing on their own side of the divisionary fences.

That the said John Turton shall, from time to time, appoint and provide a Pinner, who shall have full power to drive off and impound all sheep trespassing in the said Hay or Chace on either side of the divisionary fences.

Be it thereford enacted that Walter Chetwynd of Grendon, Crew Offley of Whichnor, Richard Swinfen of Swinfen, Albert Walmsley of the Close, Lichfield, Thomas Parker of Parkhall, Thomas Anson of Shutborow (Shugborough), Christopher Horton of Catton, Thomas Whitbey of Haywood, Edmund Arblaster of Longdon, and Isaac Teale of Tixall Lodge, Esquires, and Richard Ryder of Lichfield, and Thomas Webb of Blacknell (Blackenhall), Gentlemen, or any five of them, Commissioners appointed by this Act, are hereby fully authorised to ascertain under their Hands and Deals, where, how and in what manner the Road leading from Kings Bromley towards Street-Hay and passing through the proposed enclosure, or any other Road or Way lying now within the compass of the new enclosure, shall be turned out of the same; and to lay out in any other part other roads as they shall think meet in lieu thereof. The same shall be duly enrolled in the Court Rolls of Alrewas and Kings Bromley by their Stewards. And that it shall not be lawful for any person to pass through the new inclosure, either on foot or with any Horse, Mule or Ass, or with any Coach, Chariot, Calash or Chaise, or with any Waggon, Cart or any Carriage whatsoever.

The said Commissioners or any Five of them, shall give Notice in the Parish Churches of Alrewas and Kings Bromley of the Time and Place of every meeting of the said Commissioners, and of the business to be done, at least Seven Days before such Meeting."

This then was the major content of the Act of 1726, establishing Alrewas Hay as an Extra-Parochial Unit, and effectively separating Alrewas from Kings Bromley and preventing damage previously done to crops by deer and rabbits. Alrewas Hay was formally added to Alrewas Parish in 1885 by Local Government Board Order.

CHAPTER 17

The coming of the canal

At the end of 1765, a meeting was held, of Potters, led by Josiah Wedgwood, with Salt producers from Cheshire, and Staffordshire landowners, to discuss the construction of a canal to join the Trent and Mersey, and thus link the North Sea with the Irish Sea. Action was agreed, and at Brownhills in the Potteries, Josiah Wedgwood ceremoniously cut the first sod on 23rd July 1766. The task of constructing the ninety-three miles of canal, with all its enormous problems of acquiring land, of engineering, and the organising of labour for the work, and finding all the necessary supplies and materials, was given to James Brindley, who had recently built the Bridgewater Canal from Worsley to Manchester. When one thinks of the work, of locks, bridges, streams to divert, road diversions, a tunnel, rivers to cross, towing paths and stone edging, of the vast amount of spoil to be removed, of clay pits to be opened for lining the canal, of the transport, the lodging and employment of the Navigators (Navvies), the supply of feeders to maintain the water levels in the sections, barge building, etc., it makes one realise the enormity of the undertaking. The whole work was finished in 1777 at a cost of £300,000.

The activities of the navvies, the engineers, carpenters, stonemasons and bricklayers, as the canal was forced through Alrewas, must have created much interest and excitement for the local people. The first reference we can find to the effects of the navigation on the village, was found on the inside of the cover of the Poor Law Record, and states Oct. 22 1774, "A Memorandum of the Inhabitants, That no Officer is to fetch no more coles for the Poore of Alrewas Without he can well fetch them as cheap as thay can by them at the Navigation". For many years after that, the only mention of the Navigation is in the Parish Register, recording the fairly regular tragic drownings. Perhaps the most difficult task in this length of canal was the crossing of the Trent. This entailed the building of a long wooden bridge from the last lock, over the millstream and river, for the horses to gain the tow path on the far river bank. To maintain a level of water in the river, a weir was necessary, and fortunately for the engineers a weir was already there. This had been constructed in the 17th Century to divert a flow of water along the newly constructed millstream to the new mill, built after the disastrous fire of 1596, a stream running round the base of Wychnor hill, to drive the mill wheel, and then to flow back into the river. The canal builders deepened it, and edged the tow path, building wooden bridges to cross flood water channels and streams. The stream had cut through the middle of the site of the ruined Wychnor Moated Manor, and it is likely that the masons used stone from the ruin to strengthen the wall of the towing path edge. A cow bridge was erected over the new canal to allow cattle to use what was then called the Hall Meadow. Eventually, the long wooden "Quarter-mile Bridge" was destroyed, decay and fire probably, and it was replaced by the present iron structure, but the stumps of the original wooden pillars can easily be traced across mill stream and river to a point slightly upstream of the end of the present bridge. Between this point and along the river towing path to the turn-off to Wychnor, was, during flood time, a real hazard for the barges. Massive snagging posts were sunk into the hadge side, so that, in the event of a barge breaking loose, the tow line could be wound round the post to prevent the barge being swept into the barrier of the weir. The iron bridge has small bays let into the rails, to allow pedestrians to avoid the heavy barge horses straining to haul the barges out of the river, and up to the lock. There was some danger, too, to be faced in going downstream, for then the barges must travel faster than a swollen river, to obtain steerage, so the horses were driven swiftly down the river tow path and into the canal towpath, to bring the boat out of the river current and into the quiet canal water. The picture of the barge-folk has gone from here, the women in long, loose skirts, striding along behind plodding horses, lithe and brown-faced, like gypsies, sometimes hurrying ahead to open the lock gates.

The coming of the canal, especially at its junction with the Coventry-Fazeley canal caused the growth of a new hamlet at Fradley Junction, where a maintenance yard, a public house and grocery store, and even a small chapel for the barge folk, were built, and in 1834 there were 77 inhabitants there. Lengthsmen were needed for the control of hedges and towpaths, wharfingers to offload, load or store goods to be dispersed or transported, and in 1834 there were three wharfingers in Alrewas, and at the Junction were listed two joiners, a stone mason, a canal surveyor and James Nichols, grocer and victualler at the Swan Inn. The Navigation Inn was built at Alrewas to cater for the barge people, and on the opposite bank were warehouses and stores. The wharf, later called Gaskell's Wharf, dealt mainly with the supply of coal to the village—it had to be fetched from the wharf in wheelbarrows—while Fradley Junction dealt with commodities being transferred from the Coventry Canal to the traffic on the Grand Trunk, and great supplies of flint were unloaded there to be shipped on later to the Potteries for use in the manufacture of pottery. Between Alrewas and Fradley Junction, the Midland Counties Cement and Plaster works were built by Newton, Oswald and Co., but only the cottages, now a private residence, are left, but still referred to as the Plastermills. Here, a hundred and fifty years ago, men worked producing for the builders, "Roman, Portland, Keene's and Parian cements, Plaster of Paris, floor plaster, gypsum, terra-cotta chimney pots, glazed sanitary ware, etc., and acting as builders' merchants".

Advertisements in 1841 state: "Conveyance by water. To all parts of the Kingdom. Pickford & Co., James Sutton & Co., Kenworthy and Co., John Danks, Matthew Heath, J. G. Ames & Co., Soresby and Flack, Thomas Best, Worthington and Co., Barrow & Co., and Tunley and Hudson from the Wharf, Kings Bromley almost daily". The canals must have been crowded with traffic in those days.

In winter, when the canal was frozen, came the thrilling sight of the ice boat, towed by two huge horses, with a crew of workers holding the safety rail which ran amidships along the boat, and rocking it furiously as the boat crashed its way through the ice. At times of flood or frost, barges could be held up and tied along the bank, and the horses would be stabled in the long stable at Kent's Bridge, or accommodated in some nearby field.

One event for the young folk of the village, was when a section was emptied to carry out lock repairs. The mud and shallow water left, was full of interest, with eels to be caught, mussels, crayfish, and many small fish stirring the muddy shallows. Local anglers, indeed many coming by train from far afield, and nowadays by car, have found pleasure and not a little sport in watching their floats in the peace of the canal and its surroundings.

Nowadays, of course, the barges and horses have been replaced by pleasure craft of all description, manned by crews from all parts, indeed many from foreign countries, and once more the canal has brought a little prosperity to the shops and the public houses this time, and it still provides leisure activity, as does the river, to many anglers.

The canal's greatest effect, which lasted for a number of years, was that it made it possible, because of easy transport to Liverpool and Hull, to build a Cotton mill here, which provided more employment than the village could provide, but that we will deal with later in a study of the Mill.

CHAPTER 18

The beginning of state welfare in Alrewas

For three hundred years and more, the problem of homeless wandering families had plagued England, aggravated and increased by the destruction of villages and farms, to make way for sheep pastures. Living in the wild wastes and extensive woods and forests, these outcasts survived by begging, poaching or stealing, and their frequent highway robberies made the roads a real hazard for travellers. Attempts to rid the land of the problem by the use of stocks or pillories, by flogging and branding, were unsuccessful, indeed they aggravated the situation by turning the beggars into vicious and often murderous fugitives. The problems of poverty, sickness and old age in villages, was partly relieved by charity and bequests centred on the church, and partly by relatives and neighbours, but was only cosmetic in effect.

In 1601, the Elizabethan Poor Law was enacted, ending a series of statutes designed to try to solve the problem of the homeless vagrant population. There were three phases to be worked out, first find the vagrants and move them back to the Parishes from which they had originated, then provide welfare for them under official control, and finally to find a method of financing it all.

Every parish was to levy a rate on all owners or occupiers of land, to provide the money, and appoint Overseers of the Poor who would supervise the movement of vagrants and provide the necessary, food clothing, medical care, housing and to generally oversee the welfare of the Poor. The able-bodied men were to be found work, and severe punishment was to be meted out to wandering "rogues and vagabonds". Almshouses were eventually to be built for those needing a home, and suitable boys were to be indentured as apprentices to local tradesmen, and where possible, girls were to be found work in service. Recipients of Poor Law Relief would not be able to leave the Parish without a permit, very necessary, for in those days, strangers—unless obviously gentry—would not be allowed to pass through a village unchallenged. Life for poor folk on relief, must, at times, have been degrading and difficult, as some extracts later will show. At nearby market towns, House of Correction were to be built to house and punish anyone "on the Parish" who misbehaved in any way, and Lichfield provided this facility for Alrewas. The paupers and their families could be provided with parish care from childbirth to burial, all their requirements being provided, from breeches to petticoats, and from soap to facecloths and handkerchiefs.

Soon after the end of the last war, an old friend brought me a long, thick, leather-bound and extremely tatty book, covered in poultry droppings and feathers, which had been revealed during the demolition of the wooden floor of a Mill End poultry house, and she asked if I would like to have it, otherwise it would be burnt. I accepted it somewhat doubtfully, but on examination, after cleaning away the accumulations left by many generations of loose chickens, it was found to be an account book, or the remains of one, containing amongst other things the Rating Accounts and the Poor Law accounts from 1771 to 1818. It still contains many hundreds of entries, many of which are uninteresting repetitions, but there are still many of local and historical interest, giving a graphic idea of conditions in Alrewas at the end of the 18th Century, when rating first began to pay for the needs of the poor, and later to improve the roads and bridges, and pay for a local Constable.

As with the Manor Court Rolls, we will quote from the Rating list, then include an almost entire Poor Law Account, and then select from the years, those entries which we hope may prove of interest to the reader.

"A Rate and Afsefsment made the 2nd Day of June 1771 On the Inhabitance of the Township of Alrewas in the County of Stafford and on all others the Owners or Occupiers of Land within the said Liberty towards the Necefsary Relief of the Poor and other Publick uses at sixpence in the Pound"

	£	s	d
Adams George Esq. (The nephew of Admiral Anson, changed his name to George Anson)	1.	1.	3.
Do for Birds			6.
Athos William			3.
Baggaley John, Gent, for Roses		1.	7.
Do (Ditto)　　　for Sellerys		1.	2.
Do　　　　　for Bruck Hay Land		2.	1½
Byker John of Alrewas			10½
Byker John of Barton		2.	6.
Daggley William			6.
Dorrington Humphrey		4.	3.
Deavill Elizabeth			6.
Dolman Thomas			9.
Daniel Charles and Dolman Moses		1.	6.
Gough George for Ludgate Close		1.	0.
Goold Ralph			6.
Goold John for his House and Land		3.	0.
Gray Thomas for Birds House, Mill End House and Booths		1.	6.
Hickson John			9.
Kent Thomas		1.	0.
Ditto for Lord Middlesex		4.	6.
Lakin Samuel		1.	0.
Leavit John Esq.		13.	4½
Mary Wooley for Robeson's			6.
Shaw John		1.	9.
Smith John for Mill End House			6.
Yeld John for his farm	1.	2.	6.
From 148 Ratepayers　　The total Rate came to	£18.	17.	0.

Passed and agreed by Samuel Lakin – Church Warding
Thomas Bayley – Overseer of the Poor
and eight others including Joseph Kent and Thomas Shemmonds

Next comes an account of the Poor Law at work.

"The Account of Thomas Biker, Overseer of the Poor for the Township of Alrewas From the 25th October 1771 to the 7th day of May 1772 including 28 Wicks"

To James Pafsand	2 wicks at 5/0 p.	Wick	10. 0.
To James Pafsand	26 " at 4/6 p.	"	5. 17. 0.
To James Muse	28 " at 3/0	"	4. 4. 0.
To Jane Anson	8 " at 2/0	"	16. 0.
To „ „	20 " at 1/-	"	1. 0. 0.
To John Holyer	28 " at 2/-	"	2. 16. 0.
To Joseph Grice	7 " at 6d	"	3. 6.
To Hopkins Chield	28 " at 2/-	"	2. 16. 0.
To Ann Willson	8 " at 2/-	"	16. 0.
To Ann Willson	20 " at 1/-	"	1. 0. 0.
To Ann Tomson	8 " at 1/6d	"	12. 0.
To Dorothy Butler	6 " at 1/6d	"	9. 0.
To Dorothy Butler	5 " at 1/-	"	5. 0.
To Mary Thomas	8 " at 2/6	"	1. 0. 0.
To Mary Thomas	20 " at 2/0	"	2. 0. 0.
To our part of the Constables Account			2. 18. 7.
To the County Rates			2. 13. 0.
To my journey and Expense			1. 6.
To the County Rates			2. 4. 3.
To my journey and Expense			1. 4.
To Joseph Kents Bill for Daggley's House			7. 10.
To Joseph Fishers Bill			4. 6.
To Thomas Daggley at various times			15. 6.
To Jane Jonson in Distrefs			3. 0.
To Peter Jonson in Distrefs			6. 2.
To James Fishers family at various times			1. 6. 0.
To clothing for Hopking's child			9. 3.
To covering a pare of Steas for Do.			1. 4.
To making a slip „ „			10.
To making a patecote for Do.			3.
To shues meding „			9.

To a pare of stockings „		1.	2.
To things for mending „		1.	7½
To Mrs Austin mending for Ditto			6.
To Joseph Grice family over 21 weeks	1.	15.	0.
To a shirt for Joseph Grice		3.	6.
To a pare of shues for Do.		1.	0.
To a pare of Clogs for Do.		1.	4.
To James Pafsand for mending Shirts			6.
To James Pafsand for a pare of Breeches		3.	0.
To making them		1.	6.
To Cleing Pafsand			6.
To 6 yds of Cloth for Do.		7.	0.
To Macking them		1.	0.
To a pare of Stockings		1.	6.
To 12 Cwt Coles		7.	0.
To 3 Cwt of Coles for Dorothy Butler		1.	9.
To Ann Williamson in Destrefs		2.	0.
To Ann Williamson Do		1.	6.
To 3 Cwt of Coles for Do.		1.	9.
To Fillip Salt Going to the Justices		1.	0.
To his Examination		1.	0.
To going with Fisher to Edingal and Widenton		1.	0.
To Expence			4.
To meet Hargrave Hofficer at the Justices and Samuel Lakin		2.	0.
To Expence with them		3.	6.
To going to the Justice with Elizabeth Harding		1.	0.
To Expence with her		1.	4.
To hir Oath		1.	0.
To a Warrand for the Man		1.	0.
To Elizabeth Goold being Whith hir		3.	0.
To hir lying Hin	1.	0.	0.
To the Doctor for laying Hir	2.	2.	0.
To the Doctor for James Muse	2.	12.	6.
To the Doctor for Peter Jonson		3.	0.

To two Year Rent for Ann Williamsons House	3.	10.	0.
To thatching & Sarving the Thatcher		3.	0.
To Hay and Lugs		1.	0.
To Mr. Whighting for glazing		5.	0.
To William Bayles whyfe being at Johnsons		6.	0.
To the Woman having things from Thos. Grays		4.	5.
To Elizabeth Goold for Bear and Ale		2.	1.
To Laying the Wooman at Millingtons		3.	0.
To May Millingtons Bill		7.	3.
To Going to Whitchnor bridges for a Warrand for the New Officer and Expence		1.	4.
To Samuell Laking Going to Barton		1.	6.
To Thomas Jonson at sundry times for 10 wicks		13.	0.
To 1 cwt of Coales			10.
To a Loaf for Thos. Jonson			6.
To going to Hanslow for a warrand to sarve Rich. Heathcote		1.	0.
To expense upon the Roade		1.	6.
To expence whith my horse and self that night		3.	6.
To 4 Tole Gates			4.
To Hour Horses at Whincote			6.
To Hour Expence at Do.		3.	6.
To Hour Expence Coming Home		1.	0.
To 3 Jurneys to Hanslow		4.	6.
To 3 Days Whith the Horse		5.	0.
To Joseph Kent Bill Fetching Heathcote		6.	9.
To Joseph Kent for attending Him at Grays		1.	0.
To Attending him that night Coming		1.	6.
To Too men attending him the next night		2.	0.
To myself and my Horse		2.	6.
To Samuel Lakin and Horse to the Justices		3.	0.
To the Expence at Ridwer		1.	6.
To Expence at Barton		6.	6.
To too Horses to Tamworth & Expence		9.	0
To Thos Grays Bill	1.	4.	0.

To Hopkins Stockings and Mending forgot	2.	6.
To a Scuttle Forgot		7.
To a Spade Forgot	2.	6.
To a Peal (pail) Forgot	1.	6.
To the Midwife Forgot for Ann Wilison	3.	0.
To a pare of Hoase	1.	10.
To pafsing these Accounts	4.	0.
To Isaac Deavill Bill		4.
To a days work forgot to John Thomas	1.	6.
To a Wascote for hould Pafsand	4.	0.
To Isaac Fisher for his Brother 7 whicks	5.	6.
To James Pafsand	18.	0.

This then is a fairly typical list of expenditure and welfare in
Alrewas over two hundred years ago.

We will now extract from the accounts, those individual items which
may prove of interest, which occured between 1771 and 1818

To a Bottle of Daffies for Mary Thomas		1.	3.
To going to the Justice about Bean		1.	0.
To Peter Jonson for stoping holes at the House			6.
To Pade to George fee for making a shirt			6.
To a pare of bedsides and mat for S. Jonson		6.	0.
To a bedcord for Jonson		1.	6.
To 8 yards of hempen cloth for Jonson		6.	4½
To stuff for cleaning Mary Thomas of the Itch		4.	6.
To Thomas Austin for Bleeding S. Jonson			6.
To Doctor Leay for Muse	2.	2.	0.
To 14 Tun and 28 Hundreds of Coles for the Poor	8.	1.	9.
To the Caridge of the coles to the Poor		11.	8.
To a man for the Help to lode the Coles		2.	4.
Pd to Thomas Slater for one years rent for Wm Hill	4.	4.	0.
To a Round Frock made for Ezekial Willcox		2.	0.
,, ,, ,, ,, ,, for William Dean		2.	0.
To Knitting and Darning a Pare of Hose for Ezekial Willcox		1.	10.

To Wm. Bradshaw for making 2 shirts for John Ley		2.	0.
To a pint of Wine for Daniel Carthy		3.	0.
To Mary Dolman for attendance on Ann Ley		5.	0.
For 19 ounce of Worsted for Thomas Riley and Ezekial Willcox		4.	9.
For advertising in the Birmingham Newspaper for Parish Apprentices	1.	10.	4.
Paid cash to Susannah Turton		4.	0.
Journey to the New Inn on the Forest		3.	0.
Advertising in the Stafford Newspaper for Parish Apprentices		7.	6.
To Grice's wife for cleaning Mary Thomas		1.	6.
To the Doctor stuff for Mary Thomas		1.	0.
To a bedgown and Petecote for Ann Jonson		7.	7.
To a pare of breeches for Pafsam		2.	11½
To going to Mr. Simpson consarning Fany Badkin and expence		1.	6.
To Fany Badkin at the Crifsing (Christening)		2.	6.
To a Man found in Spelsus (Spellow)			9.
To a Warrand for Daniel Sylvester		1.	0.
To Sir Roger Newdegate signing it and a gide		2.	0.
To expence at Nuneaton, Lichfield and other places and new shoes and truble	1.	6.	8.
To Edward Gillotte Bill for eting and ale		6.	6.
For Macking and Wheshing 2 shirts for Thos. Dagley		1.	6.
To a Blanket for Joseph Grice		4.	6.
To a Shift for Ann Jonson		3.	2.
To Peter Jonson when ill		1.	0.
To fetching the Doctor sundry times		1.	0.
To Daniel Silvester attending him		1.	0.
To the wimin that lade him out		1.	0.
To Bread, Chees and Drink for the Funeral		3.	0.
To Bering Fees		3.	0.
To a Shroud		5.	6.
To a Coffin		13.	0.

To making Ann Jonsons smocke		1.	0.
To mending her shoes			8.
To a Winder frame & shutter		4.	0.
To 11 Ton of Coles at 12s p Ton	6.	12.	0.
To going to Shaneston with Sarah Baggley		2.	0.
To expences ,, Do.		10.	9.
To the Chaise for Sarah Baggley	1.	1.	0.
To a Winder Frame and Shutter and work on the 5 Hames Houses		7.	0.
To Isaac Deavill for Iorn Woork		1.	6.
To Old Glafs		1.	4.
To Mr. Nuttall for Glasing		6.	9.
To Lime and Work to point the walls		6.	0.
To Upton for taking Dilk's Child aprentice and expences	5.	3.	0.
To Straw to Thatch the Five Houses		10.	6.
To the Tatcher and his man	1.	2.	6.
To Ale for ditto		5.	2.
To Thomas Edgley for going to Wedgsbry to take Mary Rose & 2 Children with order	1.	1.	0.
To ,, ,, for taking Brooks family to Wallsal	1.	10.	0.
To taking John Nash family to Roster and expences	1.	3.	6.
To a hat and stockings for Thompsons child		2.	8.
To a coffin for Thomas Daggley		12.	0.
To a shroud for Do.		6.	0.
To the Removal of William Smith		9.	6.
To a Handkerchief for Ann Williamson		1.	4.
To expence of the Funeral of M. Roberts		4.	4.
To Mr. Evans for the Coffin and Work	1.	8.	6.
To the Bural Fees		4.	3.
To a Shroud for ditto		5.	0.
To 2 men for the Army (1797—Napoleonic War)	48.	3.	0.
To Bread for Woodword			7.
To George Jee for Lodging and expence for S. Woodward		5.	4.

To Flannel cloth and things for Sarah Woodward		3.	7.
To Sundry goods for Sarah Woodward		5.	2.
To Bread, Chees, Sugar and Tea, and Butter for Ditto		3.	11.
To Bread, Chees and Sundry things for Ditto		3.	6.
To George Jee for lodging for for Ditto		5.	4.
To Bread and Mentance for Ditto		13.	9½
To George Jee for fetching the Doctor			6.
To Saml Lakin for Straw for the 5 Houses	1.	16.	0.
To John Johnson for Thatching at Do		14.	6.
To John Wright for Wattering at Do		2.	0.
To 200 of Neails 1/0 Ale at Lakins		11.	0.
To Hay for Bonks 2/6 Lugs 1/0		3.	6.
To Eliz. Goold at Sunday times when ill	1.	5.	0.
To her Sister for Luking after her		4.	0.
To Daniel Dolman Junr. as Relief	2.	0.	0.
To Hiring Substitutes for Local Militia (1810)	17.	8.	8.
A Jackett for Jacob Fletcher		7.	0.
One years Rent due to John Tunley for Thos. Lea	5.	4.	0.
Paid the Funeral Expences for Daniel Dolman's wife	2.	0.	6.
To Mary Croft—Expence coming to Alrewas and one weeks pay for child		5.	0.
Postage of a letter to Derby (1812)		1.	2.
„ „ from „			7.
To Phineas Dolman 4 weeks at 12/— and 2 at 9/—	3.	6.	0.
A Handkerchief for Sarah Fisher		2.	3.
My Half Years Salary	5.	5.	0.
Wine and Ale for Phineas Dolman during his illnefs		11.	4.
Gilbert John Clark's Survey of Land	3.	19.	0.
Three Days journey to Coventry		10.	6.
Coach Faire		14.	0.
Expences	1.	4.	0.
Paid Joseph Saunders One Years Shaving for John Ley		5.	0.
Paid Peter Willcox for 6 leeches for bleeding Lydia Hodgets		4.	6.
Taking Account of the Population in 1811	1.	1.	0.

To a Coffin for Salts Child		6.	0.
To a Shroud ,,		3.	6.
To Funral expences		3.	5.
To going to Lichfield about Thos. May (1786)		1.	8.
To shurts and cote for Nevills child		2.	6.
To going to Hillridwar to Mrs. Webb, myself and mare		5.	0.
To Henry Smith for thathing the 5 Houses (Almshouses)	2.	2.	2.
To James Derry — sarving the thather & watring the straw	1.	5.	3.
To Bakewell, wife and child, Bed and Bord		7.	6.
To Geo. Jee, nefsaryes for Hannah Nevill when ill		4.	2.
To Buriel fees for Nevills child		3.	0.
To a Coffin for Hannah Nevill		9.	0.
To a Shroud -do-		4.	0.
To Thos. Brown for Clothing Hannah Nevills child		18.	0.
To a Bedgound for Eliz Royle and making		6.	4½
To expences with John Brookes	2.	4.	1.
To taking him and his family to Wasall		10.	0.
To 500 of Bricks for the 5 Houses		10.	6.
Paid Cash for 2 Tables and Chairs for James Fisher		4.	9.
To Will Price for Household Furniture for James Fisher		15.	7.
Two days journey to Stoke		6.	0.
Expences		16.	6.
Horse Hire		7.	0.
To Bread & chees & tobacco & Meterles & Joseph Fisher for mending Pafsands dore and Sarow Fisher for Claing him		10.	6.
To Paid Upton for taking Dilk's child Apprentice	5.	3.	8.
1771 To 36 feet of Spars		3.	0.
To laths and neals and lugs		2.	0.
To a Thather and Sarver		6.	0.
To 7 Thrave of Straw		17.	6.
To John Whiting for glazing		11.	10.
To William Lonts Bill	2.	12.	10.
To Joseph Kents bill	5.	16.	10.

To Joseph Fisher ,,	1.	18.	3.
To 8,500 bricks at 12s per thousand	5.	2.	0.
To 56 strike of Lime	2.	16.	0.
To Carige of bricks	5.	6.	3.
To carige of Sand, and Straw, and Timber		14.	0.
To 3 locks for the doors		4.	6.

These then are some sample entries from the Poor Law Accounts.

In 1771, the total cost was £88. 18. 4¾, but by 1817 it had risen to £783. 3. 11¾, and over the country many Parishes became bankrupt, and by 1834, Workhouses took over the function of looking after the poor and homeless. Here, the Enclosures of the Open Fields & Commons, complete by 1810, left many poor villagers without the means of supporting themselves with the food they had once produced for themselves. So that more of them went "on the Parish", and for much longer periods than in earlier years.

A few notes on loose pages reveal that workmen drew and spread gravel on the roads at 2 shillings a day, gravel mostly obtained from the Fradley pits.

1778 The Constables account states: —

To expence shirshing the public in Church Time	1.	6.
To ,, taking a boteman to the justice	7.	0.
To riting a list of free and Copyholders	1.	0.
To Joseph Kents Bill for mending the Pinfold	11.	6.

1780

To Joseph Adam to repairing the Stocks	15.	7.
To going to Burton to pay the Toll penny	1.	1.

1781

To a lock for the Pound		10.
To poor men and women with Passes	5.	2.
To a woman with childe		5.
To going to the Navigation Inn	2.	6.

A few remains of Church Wardens accounts are also in the book and contain the following items: —

The Accounts of Samuel Backwell, Samuel Winter and John Kent–Church Wardings for the Parish of Alrewas 7 January to 12 Dec 1778.

To a new set of bell ropes		12.	0.
To putting them up		1.	0.
To 3 pints of Ale when we lucked the Churchyard fence over			6.
To a lock for the Lightgates			9.
To Ale when the old Mill fence was put down			6.
To Wine for a sacrement		7.	4.
To John Thomas for ringing the Curfew and winding the clock	1.	12.	0.
To bread for a sacrement		2.	0.
To a Prayer for the Queen		5.	6.
To John Thomas for the moolds (Moles)	1.	15.	0.
To taking the planks and posts to the Comon		1.	0.
To Sparrows at sundry times		10.	0.
To the Shurtplis		7.	0.
1778			
To Joseph Kents bill for Tacking the dial down and putting it up and other jobs		8.	8.
To 2 quarts of Ale			8.
To Stringers bill for painting and gilding the dial	1.	5.	0.
To a prayer for the Queen		1.	0.
To taking up Statfold fence		1.	6.
1776			
To sparrows at sundry times		6.	1.
To John Thomas ½ a years moold catching	1.	15.	0.
To Samuel Lakin for 30 dozen sparrows		10.	0.
To William Smith for 10 dozen and a half		3.	6.
To sparows		6.	6.
To sparrows		8.	2.
Sparows and maending the Loft and other things	3.	11.	2.
Paid for mowing and ale (Churchyard)	1.	4.	6.
To Ale when putting Down the fens at the Hould Mill		1.	0.

These then are a few odd items of expenditure in the Churchwardens' Accounts, and include many for sparrows, but where they were caught is not stated. It may have been in the Church tower, or maybe from the sparrow-infested thatch of the cottages.

N.B. In all extracts, the original spelling has been kept, but the words are fairly easy to interpret.

CHAPTER 19

The mill

There is no mention of a mill at Alrewas in the Domesday Book, and it is possible that in early Norman times, the corn of the Alrewas peasants would have been ground at Wychnor, which had a mill in 1086. The site of this earliest mill at Wychnor was almost certainly near to the river weir, which may have been constructed to provided a mill race to drive the waterwheel. The possible short course of this millstream can still be traced as a dry ditch with no present function. The newer mill at Wychnor, built after the old mill was destroyed by fire in 1596, was built further from the river and the old Manor House, its mill stream now the course of the canal, passing through the ruin of the deserted manor house, for by this time the new Wychnor Hall had been built at the site of the present Hall.

By the 13th Century, Alrewas had an established mill, indeed the early records in 1260 speak of two mills, a grinding mill and a sieving mill. These may have been sited where the present mill stands, for early construction work on a dam, would provide a foundation for later and bigger dams, all of which would stand on a natural shallow of the river. An early agreement was made between the lord of the Manor, Thomas Turton, supported by local gentry, Sir John Needham, Thomas Curzon, William Goring, Edward Francis, John Rose and John Audley who acted as Feoffees, and John Dilks, William Baggaley, William

Charles, Thomas Oneley, John Smith, John Brown, Thomas Simmonds, John Yeld, John Cooper and Isaac Harper, representing the tenants. It was witnessed by Sir John Gresley, the Earl of Dorset, John Elson and William Shepherd of Oakley.

Some clauses of the agreement stated, as numbered in the document: —

5. Tenants to grind all their corn at the mill.
6. Tenants to repair the mill dam and the earthworks, the lord to repair the mill.
11. Heriots — the lord to have the best quick beast or the best goods.
23. The tenants shall have their fishing in the water with frike or strike three days a week, that is Wednesday, Friday and Saturday, as it hath of old times been accustomed.

The arrival of the canal drew Alrewas into the main stream of the industrial revolution, which was sweeping through England in the 18th Century, and in 1784 the new mill was opened. It was five storeys high and measured 140 feet by 30 feet, dwarfing the old mill which stood nearby, being founded by Thomas Dicken, a mercer and brewer from Burton. By the early 1790's, after some early difficulties, the mill progressed, spinning cotton and employing up to 300 workers. By 1815, although ideally situated for water power, the mill had been equipped with a 45 horse power steam engine.

The raw cotton to make the thread and cloth was purchased by Benjamin Wilson of Burton from South America, the West Indies and the southern States of U.S.A., and came to Alrewas from Liverpool via the new canal. In 1800, his first consignment of 90 bags of cotton from a Lisbon merchant, went to Joseph Greaves, a Liverpool cotton broker, who sent it to Alrewas by Grand Trunk canal. In 1801, he bought 100 bales of cotton from Charleston, Carolina, followed by 100 bales of New Orleans cotton from New York, and 150 bales of best sea island cotton from Philadelphia. Much of this must have been dispersed among other mills, but during the last three months of 1801, he bought cotton on behalf of Alrewas mill to the value of £11,000.

The local spinning mills provided thread particularly for local hosiery manufacturers and hand loom weavers, but some of the products went further afield, and even abroad. Many consignments were sent to German ports, and then distributed to the Fairs at Hamburg, Leipzig, Frankfurt and Bremen, and Alrewas mill was fully involved in this through Benjamin Wilson's Baltic connections. In 1803, he sent 2,500 bundles of cotton yarn from Manchester, and several hundred bundles of knitting yarn and cotton twist produced at Alrewas, to John Hutchinson at Altona, Germany, and similar consignments to Danzig and Konigsberg in, Russia.

Once the mills were built and the machinery installed by skilled workers, the mills could be operated by mainly unskilled workers, who could quickly be taught to operate the spinning machines. Women and children were employed in the carding and spinning sections, men being employed as overseers, mechanics, clerks, weavers and dressers. To overcome the labour shortages, and obtain cheap operators, the local newspapers in nearby towns advertised for apprentices, and these would be found by Overseers of the Poor, who would pay their indentures, but would reduce Parish expenditure in the long term, for the apprentices rarely returned to their villages. Here at Alrewas, a tenement building was erected near to the mill, to house these apprentices, usually girls, and this would almost certainly have been Elm Tree House. In addition, twelve new cottages were erected for the workers, and a "pleasant convenient messuage fit for the residence of a principal or superintendent".

Around 1810, the mill was in serious financial trouble, and Joseph Dicken, who lived at Highlands Park, Rangemore, and who had become a partner in 1808, was made a bankrupt in 1815, and the mill was offered for sale several times for £4,000, but there were no buyers, and it was abandoned soon after. It re-opened later for spinning worsted yarn, and in 1841, it employed 65 workers but in 1851, unable to compete with the northern textile industry it closed down again.

In the same years as the mill operated again, part of the mill was occupied by William Shaw who was a flour miller, and by John Wilson a corn miller, while the rest of the mill was used by M. and W. Bond & Co., for the manufacture of tape and smallware, and between 1860 and 1871 the company of W. & W. Bond were the proprietors of Alrewas Flour Mill Co. (Smallware was the name for tapes and ribbons.)

In 1818, part of the mill was destroyed by arson, and the incendiary was condemned to death, but the sentence was commuted to life imprisonment on the grounds of insanity. Small industries were carried on by various tradesmen occupying parts of the mill buildings and in 1834 wire-drawing was carried on by John Kent, Hackett and Essex who were needle makers, a corn miller, and

T. W. Haythorn, a lace-thread doubler.

There has, for many years, been the idea that the tall Trent Villas in Park Road, were warehouses for the mill, but the description of the mill in the advertisement for sale, appear to discount the idea, for after the detail of the mill and machines, it states: "Together with extensive and requisite Warehouses and other Buildings contiguous to the Mill, and a large commodious House for the reception of Apprentices, 12 cottages for work people, etc etc".

In 1888, Mr. Joseph Cartwright, who had had a steam mill erected on the canal side near to Gallows Bridge, built Alrewas House, but his venture was not a success and in 1900, it had been taken over by Herbert Bakewell Whetstone. Living opposite to him in Shugborough Villa (at this time the home of Dr. Horton) lived Mr. W. Ball, a leading Alrewas character, with his large family, and his youngest son, out of admiration for Mr. Whetstone, was christened Herbert Bakewell Whetstone Ball, whose older brother was Mr. Nelson Ball, well-loved for so many years. From 1896 to 1904, the water mill was operating as a flour mill under the proprietorship of John Lander, John Walker being his manager, and later, during the First World War, the mill was operating under Charles Watson.

It was after the First World War that the mill became a real success, under the dynamic partnership of Messrs. Egerton Orme and Frank Durose. Under them, Alrewas mill became a flourishing business, producing meal, cattle food, poultry food, seeds, etc., their lorries ranging wide through the farms of the Midlands. Huge lorries made regular trips to the Liverpool docks bringing back grain, soya beans, etc. It became an efficient and prosperous industry, operating now with electrically-powered machinery. Unfortunately, the creators of the modern mill are no longer with us, but they put Alrewas on the map. In the 1930's the name of Alrewas Mill was blazoned in huge white letters across the lofty roof, and could be seen from a great distance. Unfortunately, the steeplejack who put the name on, had to paint it out when the Second World War started, as it would provide a signpost to enemy pilots, by fixing their position. The mill is now run by a national company, and is apparently in full operation.

Before the beginning of the textile mill, some cottage industry was carried out in Alrewas, as the following inventory of the possessions of John Wilcox the elder of Alderwas, made after his death in 1633, will show.

116

	s.	d.
In the chamber over the Shop (work room)		
Linen yarn and unspun flax	10.	0.
In the Milk House		
2 (Spinning) Wheels, a reel and 4 bags	5.	0.
In the Shop		
2 Looms and implements belonging to his trade	60.	0.
Outside		
28 Sheep	110.	0
Corn on the ground	26.	8.
Corn unthreshed	25.	0.
A cart, 1 plough, horse harness and implements	66.	8.
30 Hurdles and 2 little ladders	10.	0.
5 Horses and a colt	160.	0.
3 Yearling calves and a young calf	60.	0.

Silk weaving was done at Lichfield in 1674, as the inventory of Richard Riley's possessions show, among which were: —

	£	s.	d.
In the Shoppe etc			
Three loomes with silke and working geares	1.	10.	0.
Two dozen Bothoms (Skeins of Silk)		10.	0.
In the Chamber over the house and shoppe and entrye: —			
Three dozen of Bothoms and hair sifes (sieves)	2.	5.	0.
One hackney saddle, yarne, toe, course wool etc		16.	0.
In the backside and barne and at doore			
Mucke, hey and implements, two piggs,			
two hives of bees	2.	5.	0.
Five cowes	10.	6.	8.
Twentye sheepe, young and old	5.	0.	0.
Hard corne, pease and barley upon ground	10.	0.	0.

While on the subject of the mill and the river, it might be appropriate to refer to the longstanding dispute which rumbled on for many years, over the fishing rights in the river. The freehold and leasehold tenants claimed a traditional right to fish the river from their land on three days a week, as has already been referred to, but this was disputed by the Earl of Lichfield, and the agreement, copies of which existed, simply disappeared, either never being deposited in the church chest, or being removed without permission. This, at any rate, was the theory current amongst the villagers at the turn of the century. In 1906, Mr. W. Chambers, caught fishing from the bank on land owned by Mr. E. Mellor (father of Mr. Tom Mellor of Essington Farm), was prosecuted by the Birmingham Piscatorial Society, who had leased the fishing rights from the Earl of Lichfield. Mr. Chambers stated that he had been given permission to fish from Mr. Mellor's land, and the case eventually came before the High Court, the costs of the defence being borne by Mr. Mellor, who had secured no financial help from the rest of the village. In an action dated 12th January 1907, entitled, "The Earl of Lichfield V. Chambers and another", 1906 in the Chancery Division of the High Court of Justice, judgement was given in the Earl's favour.

It was declared that the Earl is the owner of the several and exclusive fishery in and of the bed and soil of the whole stream of the River Trent, from Burway Ford to the point where the River Tame joins the Trent, except the Backwaters or Channels of the River Trent running from the Wooden Bridge at the end of Great Burlake Meadow, to the lower end of Little Burlake Meadow, and from the upper part of Longlake Meadow to the Lawn Ford, and it was ordered that the defendants, William Chambers and Edward Mellor, their servants, Agents, Lessees or Licensees be perpetually restrained by injunction from fishing in his Lordship's said several and exclusive fishery.

The whole question as to the Lord's fishing rights was fought out in the year 1752, in an action brought by John Turton Esq., the then Lord of the Manor, against one Thomas Hurdman.

The action was tried at the Stafford Assizes, and the jury found that there was no right of free fishery or common of fishery in the River Trent, belonging to freeholders or copyholders of the Manor, either at any time or on three days in the week, and Hurdman was condemned in Damages and Costs.

No person has therefore any right or is in any way entitled to fish in the said Rivers Trent, Tame and Mease within the boundaries of the said Manor, or from either bank of such Rivers, without the permission of the Earl of Lichfield, as such Lord of the Manor, or of those claiming title under him.

Signed George Birch—Steward

The Thomas Hurdman referred to previously had to pay damages of 41 shillings, and costs of £146. 15. 6d.

This was a tremendous expense for an Alrewas man in 1752, and it was the fear of such expensive costs that frightened all but Mr. Mellor, who earned great respect and admiration for his stubborn courage in trying to uphold a traditional right.

CHAPTER 20

Elizabethan goods and chattels in Alrewas

There are still some dwellings in Alrewas and Fradley which are of Tudor and early Stuart origin. Some can easily be recognised as half-timbered thatched cottages, but others have been added to and encased in brick shells, which have effectively obliterated the timbered structure, while tiles have replaced the original thatch. The timber would be of local origin, and the bricks were locally made at the brickyard at Hillyards Cross, now the site of Mr. Middleton's farm. Adzed beams are still fairly common, and much prized, and not many years ago, wattle and daub walls, and plaster and rush-layered floors in upper rooms could still be found, as well as long brick bread ovens. These are features of early housing which are well-known, because of wide survival in many other local villages. What is more obscure however, is the knowledge of furnishings, fittings, utensils and tools which were in use in those dwellings.

In Elizabethan times, as has already been mentioned, inventories of the possessions of a deceased person had to be made by responsible neighbours, with an estimate of the value of the goods and chattels in the household, and it is from these that a fair idea can be obtained of living conditions in Alrewas 400 years ago. Obviously, differences existed in the circumstances and wealth of the people living here, so to form a reasonable picture, three men's inventories have been chosen, first a blacksmith named Richard Palm, then an average husbandman, Richard Rose, and finally a wealthier yeoman farmer from Fradley, John Gilbert, whose family resided for a number of years at the Hall, and who was a churchwarden at Alrewas. He wrote in his will that, "as for my body, which came of the earth, I render and bequeath it to the earth again to be buried in the Parish Church of Alrewas neare unto my usual seat there".

First then, the inventory of Richard Palm, "the goodes and Cattelles of Richard Palm of Allrewas Deceased apased and valued the 10th daye of Aprill 1592 by John Butler, Thomas Morley, with others".

First	1 Cowe	30s.	
	1 Yearling she caulfe	14s.	
	1 Other cowe and caulfe	40s.	
	1 Pigge	3s.	4d.
	2 Towillies, 2 Littell Koverings, 4 Canvas shettes,		
	1 Boulster, 1 Pillowe, 1 matteresse		
	1 Potte of Brasse, 1 potte of yarne (iron) 2 Kettells,		
	1 Skellett, 1 Skymer, 1 Candlestick, 5 Plattes,		
	1 Sawser	15s.	0d.
	1 Coubbard, 1 churne, 1 peale, 1 lourne,		
	1 Kymnell, 1 myle (mill), 1 Barrell, 2 Cheares	5s.	0d.
	Paynted clothes, 3 coffers, 1 handyron, A peare of		
	potte houckes and Pottehangels, 1 peare of tonges	5s.	0d.
	His apparrell	6s.	8d.

Total £6. 8s.

In his will he states:

"I give and bequeath to my sonne Jhon Palm all my tooles that are belonging to my occupation of yorne and of woode and are in the Shoppe"

An inventory of the goodes and cattelles of Richard Rose the Elder, deceased, preased and valued the 18th daye of October 1596 by Walter Bury, gent, Jhon Butler, and James Geninges.

		£	s.	d.
First	4 Cowes	6.	13.	4.
	2 Winter heffers		53.	4.
	1 Yearling bullocke		20.	0.
	2 Weaning Calves		20.	0.
	2 Mares	3.	0.	0.
	2 Swynne		13.	4.
	3 fether beds, 3 matteresses, 3 Koverings			
	5 Blanketes 4 Boulesters, 6 pilloes 3 Bedsteades	4.	0.	0.
	3 Peare of flaxen shettes, 2 peare of shakedown			
	3 Peare of Nogen shettes, 3 pillowe Beares,			
	5 Bourd cloths, 3 Towelles, 12 Napkins, 8 Cushions		36.	0.
	1 Cubbord		13.	4.
	1 Foulden Table		10.	0.
	1 Bason and yrons of mastelon		3.	4.
	5 Voyders, 5 Puterdishes 7 porringers, 5 Sawsers			
	3 Saltes 4 Candelstickes		10.	0
	2 Coffers (chests) 2 whitches ? 2 Table bourdes			
	2 Formes 3 Cheares 4 Lournes 2 Barrels		24.	0
	1 Chaffing dishe and frying panne		25.	0
	1 Handyron (Poker), 1 Fyer shovell, 1 pair of			
	Tonnges, Potte hengels, potte houckes and gridyrons			
	1 Bill and axe, a hatchett, 2 Spittes, I peare			
	of cobards with other yorne ware		10.	0.
	4 peals (pails), 2 Bowels with silver and 30 wodden			
	dishes and other woddon stuff		5.	0.
	Hennes and Geese		4.	0.
	Corne and hey in the barne and field		50.	0.
	His aparrel		10.	0

Sum £29. 10s. 8d.

Lastly, "An inventory of the goodes and cattels of Jhon Gilbert of Fradley within the P'she of Alrewas deceased, aprased by Jhon Byker, Jhon Butler, Robert Duffield, Henry Dowell, the 23rd day of September 1591".

	£	s.	d.
Fyrste VI Oxen (For ploughing)	21.	0.	0.
9 Cowes and a Bull	20.	0.	0.
10 Winter beastes	23.	0.	0.
10 Yearlinges	8.	0.	0.
8 Weaning Calves	3.	0.	0.
3 Mares and 3 Coltes	7.	0.	0.
1 Horse coulte and 1 filly	5.	0.	0.
2 other coultes	11.	0.	0.
6 Score shep with lambes	33.	0.	0.
4 Olde Swynne, 1 boore & 6 young score		30.	0.
Wheate, Rye, Barley and Ottes	20.	0.	0.
Item— Hey		40.	0.
1 Yorne bounde Weane, 2 Harrows, 3 yorne teames			
2 Ploughes with such stuff	6.	13.	4.
An Axe, 2 Billes, 1 mattocke, 2 Yorne wedges		3.	4.
4 Brasse pannes, 6 Brasse pottes, 4 Kettels, 1 Skeller		6.	8.
29 peces of puter, 7 sawsers, 12 Counterset dishes			
2 chaffing dishes, 6 Candelstickes, 2 Saltes		42.	0.
2 Coubbards, 2 Table bourdes with frames			
3 Fourmes, 1 pair stoolles, 3 cheares		33.	4.
2 Standing beddes with testers, 6 peare of Bedsteades			
1 presse, 4 Coffers		43.	4.
3 Featherbeddes, 4 Mattereses	3.	6.	4.
1 Kovering, 7 Koverletes	3.	0.	0.
6 Blankets, 8 twil shettes		30.	0.
8 Boulsters, 4 Pillowes		29.	0.
30 Peare of Sheettes (10 of flaxen, 20 of canvas shettes,			
4 Table clothes, 2 Dossen table napkins 8. 0. 0.	8.	0.	0.
5 Stone of wolle	3.	6.	8.
Wodde and timber		5.	0.

4 Barreles, 4 loommes, 6 peales, a kneading tubbe			
1 Churne, a dishe bourde, 2 Spinning wheles,			
2 littell whelles, a Boulting tube	3.	13.	4.
4 Silver sponnes		20.	0.
paynted cloths with silver dishes and stuff		10.	0.
6 Cushens 2 benches		3.	4.
3 Broches, 1 peare of cobbardes, 1 Frying panne,			
2 handeyornes, 1 fyer shovell, 1 peare of tonnges			
potte houckes and potte hangels and iron ware		10.	0.
Hennes, Geese, duckes and capons		10.	0.
His aparrel		40.	0.

Some idea of the frugality of Elizabethan homes can be gleaned from these lists, which contain few items catering for luxury or comfort as we understand it today. There was nothing superfluous in the homes, there was not space for anything which was not purely functional, and the chief features of the furniture, utensils, etc., most of which were locally manufactured, were simplicity of design and durability.

CHAPTER 21

Schooling in Alrewas

For many centuries, children were schooled in the home, in the fields or in the workplace by their parents, learning to take on the work when time made it necessary. A very few served as apprentices to learn a trade, while still fewer went to Grammar Schools or Universities.

The early records of the 17th and 18th centuries revealed that many of the responsible villagers, called upon to witness accounts, were unable to sign their names, having to make a cross, countersigned by a witness to the mark made.

Reading and writing were for the few, most villagers lacking the opportunity, or having little time for book-learning, being fully occupied in the daily struggle to feed, clothe and house themselves, at a time when even the youngest members of a family were found plenty of work by fully occupied parents. Some teaching of reading and writing was available to the better off families, when, for a small weekly fee, they would be taught in private houses, which were fashionably styled as academies.

In 1815, a National School was founded by private subscription, at what is now called the Old School House in Park Road, opposite the end of William IV Lane. In 1840, this school was run by Thomas Longhurst, master, and Jane Longhurst, mistress, and in 1851 by Mr. and Mrs. Robert Nettleton. In 1834, there were three academies in addition to this school, run by Gilbert Clarke, Sarah Ellis and Samuel Lyon, and not long after this, it is recorded that small local boarding schools were operating, two at Barton in the charge of Ann Nichols and Stephen Hawksworth, and one at Yoxall run by Emma Garner. These small privately run "academies" were to continue in Alrewas long after the old village Church school was built in 1855. This school, which served Alrewas well for over 100 years, was built on a piece of land which was the site of old Manor Dovecote piece, being purchased from the Earl of Lichfield for the sum of £40, and made over to the Rev. R. K. Hazlehurst, and to his succeeding Vicars—"for a school for the education of children and adults, or children only, of the labouring, manufacturing and other poorer classes of the Parish of Alrewas". The school was—"to be conducted according to the principles of the National Society for Promoting the Education of the Poor in the Principles of the Established Church throughout England and Wales".

The appointment and dismissal of the Schoolmaster, Schoolmistress and assistants, and the general control of the school were to be exercised by the Vicar, his curate and four other persons chosen from members of the Church of England, and who were annual subscribers of 20 shillings each at least, to the funds of the school. The original members were Rev. R. K. Hazelhurst, Thomas George the Earl of Lichfield, Morton Bond and William Bond (described as Smallware Manufacturers) and Thomas Winterton, farmer of Alrewas Hayes.

Five years later, the Rev. Alfred Ainger, on his appointment as curate, joined the committee. He later became Canon of Bristol Cathedral, Master of the

Temple and a notable writer—he wrote the volume on Charles Lamb in "The English Men of Letters" series, a volume of humorous essays, and many hymns the best known being "God is working His purpose out". He was a friend of Charles Dickens, acting with him in amateur performances at Tavistock House. It was in the new school that he delivered a series of lectures on Shakespeare, which attracted a wide audience from surrounding districts.

From funds raised locally and from grants by the National Society and the Exchequer, the school and schoolhouse were built and opened in 1855. The school consisted of three rooms, two large ones, one of which was the Infant Room, and a smaller one, fitted with a gallery along one side. It was heated by open fires, lit by oil lamps, and had the usual primitive sanitary and drainage systems common at the time. From then onwards, its story is one of extension and improvement, to try to keep pace—within the limits of the funds at its disposal—with the development of Educational practice. These funds came from private subscriptions and voluntary fund-raising efforts and grants from the Exchequer

(a)   towards the maintenance of the building—up to one half of the cost in the case of efficient schools

(b)   towards the teachers' salaries

(c)   Capitation grants from 3 shillings to 6 shillings on each pupil, and the weekly charge on the parents of pupils, which varied from 2 pence to 6 pence per child according to the family's circumstances.

Later in 1862, came the system of payment on results—based on the efficiency of the teaching of Reading, Writing and Arithmetic, as assessed by Her Majesty's Inspectors. This system lasted until 1895, and on only one occasion did the Inspector threaten to withhold the grant unless the results were better the following year. Attendance, however, was not compulsory and it was not until 1876 that School Boards—statutory bodies set up by the 1870 Education Act— were empowered to make bye-laws fixing the age at which education was to be compulsory.

The first school-master was Edwin Sellick and Miss Ann Lea was his assistant for the infants. During Mr. Sellick's time, the school was used for Church service while the north aisle was being built on to the Church, and re-seating being installed. At this time too, and until the Village Hall (Oddfellows Hall at first) was built, the school accommodated many village functions, concerts, dances, tea parties and public meetings. On his retirement in 1875, Mr. Sellick became a member of the School Committee, and was connected with the Church and choir for a number of years.

The Committee then decided to form two separate schools, each under its own head teacher—an Upper School, which continued to be known as the Alrewas National School, and an Infant School, the Alrewas National Infants School. Mr. H. W. Brierley, who up to that time had been in charge of the small school in Park Road, became the new headmaster of the upper school. He occupied the position for the next ten years, when he resigned, to become clerk and rate-collector to the Overseers of the Parish—a sad comment on the status of schoolmasters at that time, still "passing rich on £40 a year". He maintained his interest in the school, becoming first a member of the Committee, and later acting as correspondent to the Staffs. Education Committee when that Authority came into being as a result of the Education Act of 1902. He only relinquished this position in 1933, so that for 58 years he was connected officially with the life of the school. Indeed, until his death in 1937, he continued to show a lively interest in the School's activities.

The first headmistress of the Infant School was Miss Minetta Harris, who, with only a girl monitor, and later with a supplementary as her assistant, struggled for 27 years with classes of infant boys and girls whose numbers ranged from 50 to 65. The two schools helped one another out during the absence of teachers.

Overcrowding was then, as it was in the future, one of the disturbing features of the school. To cope with the increasing numbers attending, extra accommodation was obtained by erecting two more galleries, one in the Infant room, and the other in the large classroom of the Upper school. The last of these galleries was removed from the Infant room in 1905. During the winter months the accommodation problem as a little easier, as it was the custom for a number of children to go, as it were, into hibernation in October, and present themselves again the following April. It meant a hard Summer Term for the teachers trying to bring these children to the standard to satisfy the Inspectors. In 1880, a definite enlargement was made to the building, by extending the large classroom of the Upper School, and in 1890, the small classroom was doubled in size and boys' and girls' cloakrooms added. It was now possible, by means of a partition and curtains to make four classrooms in the Upper

School. Even so, the overcrowding continued—at one time there were 81 children on the Infant registers, and all children under five years of age were refused admittance.

Mr. Tillett succeeded Mr. Brierley, in recent years, some of our older inhabitants who have now passed on, could well remember Mr. Tillett. During his tenure in addition to building enlargements, it was found necessary to improve the sanitary arrangements. There were no available grants, and the Managers under their Chairman Rev. W. A. Webb, made an appeal to the village for the sum of £70 which was needed to carry out the work. A generous benefactor was forthcoming in the person of Mr. Crossman of Orgreave Hall, who contributed £35, the remaining half being made up of subscriptions varying from £5 to 3 pence. Only a few months before, the Alrewas Parish Relief Fund had been launched, to relieve the distress caused by the unusually severe winter of 1893 to 1894. Here again Mr. Crossman headed the list with £33. 12s. 6d. In addition to cash subscriptions, there was a gift of 10 tons of coal, and another of 60 gallons of Soup. This severe weather had caused much illness, particularly among the children, so school attendance suffered considerably. But even in normal times, year after year came outbreaks of epidemic diseases like scarlet fever, measles, chicken pox, mumps, etc., causing the closure of the school from three to four weeks at a time, sometimes twice a year. It says much for the Welfare Services and medical advancement, that since 1934, no epidemic has been severe enough to cause the school to close.

Some extracts from the Parish Magazines of these early days will reveal how Mr. Tillett tried very hard to improve school attendance. Many of the names mentioned will be those of departed villagers, but many will be recognised, and some will be relatives of readers, many of the same name.

1888 The Reports of H.M. Inspector have been received.

Jan. Each of the three Departments have earned the 'Good' merit grant. The percentage of passes in the Mixed School is 82. The Total Grant amounted to £179. 7s. 2d. Diocesan Inspector's report

Feb. Alrewas Mixed— Each division passed a satisfactory examination: The knowledge of Holy Scripture and Catechism was accurate and definite, but the Liturgy was not so good—scholars orderly and attentive.

> Alrewas Infants— The instruction is carefully imparted and the elder children answered creditably. Classed Good.
>
> Fradley Infants— Religious knowledge and repetition very satisfactory. School classed as Excellent.

October— Miss Harris has begun her work as Mistress of Alrewas Infant School, in succession to Miss Grantham. Her Fradley friends presented her with a handsome leather writing desk as a momento of her sojourn in Fradley, and as a token of esteem she has won by the faithful discharge of her duties during the past nine years.

September 1890

Notice issued by the Lichfield Union School Attendance Committee

a. No child under the age of 14 years shall leave school without having passed the 4th Standard, or without having made such regular attendance as is required by Act of Parliament.

b. Every person employing a child in contravention of this Act, shall be liable, on conviction, to a penalty of 40 shillings.

c. Parents must notice that full attendance every day is required.

d. The evils of irregular attendance are so serious, and causes frequently so trifling that the School Attendance Committee are compelled, however, reluctantly, in the interests of the children themselves, to prosecute persons in default.

e. Parents should understand that it is to their own interests to see that their children attend school punctually, and that they do not change school except for a good reason, as from these causes a full year's time is often lost in obtaining the certificate of employment in accordance with the Bye-laws of the Committee.

Mr. Tillett tried an idea to improve attendance by issuing a "Regular Army" of scholars who had put in full attendance for the month. Here is his account for the month of February 1897—

Our 'soldiers' number altogether 236, but only 47 responded to the 'bugle' or bell.

In December, the school opened 34 times, but only 33 scholars attended on every occasion

Regulars— Wm. Ryde, Wilf. Brough, Lucy Cartwright, Frances Ball, Ethel

Bartram, Evelyn Ball, Edward Wallis, Lucy Newman, Nellie Aston, Bertha Salt, George Thomas, Ernest Brough, Hilda Ball, Clara Jones, Fanny Bent, George Smith, Charles Mycock, Reginald Yates, Edward Millington, Thomas Shemmonds, W. Hives, Blanche Houghton, Irene Ball, Mary Woodburn, Hannah Ward, Ellen Heathcote, Edith Brian, Gert. Bartram, Fanny Swann, Mabel Dolman, Nelson Ball, Chas. Smith, Olive Morrey, and Maud Green, Joseph Cartwright.

Infant Department— Willie Hives, Cecil Chandler, Reuben Dolman, Edith Dolman, Charlotte Dolman, Irene Ball, Agnes Woodburn.

Similar lists were printed each month until Mr. Tillett resigned in that same year, with one variation, when he issued a list, and it was a long one, of those who were unpunctual, a black list which only consisted of initials, like E.H., R.W., etc.

Mr. Tillett was succeeded by Mr. J. H. Job, whose father was Headmaster of Christ Church School, Lichfield. During his long headship of 26 years, great changes took place in education, and the school benefited enormously. The 1902 Education Act did away with School Boards, and constituted the County Council as the Local Education Authority, and from then onwards came a steady improvement in the provision of furniture, books and apparatus for teaching purposes, for the cost of these and also of teachers' salaries, which by now had shown improvement, was met out of the Education Rate, imposed by the County Council. The managers of the school, however, remained responsible for the upkeep of the fabric, heating and lighting, sanitary arrangements, the appointment of teachers, including the headmaster, and the maintenance of religious instruction. Many of the clergy gave regular weekly lessons in the Scriptures for many years.

Dual desks were introduced in place of the long heavy uncomfortable ones which held six to eight children, and writing books, with pens, ink or pencils took the place of the slates. A full-time attendance officer was appointed in the person of Mr. T. Reynolds, who became a familiar, if feared, figure to many people in the local villages for over 30 years. Officers of the Education Committee now made frequent visits, to advice on procedures and further improvements.

In 1905, the two schools reverted to the position they occupied before 1875, the Infant School coming under the direct control of Mr. Job, and an assistant mistress, responsible to him, put in charge of the infants. Next year, the official name of the school was changed, and was now to be known as the "Alrewas Church of England School", a name it kept until 1955 when it was renamed "All Saints Church of England School (Controlled) Alrewas". The 'controlled' addition meant that the Education Committee assumed responsibility for the whole of the expenses incurred in maintaining and improving the school. 1907 saw the inclusion of Gardening into the curriculum for the boys, and Cookery classes for the girls, held at first in the School House, but later in the Schoolroom of the Wesleyan Chapel, and later in 1949 in the School's own Domestic Science Room. Medical inspection of children began in 1907, but it was not until 1936 that Dental Inspection and Treatment was introduced. In 1911, new doors were installed in the main entrance, hat and coat rails, fitted with pegs, were fixed in the porches, which were enlarged two years later, and at the same time, hopper windows were fitted to improve ventilation.

In 1923, Mr. Job resigned. He had been a very active Headmaster, conducting an Evening School for some years for adults, and training prospective teachers under the Pupil Teacher System, several of whom entered Teachers' Training Colleges. For 18 years he was Secretary and Treasurer of the Lichfield Teachers' Association, was a member of Alrewas Parish Council for 16 years, and Worshipful Master of St. John's Lodge of the Freemasons in 1921.

Mr. C. P. Smith succeeded Mr. Job, and during the next 10 years, under his guidance, the school built for itself a sound reputation, particularly in the work done in Art and Crafts, and in the science and practice of Gardening. During Mr. Smith's time, the School began to send educational exhibits to the annual Staffs. County Agricultural Show, a practice which was continued, after Mr. Smith left, until 1939. Until 1931, Mr. Smith's assistant was Mr. J. C. Shannon, who founded the Alrewas Scout Troop, and who left to take up the headship of Kings Bromley School. He was succeeded by a young 20-year-old teacher who was faced with a huge class of 53 boys and girls, augmented for a few music lessons (until the noise disturbed the whole school) and by the regular twenty extras each morning for Scripture, most sitting three to a dual desk. This young fellow eventually settled to the work, and except for the war years spent in the army, remained until 1957, when he took the Alrewas seniors to

John Taylor School at Barton, where he remained until 1976, when he set himself to write this history. Some of Mr. Shannon's original troop are still on patrol doing their good deeds amongst us in 1985, Frank Kent, Walter Smith, Basil May, Norman Ward, Jock Taylor, Jack Bannister and Fred Durose (who, in 1929 and 1932, rescued two children from drowning in the canal). In 1925, the sanitary arrangements and the playground were proving inadequate, the latter with it's tree stump getting in a sorry state—an uneven surface of loose gravel, and new heating system and lighting facilities were needed to replace the stoves, open fire and paraffin lamps. The cost of these changes was heavy and again the village was appealed to for funds to supplement grants. The Rev. J. S. Caiger, Vicar and chairman of the managers worked indefatigably to raise the money, and a start was made in 1931, when the central heating system was installed. In 1933, the old lavatories were removed and W.C.s substituted—the school was really getting into the 20th Century!—for the porches were enlarged, new wash-basins installed, and the school redecorated inside and out. The following year, the school was fitted with electric lighting, and the playground resurfaced. The lighting installation was paid for out of the proceeds of a School concert, given in the Oddfellows Hall on two successive nights.

Mr. Smith did not remain to see the completion of the improvements, for in 1933, he was appointed Headmaster of Uttoxeter Secondary Modern Boys' School until he retired to Grange-over-Sands, where he lived to be over 90 years old. He was succeeded by Mr. J. R. McKnight, and for six years the work of the school was consolidated on a much more liberal and broadly based approach. He was deeply involved in the life of Alrewas, in the Church, as a chorister and reader, he was Parochial Councillor, on the Parish Council, the Workers' Education Association, Playing Field and Village Hall Committee, and most functions which occurred from time to time. He was a keen member of the Bowling Club and an enthusiastic member of the Johnson Society in Lichfield. The outbreak of war in 1939 brought many problems and difficulties, especially when the majority of children from Holy Trinity School and Bratt Street Infant School were evacuated from West Bromwich, arriving on the 6th September, 1939, to be billeted with foster parents, who showed great kindness, tact and forbearance to the children placed with them. A double shift system of school attendance had to be adopted, the Alrewas children attending from 9.0a.m. to 1.0p.m. and the West Bromwich pupils from 1.0p.m. to 5.0p.m. The arrangement was not of long duration however, for after the first shock of the threat of air-raids was over, many children began to return home and by November, only 22 remained, and most of these remained here until the end of the war. There were, however, a number of privately evacuated children, a number which increased when the Flying Bomb attacks on London began in 1944, and the number attending school that year, rose to the record total of 286. The village was fortunate in escaping the enemy bombs, and except for the later opening of school after all night raids on midland towns, the work of the school was never seriously interrupted. One feature, which those who were at school at that time will remember, was the two week release of children over 12 to help with the potato harvest on local farms.

At the end of the war, school meals were introduced and in 1949 came a major change—the raising of the school-leaving age to 15. To meet the expected increase in numbers, and to provide more education of a practical nature, a new classroom, a woodwork room, and a domestic science room were built on the site of the garden of the school and the long air-raid shelter, which had to be demolished.

In 1957, the new Secondary Modern School was completed, and all the 11-plus children were transferred there. At the same time, Mr. McKnight retired and he was succeeded, as Head of the Junior and Infant School, by Mr. A. Hayton, who eventually moved with the scholars and staff to the new school in Furlong Lane, with a Playing Field, something the old school had never had, though some excellent footballers and cricketers had their early training on what is now the new cemetery, and where Alrewas and Fradley children spent many happy hours (as did at least one of their teachers). The introduction of school dinners came after the war, the meals being brought in containers from Barton, but before that except for a very few pupils from Fradley and the Junction, children would walk home to Fradley across the fields, or to Fradley Junction along the canal towing path, have their dinners, and return, though severe winter days would necessitate the bringing of sandwiches, often being eaten in the porches. No bicycles appeared to be in evidence and the distant children certainly carried the nickname of the "Fradley Bulldogs". There were some rivalry between Alrewas and Fradley children, and there were regular "scraps" in Walkfield when school was over. It is certain that most old Alrewas folk look back with many happy memories of their years at the 'Old School', which is now fulfilling a different function as 'Alrewas Outdoor Education Centre', with groups of children spending a few days enjoying outdoor activities, mainly in contrast to the urban districts from which they come.

There are some interesting extracts from the old School Log Books—

20 January 1892	Today being the Oddfellows Fete, the morning school closed at 11a.m. The afternoon meeting was poor.
27 July 1892	A whole holiday, it being Flower Show Day.
13 May 1893	A--- P--- marked left. She has not been to school since 19 October. She has gone on the boat with her parents.
18 May 1893	Several children stayed away to see the Yeomanry pass through the village.
23 June 1893	A whole holiday on account of the Choir Trip.
8 January 1894	Only half the children present on account of the severe weather.
9 November 1894	Admitted a little girl of 7 who has had to be placed with the babies as she does not know her letters.
24 April 1896	A great many absent all day today—it generally being the case on a Friday.
22 June 1897	A whole holiday on account of the Queen's Diamond Jubilee.
2 July 1897	No school today—Choir excursion to Brighton.
23 June 1899	Choir excursion to Blackpool. Holiday for the day.
27 April 1900	Registers not marked this morning, children going to see a procession of motor-cars which was passing along the road to Burton.
20 January 1902	Half holiday, on account of the room being wanted for an "Old People's Tea".
2 June 1902	A half holiday in Commemoration of the Proclamation of Peace, at the end of the South African War.
22 October 1909	Mr. Mallaber sent two large hampers of pears for distribution among scholars. (These from the Sittles.)
29 September 1910	Aeroplane race from Lichfield to Burton.
12 June 1912	Death of Miss Lilian Dolman, part-time sewing mistress since 1882.

18 October 1912	Mr. Thompstone, Elford Park sent two large baskets of apples, and Mr. E. H. Mallaber two large baskets of pears.
1 February 1916	Zeppelin raid over Burton, and other midland towns.
16 September 1916	Another Zeppelin raid.
16-23 October 1916	School closed for children to help with potato harvest, as there is a great shortage of labour in the Parish—nearly 200 men having joined the colours.
1 October 1919	No cookery class today, as the Instructress is prevented from travelling by the National Railway Strike, which commenced on 27th Sept.
24- November 1919	Lieut. F. J. B. Powell, R.A.F., a former scholar, has been awarded the O.B.E. (Military Division.)
15 March 1920	Heavy blizzard. Only 87 present out of 216.
13 April 1921	Holiday on account of the South Staffs. Hunt "Point to Point" Races at Fradley.
18 April 1921	Suspension of certain trains to Burton in consequence of the miners' strike.
9 & 10 January 1934	School Concert in Oddfellows Hall.
6 & 7 May 1934	School closed for two days on the occasion of the Silver Jubilee of King George V. The children took part in a procession to the Church, and at the War Memorial sang Kipling's Hymn "Land of our Birth". After the service each child was presented with a Jubilee Beaker. In the afternoon they took part in a sport programme, and were afterwards entertained to tea in the Oddfellows Hall.
28 January 1937	School closed—it being the day of the funeral of King George V.
12 May 1937	School closed for the Coronation of King George VI. In a village procession, eight girls representing children of the Empire supporting "Britannia", formed one of the tableaux. After the service, the children attended at School to be presented with Coronation Beakers by Mr. W. E. Ward, Chairman of the Celebrations Committee.
29 Jan 1939	Heavy fall of snow during the weekend—the heaviest for

40 years. Road and rail transport disorganised. Only 78 children present.

3 September 1939	Declaration of War by Great Britain on Germany.
21 August 1940	Air-raid warning at 10.25a.m.
26 August	School opened at 9.30a.m. following a night when the Air-raid siren sounded at 10.0p.m. and the all-clear at 3.10a.m.
28 August 1940	School opened at 10.0a.m. following an air-raid alarm from 10.0p.m. to 3.55a.m.
29 August 1940	School opened at 10.0a.m. following an air-raid alarm from 10.l0p.m. to 4.0a.m.
30 August 1940	School opened at 10.0a.m. following an air-raid alarm from 9.45p.m. to 2.0a.m.
16 June 1941 War	40 children on the recommendation of the Agricultural Committee allowed to help pea-picking during school hours.
15 October 1941	Children over 12 allowed to be absent from school for a fortnight to help with the potato harvest.
8 May 1945	V.E. Day—School closed for two days.
1 & 5 June 1953	School closed for Coronation Celebrations of Queen Elizabeth II. The children assembled in school, at 10.0a.m. on Coronation Day 2nd June, for a special service, at which the Headmaster spoke of the significance of the Coronation. Following the service Mrs. P. Turner of Westgate House, presented each child with a coronation medal generously given by her husband. The design—a pictorial representation of the Village—had been executed by Mr. R. N. Stubbs, the senior assistant. Also present were the children of St. Christopher's School, with their Headmistress Miss M. Hunter, the Rev. J. Griffiths, Vicar, and Mrs. Griffiths, Mr. M. Hearley H.M.I., and Mrs. Hearley, and the Staff of the School. In the afternoon the children took part in a procession through the village, and later took part in a sports programme, being served with tea at the interval, by the

ladies of the Celebrations Committee. Unfortunately, the event was somewhat marred by strong winds and rain.

List of Assistant Masters and Mistresses to 1957

Miss A. Lea; Miss Minnie Durose (Monitor); Miss Ethel Warrington (Monitor); Miss Lilian Dolman; Mrs. Hooker; Miss Gale; Miss Gray; Miss Margrave; Mr. A. Selvidge; Miss Parkinson; Mrs. Garner; Miss J. Nettleton (Mrs. May); Miss A. Woodburn; Miss A. Smalley; Mrs. J. Lander; Miss A. Goddard; Miss E. Besley; Miss E. Parker; Miss A. Carter (Mrs. Nelson Ball); Miss Z. Olsonn (Mrs. J. Whitfield); Miss E. Olsonn; Miss M. E. Siddals; Miss Reynolds; Miss G. M. Hartland; Miss E. Lomas; Mr. Frank Sanders; Miss L. Tregillus; Mr. Walter Jackson; Miss H. Fearn; Miss McGarry; Miss E. Moorcroft; Miss E. Jones; Miss E. Cartwright; Miss D. Woodfield (Mrs. W. Whitfield); Miss A. Lakin (Monitor); Mrs. D. Thompson (Cookery); Miss A. Bates (Monitor); Miss H. M. Moorby; Miss E. N. Fry; Miss E. Culley; Miss F. Bills; Miss E. Guest (Monitor); Miss W. Garratt; Miss G. Kirkland; Miss C. Woolley (Mrs. Newbold); Mr. L. P. Marler; Mr. T. G. Graham (Temporary Head); Miss J. Gartside; Miss C. M. Jones; Miss Tunnadine; Miss M. E. Naylor; Miss M. Pillinger (Mrs. Shannon); Mr. J. J. C. Shannon; Miss C. M. Parry; Miss I. Stokes (Mrs. Constable); Mr. R. N. Stubbs; Miss M. Davies; Miss K. Mould; Mrs. L. E. McKnight; Miss B. Hobley; Miss M. Jones (Mrs. L. Leavesley); Miss Francis (Cookery); Miss M. Ward (Mrs. Bunting); Mr. W. J. Mead; Miss Waller (Cookery); Miss M. Harrison; Miss A. E. Williams; Miss Howie (Domestic Science); Mr. A. Jones; Mrs. L. A. McKnight; Mr. W. A. Malbon; Miss F. Lakin; Mrs. M. Wilkins, Mrs. Brown (Domestic Science), Mr. W. Hares (Woodwork); Miss B. Cluloe.

CHAPTER 22

The Manors and their lords

The first recorded holder of the Manor of Alrewas was a Maur Wulsye in 942 A.D., but soon after, it passed into the hands of the Earls of Mercia. From 1066 until 1204, Alrewas was held by the Kings of England, when, in the reign of King John it was given to Sir Roger de Somerville, the baron of Wychnor, on payment to the King of 60 marks and 2 horses. The Somervilles had held Wychnor, and Parva Ridware (now the village of Netherton) since Norman times, and had built their moated manor house on the meadow below where the Church was later to be built. It is probable, that the site of the early fortified Manor House was chosen, to maintain, and if necessary, guard the river bridge and the several fords which allowed passage over the Trent. Until 1661, Alrewas was never to have a resident lord here, and this absence of a rigorous resident authority, was to foster an independent spirit in its people lasting over many centuries. Amongst its tenant farmers was a generous sprinkling of free men, with others holding land here, yet resident in neighbouring manors, like Elford, Ridware, Curborough, Croxall, Streethay or Sutton. There were also soc men, men who had been royal retainers or the descendants of the same, who claimed exemption from the servile duties and services owed to the lord by the lower villeins as part payment for their land.

In 1287, Sir Robert Somerville, who by that time held Alrewas, Wychnor, Dunstall, Newbold, Brideshall, Sirescote, Curborough, and Edingale, was granted by the King, the right to hunt on his lands, to hold a weekly market at Alrewas on Tuesdays, to hold an annual Fair on the eve, day and morrow on the Feast of St. Margaret the Virgin and the authority to erect a gallows for the hanging of criminals. An earlier Somerville, Sir Walter, had been the sworn brother of Sir Robert Marmion of Tamworth Castle, who had, at one time, dispossessed some nuns of their abbey and lands at Polesworth. Soon after this, following a roistering feast with his friends in the castle, the guests were roused by the yells and screams of a frightened Sir Robert, who told his startled friends and servants that he had seen a vision of St. Edith, who, after upbraiding him for his treatment of the nuns, threatened him with a cruel death and hell, if he did not make amends and restore the nuns to Polesworth. The spectre then ended her materialisation, by striking the terror-stricken baron in his side with the crozier which she carried. It was found that the blow had drawn blood, and the next morning, Sir Robert, accompanied by Sir Walter Somerville, rode to Oldbury where the nuns had found refuge and begged them to return. He asked the Abbess later if he and future Marmions could, on their deaths, be buried in the Chapter House of the abbey, while Sir Robert Somerville requested that in future, his family could be interred in the Cloister. The success of the request explains why the numerous graves of dead Somervilles are not to be found at Alrewas or Wychnor, and why the Abbey of Polesworth held land near Wychnor Bridge for many years, which was held on condition that prayers were offered for the souls of dead Somervilles.

Sir Robert Somerville was succeeded by Edmund, who was a clerk in Holy Orders and had little to do with his estates, and in 1322, he was followed by his brother Roger, who had fought against the Scots at Bannockburn and probably saw little of his manor here, for when his son Philip came to Wychnor in 1337, it was to find that the Manor House had been raided by thieves. At this time, the countryside was always under threat from bands of discharged soldiers from the armies fighting in France or Scotland. This Sir Philip, the last and most powerful of the Somervilles, was to extend his estate and authority to Draycott, Highlands Park, Barton and Callingwood, mainly because of his close friendship with John of Gaunt, Duke of Lancaster, the fourth son of Edward III, who rebuilt Tutbury Castle as his courtly seat.

Under Philip, Alrewas obtained the status of a Borough, and was obviously recovering from the dreadful losses sustained in the Black Death plague of 1349, helped almost certainly by the influx of families from surrounding villages like Catton and Croxall, whose populations had been decimated by the plague. With so many deaths, there was land to spare, and the period is notable for the institution of some strange customs for holding land, one of which was Sir Philip's own holding of his lands, in return for the donation and maintenance of the Flitch of Bacon in the hall of his manor house, as has already been described in a previous chapter.

Sir Philip, probably the 11th baron, died in 1355, and his extensive estates passed to Sir Rees ap Griffith, who had married Joan Somerville, for there was no male heir. The descendents of this marriage, the Griffith family, were to hold Alrewas until 1661, dividing their residence between Wychnor, Wales and Yorkshire, where their scattered manors were situated. Some of the early Griffiths were buried at Polesworth, others at Annesburton in Yorkshire, but most of the later burials took place in Tatenhill church. Only one, Thomas Griffith, was buried in the Chantry of the Blessed Virgin in Alrewas Church in 1431.

By 1540, the old moated manor house below the church at Wychnor, was unoccupied, in poor repair, and liable to flooding, and in 1584, work began on the construction of a new hall on the high ground of the Park, overlooking the Trent Valley, on a site which in Saxon times may have been a defensive burgh against the Danish invaders. The site was called the Trent Yeat, which meant the Trent Gate, meaning either a gate into the Hunting park, or a narrowing of the river, and by 1621, the Hall was commodious and splendid enough to accommodate King James I and his court. This was not the present hall, but an inventory of 1599 gives some idea of its original size. It contained a Hall, a Great Chamber, the Ladies' or Inner Chamber, the Lyston Chamber, chambers for waiting maids, servants, the brewers, the gardener, the curate and the steward. It had a gallery, a great and lower parlour, a buttery, a nursery,. a kitchen, a pastery and larder, a brewing house and bakehouse, a day house, a chapel, a washing house, a candle house, and many small rooms. It was, therefore, the home of typical Elizabethan gentleman's family. In 1646, the last Griffith died, and the manor passed to a nephew, a Francis Boynton of Brampton in Yorkshire, who in 1660, sold the Alrewas part of the estates to the Turtons of Alrewas. William Turton had been agent to several local lords, and had prospered well during the Civil War, increasing his wealth and land by marriage to a Miss Holmes, the daughter of a wealthy yeoman farmer of Orgreave. It is possible that he arranged the purchase of Alrewas Manor, though the indenture for the transfer, quotes his two sons John and Philip as the purchasers, though John was only 23 years old at the time, young for such a deal. The Turtons paid £3,130 for the manor, containing: "One capital messuage with appurtenances, 12 other messuages, 2 cottages etc in Alrewas, 5 messuages and Loopin Chapel at Orgreave, and a messuage in Fradley, with divers lands etc belonging to the respective tenants, and also those streams and rivers within and belonging to the said manor, known as Trent, Tame, Mease, Pipebrook and Marebrook, with the free fishery and all swans upon the same; and all other Messuages, lands, etc in Alrewas, Fradley, Orgreave, Edingale and Kings Bromley; also the Hay of Alrewas within the Forest of Cannock, with the lodges and other appurtenances, and a water mill within the same called Woodmill (built in 1614).

John Turton, who was later knighted, became a Baron of the Exchequer, and a Justice of the King's Bench, living much of his life at the Manor House, which the Turtons built at Alrewas, which is now the Manor Farm. He died in 1707, at the age of 71, having survived his son and heir, and the estate passed to his grandson, another John Turton, who held the manor for nearly 50 years. During his time, Orgreave Hall took the place of the Manor House as the family seat, and to provide the privacy required in such a residence, the old Salters Way (or Overley Lane), which had been the main highway from Alrewas to Kings Bromley, became secondary to the new straight Orgreave Road running by the Hall Lodge, at the end of the Avenue approach to the new Hall. Many Turtons are buried in the Church at Alrewas, and the will of Sir John in 1707 states: "my body to be decently interred without great funeral pomp, in the chancel of the church at Alrewas (the place of my birth) called the lord's chancel, which solely belongs to my family, and where my late honoured father and mother, my wife, my two sons, my brother and others of my family, and relations have been interred".

In 1752, John Turton sold the manor of Alrewas to Admiral George Anson. This famous sailor, in completing the second voyage to circumnavigate the earth by an English captain took vast treasure from the Spaniards, with whom England was at war, and on his return in 1744, so much treasure was contained in his remaining ships, that it was said to have taken 32 wagons to haul it to the Bank of England. In 1747, he captured six French warships and four East India merchant ships, and was rewarded by being created Lord Anson. He had estates in Hampshire and Hertfordshire, and it is unlikely that he spent much of his remaining years at Orgreave. When he died in 1762, he left Alrewas manor and Orgreave Hall to his nephew, George Adams, who later resided for some time at Orgreave, and changed his name by deed poil to George Anson, and represented Lichfield as its Member of Parliament from 1774 to 1784. His son,

Thomas Anson, inherited all the extensive Anson estates, and enlarged Shugborough Hall, which housed many of the treasures brought back by the Admiral. In 1806 he was made a Viscount, and like his father before him was the M.P. for Lichfield. He had married the daughter of Thomas Coke of Holkham in Norfolk, whose name will always be associated with the improvements in agriculture in the 18th Century. In 1818, his son Thomas William Anson succeeded him, who was later to be made Earl of Lichfield. Thomas George, 1884 to 1892, Thomas Francis 1892 to 1918, and Thomas George 1918 to 1960 followed him, the title at the time of writing being held by Thomas Patrick, Earl of Lichfield.

On 11th June 1953, the Ranton Estates Co., formed to control the Earl's estates put up for auction the major part of the Alrewas Estate, when 15 farms, 16 houses, and cottages—a total area of 2,656 acres, with all fishing and sporting rights—were dispersed under the auctioneer's hammer, and Alrewas manor, which had existed for a thousand years, was no more.

The Wychnor part of the Somerville manor, has a different story, for Sir Henry Griffith, the last of the Somerville line there, had been a loyal supporter of King Charles during the Civil War, and because of this, after the King's defeat in 1645, he was heavily fined by the Parliament as the following extract shows: "Oct 1646, Sir Henry Griffith, of Agnes Burton, Co. York, to settle £178 per annum for two lives, upon such places as Parliament shall appoint, for which is deducted £1246, and so the fine of £8793 is reduced to £7547." When Sir Henry died, his nephew Sir Francis Boynton inherited the estates and the huge debt which accompanied his inheritance. It was this which forced him to sell Alrewas to the Turton family and the following year, he sold Wychnor to the widow of John Offley of Madeley, and it was her grandson, Crew Offley, who built the present hall on the site of the Tudor hall which had been built by Henry Griffith in 1584.

In 1765, John Offley sold the estate to John Levett, from whom it passed to Theophilus Levett, whose brother was Vicar of Whittington and minister at Wychnor. This family held Wychnor for many years, and in 1890 it was occupied by Colonel Theophilus Levett, whose wife, Lady Jane, was the daughter of the Earl of Denbigh, and was related to the Hapsburg family, whose head was the Emperor of Austria. The writings of the Colonel's contemporaries show him to have been a kindly and benevolent landlord, with a keen and kindly interest in the welfare of his tenants, and a generous patron of local affairs, an example of the type of land owner which has, regrettably, largely vanished from the rural scene.

At the beginning of this century the estate was bought by Colonel Harrison, who moved from Orgreave Hall to Wychnor, where his family resided until the death of his son, Mr. W. H. Harrison. After standing empty following the auction of the contents, it was occupied for a time until the tragic death of Mr. Alec Mercer, the new owner. Much of the estate has been taken over by a finance company, but the Hall and Farm are now occupied.

The three very old names of land towards Wychnor Hall, though on the Alrewas side of the river, Burlake, Burway and Burhay, would seem to indicate the presence of an Anglo-Saxon Burgh or fortress, which could possibly have been the hill on which the present Hall stands.

In December 1985, the Earl of Lichfield put up the Lordship of the Manor of Alrewas for sale at an auction in London, and it was bought for £10,500 by a Mr. Tahir Khan-Lodhi, who is a banker from Kenya, and who declared himself "proud to have acquired a piece of English history".

Croxall and Catton

Like Alrewas and Wychnor, Croxall has a very long history, dating back to prehistoric times, and for much of this account, I am indebted to Mrs. Rose and her daughter Mrs. J. Orme, who kindly lent me a rare book on the "History of Croxall, Catton and Oakley", (written in 1881 by Rev. Richard Usher) some time before they vacated Croxall Hall.

The manor dates back to Anglo-Saxon times, and after the Norman conquest, it was held by a Breton, Giraline de Curzon, from whom it passed to his son Richard. Robert Curzon succeeded him, and his wife, Alice, who was later to marry Sir Roger Somerville, gave to the Curzon family three sons, Richard, Thomas and Robert. Richard married Petronella of Campville and set up his household at Croxall, while Thomas took another manor at Kedlestone, near Duffield in Derbyshire. He unfortunately died young, leaving a son, another Thomas, who was later to be prevented from his inheritance by his greedy grandmother, Alice de Somerville, who claimed Kedlestone as her dower. After years of legal dispute, Alice eventually gave up the estate, and was given land at Croxall as compensation. The third brother, Robert, entered the church and became Cardinal Curzon, the great friend of Pope Innocent III, and was made papal legate to Paris. He went on a Crusade against heretics in the south of France, fighting at the side of the father of the famous Simon de Montfort, Earl of Leicester. He died at Danetta in Egypt in 1218.

During the following centuries Croxall was held by the Curzons, many of them being buried in the Church there, and by 1421, John Curzon had sold all his manors except Croxall and part of Edingale which did not belong to Alrewas manor. In 1513, a John Curzon was fighting at the side of Henry VIII in France, the same John Curzon who in the 1521 Rental, held the "Studmare Holme for a yearly rent of 1 lb of pepper, and the Mill Pool for 2 shillings", these rented from Walter Griffith of Wychnor Manor. His son, Thomas Curzon, married twice, first to Anne Aston of Tixall, who had numerous children, among whom was Joyce Curzon. This daughter married a George Appleby, and on his death married Thomas Lewis of Mancetter near to Atherstone. Here she came under the influence of a strict Protestant family named Glover, who were zealous reformers, a dangerous thing to indulge in during the reign of Mary Tudor. Joyce Lewis, as she now was, was arrested and appeared before the bishop of Lichfield, where she refused to recant and accept Roman Catholic doctrine on transubstantiation. For this, she was condemned as a heretic to be burned at the stake, and the sentence was carried out in Lichfield Market Place, where a tablet still tells of her martyrdom on 18th December 1557.

A George Curzon succeeded to Croxall, and his grandson, the last of the male line, died in London in 1622, and his daughter, Mary Curzon, transferred Croxall to her husband, Sir George Sackville, who later became the fourth Earl of Dorset. He became Lord Chamberlain to King Charles I, and Mary Curzon, now the Countess of Dorset, became governess to the Royal children. She was so universally well-regarded, that when she died in 1645 during the time of the Civil War, the Lords and Commons granted £600 to provide a public funeral for her, the only time that a woman had been given such an honour in London. In 1613, at Croxall, the young Earl had been challenged to a duel by a Lord Edward Bruce, and the fight took place at Tergooze in Holland, where Bruce was killed, and Sir George (as he was then) sustained a wound from which he recovered. He was a devoted Loyalist in the Civil War and fought at the Battle of Edgehill in 1642.

Richard, the fifth Earl, succeeded to Croxall and supported Charles II, being one of the judges at the trial of the men responsible for the execution of Charles I. His son, Charles, the sixth Earl of Dorset, was a very accomplished scholar, and was a great friend of the Poet Laureate, John Dryden, who was a frequent visitor to Croxall. The poet's favourite walk was said to have been along the crest of the long hill towards Catton and Walton. This walk provided picturesque and extensive views across the Trent valley, and the path is still called Dryden's Walk.

The seventh Earl, Lionel, invested King George I with the Order of the Garter in Hanover, and brought him to England in 1714, being later made Lord Lieutenant of Ireland and first Duke of Dorset. His son, Charles, the second Duke, died unmarried, and his nephew, John Frederick, sold the neglected Croxall manor to Thomas Prinsep in 1779. By 1794, the new owner had become famous in the farming world, for his breeding of long-horned cattle, a hobby which was imitated by his friend and neighbour the Marquis of Donegal, who lived across the river at Fisherwick Hall. The next Thomas Prinsep died without issue, and Croxall was willed to his nephew, Thomas Prinsep Levett, the son of his sister Frances, who had married Theophilus Levett of Wychnor. He assumed the arms and name of Prinsep with that of Levett, and in 1868, the Hall was restored by the new occupant, now Thomas Levett Prinsep. An old drawing of the Hall when it was used as a farmhouse, shows that the main fabric of the Elizabethan structure was retained in the restoration, and it still presents its charm and character as an example of an Elizabethan manor house. The scars of the tragic fire which destroyed a wing of the Hall during the Second World War, have long been erased and Croxall Hall in the glow of evening sunlight is a picture not soon forgotten.

Not far from Croxall lies Oakley Farm, all that remains of an ancient manor dating back over a thousand years, for many years—from 1400—the home of the Dakins. The Midland Railway cut through the heart of the manor, but in the early days of the railways, provided a station for passengers from Alrewas, a station reached by a long flight of steps up the embankment, near to the bridge which crosses the road. No trace of the station remains, as it had little use after the building of the South Staffs line through Alrewas, though it was still in regular use during the First World War.

Catton

It is not our intention here to write an account of Catton history, and the long line of Hortons who were lords of the manor there for many centuries. It was a well inhabited manor in the 11th Century, and around 1100 a chapel was built there by Nigel de Albini, who eventually married the daughter of the great Henry de Ferrers. He had built a Cluniac Priory at Tutbury, and because of this, the chapel was put within the authority of the Priory. Later, in 1279, the Archbishop of Canterbury took it away from Tutbury, and gave it, along with Croxall, to the Priory of Repton. The chapel at Catton disappeared, probably destroyed by fire, and only a few pieces of carved masonry in the grounds tell of its existence.

There were two ladies of the Horton family who deserve mention in the Catton story. Many readers will be familiar with the poem by Lord Byron called "Hebrew Melodies", which contains the following famous lines quoted so well in the film of the book "Jamaica Inn" by Daphne du Maurier:

"She walks in beauty, like the night
Of cloudless climes and starry skies,
And all that's best of dark and bright
Meet in her aspect and her eyes."

The lady whose beauty inspired Byron to write these lines was no other than Lady Wilmot Horton, the daughter of Eusabius Horton of Catton.

In 1769, the Duke of Cumberland, brother of King George III, fell in love and married a commoner, a Madame Horton, the widow of Mr. Christopher Horton of Catton, and the marriage caused a national scandal and a constitutional crisis, which ended with Parliament passing the Royal Marriage Act, which was to control future royal marriages.

An interesting record deserves inclusion, which relates the method of establishing the age of the heir to an estate. There were no written records of births, and when parents were deceased, the proof of the age of the next in line depended on the sworn statements of 12 witnesses as to the time of the new lord's birth. The witnesses in this case, who made their depositions before the Court at Repton, make a wonderful list of men with wonderful memories, but the year was 1439, when events and incidents probably made a greater impression on the minds of men than they do today.

"Taken at Repton 29th June by witnesses to say on oath that William Horton was born on 1st May in the 5th year of the rule of Henry Vth. (i.e., 1418, making him 21 years of age.)

John Hugge, being of 60 years of age, knows this well, because he says he bought from John Rawlyn, for himself and his heirs, I virgate of land on the same day he was born and baptized.

John Whyttyng, being of the age of 58, knows this well, because he says that a certain Robert, son of the same John Whyttyng was born on the same day and baptized in the same church.

William Irpe, being of the age of 59 years, knows this well, because he says he himself was made Parish Clerk on the same day William Horton was born.

Henry Ampe, being of the age 61 years knows this well, because he married Joan, his wife, in the church of Maysham on the same day.

John Bayly, being of the age of 63 years, knows this well, because he says that he had a certain house in Catton burned on the same day that William was born.

William Smythe, being of the age of 67 years, knows this well, because he says that John Smythe, father of the aforesaid William Smythe, entered on the way of all flesh on the same day that William was born.

William Huckyne, being of the age 68 years, knows this well, because he himself carried the chrismatory (Holy oil vessel) at the font of the Chapel at Catton at the Baptism.

William Maylour, being of the age 62 years, knows this well, because he says that Henry, the father of William Maylour, was Godfather to the aforesaid William Horton, and the aforesaid William Maylour was present with his father, by his command in the Church.

William Jenkynsone, being of the age of 59, knows this well, because he says that John Batte severely beat and wounded him at Catton on the day of the birth.

Richard Taylour, being of the age 65 years, knows this well, because he says that Alice, his daughter, married John Boldynge in the church of Catton on the same day William Horton was born.

John Pryst, being of the age 64 years, knows this well, because he carried a taper before the said William Horton, when he was carried into the church of Catton.

John Lessone, being of the age 66 years, knows this well, because he says he fell from his horse to the ground at Catton, and broke his leg on the day William Horton was born.

There are some interesting surnames contained in these early Croxall and Catton records. There are Dakins in Alrewas today, and there were Dakins at Oakley Manor for some centuries, the first recorded that we found was of Adam Daykin in 1423, and long lists of Dakins at Croxall from 1600. In 1591, a John Malaber was married in Croxall Church to Ales Taylor on 6th February, and in 1626 in the will of Walter Horton at Catton, amongst other debtors was £10 owed by Ann Malaber. In 1703, a Botham Orme of Burton married Elizabeth Holland of Caldisell at Croxall, and in 1699, Anna, the daughter of Richard and Maria Startyn was baptized, and in 1711, Maria, the daughter of Richard Startyn of Curborough was buried in Edingale Cemetery.

In 1765, Thomas Hollier of Mytholm House was buried. This was at one time an inn, and the old Salters Bridge crossed the Tame nearby, the road continuing straight on over the hill to Edingale. Its point of crossing the hill can be clearly seen.

CHAPTER 23

Alrewas in the County Directories

In 1801, there began the taking of the National Census, to be repeated each following ten years, and the release of the resultant statistics stimulated great interest. To satisfy this interest, various publishers compiled and issued County Directories, which were brought up to date and re-issued at roughly ten year intervals. The early directories are rare today, and are much sought after by collectors.

The different publishers followed a similar pattern in the presentation of the facts about each town and village throughout the five Hundreds of the County of Stafford. First came a short history of the place, then brief facts about churches, chapels, schools, postal services, carriers to local market towns, canals and railways, populations and rateable values. Then followed a list of local gentry, clergy and private citizens, concluding with a list of farmers, master tradesmen, shopkeepers, inns and innkeepers, retail ale-houses, doctors (then called surgeons) and other special occupations

In 1841 Alrewas is quoted as: "being situated on the southern bank of the River Trent. The Grand Trunk Canal passes through the parish. A mile and a half from the village is Oakley Station on the Birmingham and Derby Junction Railway. The places of worship are the Parish Church of the Saxon style of architecture, and chapels each for Primitive and Wesleyan Methodists. The Parish includes the hamlets of Fradley and Orgreave, and contained in 1831, 1,607 inhabitants, and in 1841 1,750. Post Office at the Crown Inn, William Lakin, Postmaster. Letters from London and all parts south arrive from Lichfield every morning at nine, and are despatched every afternoon at 4. Letters from Burton and parts north and east arrive every day at twelve and are despatched every morning at eight."

Bakers	—Thomas Edgley and George Thomas
Basket Makers	—Moses Dolman, Moses Dolman Junior, William Dolman
Blacksmiths	—Joseph Bean, William Bean
Boot and Shoe Makers	—Thomas Green, John Lakin, Thomas Langley, George Roberts
Bricklayers	—James May, Joseph May, Thomas May
Butchers	—James Green, Joseph Green, Thomas Shakeshaft, William Tunley
Coal Dealers	—Joseph Kent, Thomas Langley
Coopers	—James Graham
Grocers	—Charles Marshall, Maria Fox, Thomas Grey, Thomas Langley, Henry Slater, George Thomas
Linen Drapers	—Charles Marshall
Maltsters	—Thomas Lakin, Thomas Shakeshaft
Millers	—William Shaw

Nailmakers	—William Green
Saddlers	—Thomas Green
Surgeon	—John Osborne
Tailors	—Samson Bannister, John Dakin, Richard Hurdman, Joseph Liversuch, John Mattock, Thomas Stokes
Taverns and Public Houses	—Bell—Isaac Fisher (Fradley), Bulls Head, Fradley—John Paskin, Crown—William Lakin, Crown (Fradley)—Thomas Lester, George and Dragon—Thomas Shakeshaft, Paul Pry—Thomas Dugmore, Swan (Fradley)—Joseph Radford, White Hart—Henry Bladon
Beer Retailers — (or Ale Houses)	William Eaton, Maria Fox, John Gildart, Mary Hanson, William Lucas, Thomas Morgan
Timber Merchant	—Joseph Kent—and Iron monger
Wheelwrights	—Joseph Kent, John Shakeshaft
Worsted Spinner	—Thomas Hitchcock
James Mottram was a Woolstapler	
Clog and Patten maker	—William Thomas
Sheet and Bar iron	—Benjamin and William Tyler at Wychnor Forge Manufacturers

Farmers were not included in this 1841 Directory.

In 1851 it states that it is a district "which comprises of the three townships of Alrewas, Fradley and Orgreave, which had 1658 inhabitants in 1841, of whom 1173 were in Alrewas township. Here is a Wesleyan Chapel built in 1805 and enlarged in 1846, and a Primitive Methodist Chapel built in 1828, the former has a Sunday School and Library.

Fradley is a small village comprising within it's township about 1,300 acres of land, and 362 inhabitants.

Orgreave is a small village and township half a mile west of Alrewas. It has about 700 acres of land, and 123 inhabitants, viz 96 at Orgreave and 27 in Overley hamlet. The Hall, now a farmhouse with a fine avenue of lime trees, was formerly the home of the Adams family.

Alrewas Hay is an extra Parochial liberty of 132 Souls and 1680 acres, and containing the small village of Fradley Junction, so called from the Fazeley and Trent Mersey Canals, who here unite.

Alrewas Private Citizens and Commercials

John Baggaley	—gent, The Cottage
Thomas Bagnall	—Millwright
Thomas Battelle	
Samuel Beech	—Gardener
Morton and William Bond	—Tape Manufacturers
Ann Buckley	—Dressmaker
George Cook	—Plumber and Painter
Wm. Dannofy	—Hay and Corn Dealer
John Day	—Station Master
Mrs Sarah Gillott	
James Graham	—Cooper
Edith Green	—Saddler
William Green	—Nailmaker
Richard Harrison	—Carrier
Joseph Kent	—Wheelwright
Sarah Lakin	—Draper
Edw. Langley	—Lock and Whitesmith
Robert Leggett	—Gardener
Rev. J. Moore	—Vicar
Parkinson Oates	—Surgeon
J. Winter Pycroft	—Gent
Joseph Sanders	—Hairdresser
Joseph Shemmonds	—Farrier
Thomas Shemmonds	—Nurseryman
Simon Sketchley	—Horse breaker
J. Smith, W. Symnett	—Keepers
Wm. Thomas	—Clogger, Parish Clerk
Wm. Turner	—Sawyer
John Weldon	—Gamekeeper
George Whiting	—Drill and Machine Owner
John Wilson	—Corn miller

Inns and Taverns

Crown   — Jane Lakin and Post Office
George and Dragon   — Thomas Shakeshaft
Paul Pry   — Emma Edden
White Hart   — Ann Bladen

Beer Houses

William Edgley, William Genders, William Roberts and John Thomas

Bakers

Joseph Edgley, Joseph Liversuch, William Moorley, George Thomas

Basket Makers

John Carthy, William Dolman, William Dolman Jnr., John Dolman, Thomas, Moses and Phineas Dolman, William Fletcher, Isaac Gray

Boot and Shoe Makers

Daniel Dagley, William Gaskell, Thomas Genders, Thomas Green, John Lakin, Thomas Langley, George Roberts and Thomas Turner

Bricklayers

John Lacey, James May, Thomas May, Thomas Taylor and Philip Wood

Blacksmiths

James Bean, William Bean

Butchers

William Ganes, Joseph Green, James Green, Thomas Shakeshaft

Farmers

John Bailey, Henry Bladen, Thomas Dolman, James Dutton, James Beech (Hill Cross), Edward Hastilow, Mary Lakin, Ann Lees (Sittels), William Lucas, George Merry (Bailiff), Thomas Parr, Thomas Shakeshaft, J. Shemmonds, Wm. Shemmonds, Jas. Thorniwork, Jas. Tomlinson, William Tunley, John Upton

Joiners and Builders

William Harris, Isaac Kent, Joseph Parker

Maltsters
Mary Lakin, Thos. Shakeshaft, William Sylvester

Shopkeepers
William Betts, William Genders, Thomas Gray, Eliz. Johnson, Thomas Langley, Joseph Liversuch, Mary Marshall, William Moorley, George Thomas, Eliz. Slater, David Wilcox, Thomas Woodward

Tailors
Richard Hurdman, John Mattock, Adam Port, Thomas Stokes and James Wilkins

Wheelwrights
Joseph Kent, Thomas Pallet, John Shakeshaft

Post Office — at Crown Inn, Letters depart 7.30 evenings via Lichfield
Carrier — Richard Harrison to Lichfield on Fridays at 9.0 a.m.
to Burton on Saturdays at 9.0 a.m.

At Fradley
Bannister William	— Wheelwright
Dolman Daniel	— Baker and shopkeeper
Dolman Thomas	— Basket maker
Fisher Mary	— Beer house at Bridge, Fradley
Lester John	— Shoemaker and Shopkeeper
Lester Thomas	— Victualler at Crown Inn
Nichols James	— gent, The Cottage
Paskin John	— Bull's Head
Rowe Thomas	— Tailor
Sharratt John, Upton W.	— Blacksmiths
Watson James	— Gamekeeper
Yeomans Thomas	— Wheelwright

Farmers
Baxter James, Dakin John, Dolman Joseph, Edwards Nathl., Finney Moses, Heath Daniel, Lester Thomas, Paskin Samuel, Paskin Thomas, Paskin John, Riley James, Robinson William, Shaw Eliz. (Hall), Sherratt Thomas, Upton John, and Winter Richard

At Orgreave

Cook John	—Shopkeeper
Eccleshall John	—Farm bailiff
Lancaster Mr. John	

Farmers

Collett Thomas	—Knowle Bank
Gould Ralph	—Lupin Bank
Eliz. Kent, Green Chas	—Lupin Bank

Lakin William, Sylvester John, Smith John, Smith William, Shipton Thomas (Orgreave Hall), Sylvester John (Overley), Wright William

Total number of Farmers 46, as named in the Parish. **In 1884** roughly 100 years ago, the list begins to show changes, old crafts disappearing and improved contact with the towns by railway, bringing a decrease in some local commerce. There were 955 people in Alrewas, 380 in Fradley, 113 in Orgreave and 115 in Alrewas Hayes, including Fradley Junction. The Post Office was kept by Mrs. Mary Emily Eggleston, and the station master was Jabez Butler, still there in 1896. In 1876, the station master had been Bernard Ball, who was grandfather to the late Mr. Nelson Ball.

Two carriers were operating, Joseph Smith to Lichfield on Fridays and to Burton on Thursdays and Saturdays, while Frederick Colclough carried too, to Lichfield on Fridays and to Burton on Tuesdays, Thursdays and Saturdays.

Inns and Taverns

White Hart	—John Bradshaw
George and Dragon	—William Crabtree
The Bell	—Mrs Ellen Fisher
Navigation	—Joseph Greenwood
Crown	—Alfred Lakin
Bulls Head	—Thomas Paskin
Royal Oak	—William Pott
Paul Pry	—John Taylor
Crown (Fradley)	—Thomas Tomlinson

Beer Retailers —John Lester (Fradley), Elizabeth Tyler

Bakers	—Richard Brain, Joshua Garratt, John Gilbert and John Morris
Basket makers	—Edward Dolman, Henry Dolman, Phineas Dolman, Thomas Dolman and William Dolman
Boot and Shoe makers	—Daniel Dagley, Thomas Genders, Charles Harris, William Jenks, Thomas Turner and Robert Warrington
Bricklayers	—Thomas May
Brick maker	—Richard Pegg at Hillyard Cross (Pegg's Hill)
Blacksmiths	—William Bean, Alfred Cross, John Sherratt (Fradley), Edwin Upton (Fradley)
Butchers	—William Dumolo, Joseph Green, Joseph Statham
Farmers	—Joseph Adams, Charles Bailey (Hayes), Henry Bailey, George Beech (Hillyards Cross), William Booth (Bears Hay), John Cotton Cliff (Dunstall Farm), Isaac Deville (Orgreave Gorse), Daniel Dolman, William Edwards (Fradley), William Evans, Thomas Ford (Fradley), Richard Grey, Henry Hackett (Fradley), Jesse Hollingworth (Fradley), Thomas Jones (Fradley), William Lakin (Orgreave), William Mason, Joseph Reynolds (Orgreave), John Richardson (Overley), William Shaw (Fradley Old Hall), Elizabeth Sherratt (Red House), Joseph Smith (Butt Croft), Joseph Smith (West Hill), Carolyn Sylvester (Overley), Richard Taylor (Hayes), Thomas Tomlinson, William Tunley, Thomas Turner (Fradley), John Upton (Manor Farm), Thomas Yeomans (Fradley) Total number of farmers named—31
Wheelwrights	—William Shakeshaft, George Tomlinson, Thomas Pallit
Mole Catcher	—John Woodburn

In 1896 the list appears to be much more complete, with more introductory detail and a wider inclusion of people.

Police Station	—P.C. John Morrey
Railway Station	—Jabez Butler—station master
Carriers	—Thomas Yeomans to Lichfield on Friday—to Burton Thursday
	Thomas Turner—to Burton daily
Post	—Mrs Mary Emily Eggleston—sub-postmistress.

Letters from Burton arrive at 7.30 a.m. and 5.15 p.m. Dispatched at 10.45 a.m. and 6.20 p.m. week days only.

Telegraph office open on Sundays from 8 to 10 a.m.

Wall Letter boxes—Fradley Junction cleared at 6 p.m.

Fradley Green cleared at 6.5 p.m.

Royal Oak (Alrewas) cleared at 6.25 p.m.

Orgreave cleared at 5.45 p.m.

The population in 1891 was 1,512 for Alrewas, Fradley, Alrewas Haye and Overley, and Orgreave.

Inns and Taverns

White Hart	—John Bradshaw
Royal Oak	—Charles Draper
Navigation Inn	—Joseph Greenwood
Crown Inn	—Alfred Lakin
Bull's Head	—Thomas Paskin
Paul Pry	—John Taylor
George & Dragon	—Amos Whetton
Beer retailers	—Alban Aston, Ann Maria Lakin, Wm. Mansell (at Fradley Junction), Thomas Sommers
Basket Makers	—Edward Dolman, Elizabeth Dolman, William Dolman
Plumbers & Painters	—Edwin Houghton, Thomas Brown
Bakers	—Richard Brain, Joseph Greenwood, Frank Rochford, Samuel Smalley

Boot Maker	—John Harvey, Charles Harris, William Jenks
Brickworks	—Hillyard's Cross (William Bagnall—manager)
Bricklayers & Builders	—Henry Littler, Henry May, Thomas May, Henry Kent
Blacksmiths	—Mrs Ann Cross, Edwin Upton
Butchers	—William Dumolo, Joseph Green, Edwin Mallaber
Grocers	—Richard Brain, Francis Arthur Lowe, Elizabeth Lucas
Drapers & Milliners	—Thomas Durose, Mary Eggleston, Elizabeth Lucas, Annie Tait
Dressmakers	—Mary Tipper, Kate Wells, Tailor—John Dakin
Mole Catcher	—John Woodburn
Vermin Destroyer	—Frederick Tipper
Farmers	—David Brough, Thomas Carter, Harry Chandler, Will Chawner, Joseph Clarke (Sandyhill), John Coxon, (Hayes), Charles Dolman, John Fellowes (Roddige), Hannah Ford, George Garratt, Charles Gough (Sale), Richard Gray, Charles Greaves (Hillyards Cross), Thomas Greaves (Easthill), Mark Hackett (Overley), Will Hackett (Overley), Jacob Hammersley (Orgreave Gorse), John Hiley, Trevor Holland, Charles Howitt, Daniel Hulme (Sittles), William Johnson (Lupin), Mary Jones, William Lakin (Orgreave), Daniel Mallaber, William Paskin, Thomas Ratcliffe, Joseph Reynolds, William Shaw (Old Hall), Elizabeth Sherratt (Fradley House), Caroline Sylvester, John Timmis (Westhill), Richard Tunley, Benjamin Turner, Job Wilkes Turner, John Whitfield (Mill Farm), Thomas Yeomans. Total Farmers—37.

The Post Office in early times

We are indebted to the late Mr. Wilfred Fisher for the following account, reproduced in total from his account.

"The 1851 census shows the road, which is now Post Office Road, as being called Market Street. It is probable that a village market was held on and around the village green, which in living memory, was larger than it is now. It could also in early times, have been down each side of the road. Early records say that the repeal of the Corn Laws was marked by the erection of a maypole on the green.

In the early days of the Post, the mail was collected from the Crown Inn. Some time after that the Post Office was run by two elderly ladies, who lived either at No. 3 (Mrs. Yardley's) or No. 5 (Mr. Orme's). In 1871, the office became vacant and Mrs. Eggleston was, in June 1871, appointed postmistress, a post which she was to hold until her death in 1935, after which her grandson, Mr. W. Fisher, was appointed postmaster, a post which he held until his retirement in June 1970.

The telephone came into the village in April 1923, with 8 subscribers, and two call officers, one being at Elford Post Office. Previous to the arrival of the telephone, telegrams (6 pence for 12 words) were sent from Alrewas to Tamworth by "ABC", an instrument like a clock, but with letters round the face, and keys to press. On the turn of the handle, the needle moved to the letter of the key you had pressed, and was equally received at Tamworth, and vice versa, when Tamworth forwarded the telegram on to where it was addressed.

The telephone went automatic in September 1939, just before the war."

Many old villagers will remember Wilfred Fisher with affection, for his sympathetic and helpful service during his long period as Postmaster.

CHAPTER 24

Between the wars

By 1932, the population had reached 1,636, and like the remainder of the country at the time, was suffering from the industrial depression. The effects of this were not so keenly felt here as in the industrial centres, for agriculture provided employment, and the Mill and local building firms provided work. There were then seven such firms of building and allied trades, John Bannister, George Kent, Arthur Kent, John E. May, W. Raworth, Edwin Houghton, and W. E. Ward, with Henry Lakin carrying out painting and decorating. Other occupations were:—

Baker	—Thomas Turner
Basket maker	—John Dolman
Boot repairer	—Thomas Guest
Blacksmith	—Charles Eyre
Butcher	—Frank W. Coates
Shopkeepers	—Sarah Allsop, C. H. Averil (Chemist), R. J. Barker, Ada Dolman, Mary Egglestone, Joseph Green, Annie Hopper (Draper), T. Turner, John Whitfield, E. Williams, A. Hardy (Fradley)
Dressmakers	—Mary Tipper, Mrs. and Miss Budgeon
Wheelwright	—David Cartwright and Son
Caterers	—Ernest Albert Revell
Garages	—Hart Bros., J. T. Leavesley (Cycle repairer, Motor engineer and haulier), W. Taverner (Pyford Brook)
Mole Catchers	—C. J. Woodburn and Sons

By far, the largest number of workers were involved in agriculture, either as individual farmers with their families, or as farm labourers, and included the names of well-known farming families.

Frank Beech (Hillyards Cross), Ernest Byrne, John Dolman, Will Heath (Whitemoor Hay), Percy Mallaber (Home Farm), Edward Mellor (Essington House), Albert Shaw (Mill Farm), George Smith, Thomas Smith, Arthur Swinfield, Chas. Sylvester (Furlong Farm), A. Tatlow (Bagnalls), G. Mycock (Manor Farm), J. Archer (Roddige), George Beech (Bridge Farm), Thos. Deville, Wm. Elson (Crown Farm), Chas. Greaves (Easthill), Philip Hill, Hy. Johnson (Pit Farm), W. J. Shaw (Old Hall), Fred Sherratt (Red House), Edward Timmis (Westhill), Tomlinsons (Dunstall), J. Watson, Charles Woolley, Charles Archer (Orgreave Gorse), Fred Cliffe, A. F. Coates, Geoff Hill, Thomas Lakin, Albert Peach, Doug. Shaw (Overley), George Smith, Chas. Weaver, D. Alsop, F. Turner, and may be a few more odd ones. This gives a total of at least 37 farmers in the Parish.

Today in 1986, the reader would find difficulty in counting ten farmers in the parish, for all the small land holdings have been absorbed into large farm units.

There are fewer opportunities for employment now, even though the Parish has doubled its population, and only one local building firm exists today.

CHAPTER 25

The village at war

The names of those men who sacrificed their lives in the First World War are well recorded, but the names of those who fought and suffered should also be recorded somewhere, and this book seems the appropriate opportunity to remember them. The list is drawn from the Walsall and District Roll of Honour, and contains the following names:—

L/Cpl. C. H. Archer	Staffs Yeomanry	1914-1919 Orgreave
Pte. G. Bailey	West Yorks Regt.	1916-1919 Alrewas
Cpt. N. Ball, M.M.	Kings Royal Rifles	1915-1919 Alrewas
F/Sgt. J. Bannister	Royal Air Force	1916-1919 Alrewas
Pte. S. Bates	Royal Guernsey Lt. Inf.	1917-1919 Alrewas
Sapper T. Bates	Royal Engineers	1915-1919 Alrewas
Pte. R. J. Bentley	Lincoln Regt.	1918-1919 Wychnor
Gnr. Josiah Brown	Royal Artillery	1917-1919 Fradley Jntn.
Pte. John Brown	South Staffs.	1915-1919 Fradley Jntn.
Pte. A. Collingwood	Royal Berks. Regt.	1916-1920 Fradley
Gnr. H. A. Dagley	Royal Artillery	1916-1919 Alrewas
Cadet R. W. N. Dawe	Royal Air Force	1918-1919 Alrewas Hys-.
Sgt. A. F. Dodd	Duke of Wellingtons	1915-1919 Alrewas
Cpl. T. Dyer	1st Res. Batt. R.E.	1915-1919 Alrewas
Pte. G. Elson	3rd N. Staffs.	1915-1917 The Sale

Sign. P. Elson	7th S. Staffs.	1914-1919 The Sale
Pte. T. Fisher	2nd N. Staffs.	1915-1920 Fradley
Driver C. Garratt	R.A.S.C.	1916-1919 Alrewas
Sgt. E. Gray	2/5th Gloucesters	1918-1920 Alrewas
Gnr. C. Hackett	Royal Artillery	1915-1919 Fradley
Pte. A. Howard	1st Manchesters	1912-1919 Fradley Jntn.
Pte. C. Hallam	R.A.S.C.	1916-1919 Fradley
Gnr. A. Hardy	Royal Artillery	1915-1919 Fradley
Cpl. S. Hartopp	Royal Engineers	1915-1919 Alrewas
P/O R. A. Bull	Royal Navy	1897-1916 Orgreave
Sgt. E. Houghton	Royal Engineers	1914-1919 Alrewas
Sapper T. Houghton	Royal Engineers	1916-1919 Alrewas
Pte. G. W. Jackson	Leicester Pioneer Corps	1918-1919 Fradley
Pte. R. B. Johnson	4th Lincolns	1918-1919 Fradley
Driver J. T. Leavesley	Royal Engineers	1915-1919 Alrewas
2nd/Lt. F. Livesey	Machine Gun Corps	1911-1919 Alrewas
Pte. W. J. Lucas	2/5th West Yorkshires	1916-1918 Fradley Jntn.
Sapper F. Lunn	Royal Engineers	1916-1919 Alrewas
Drummer. A. Mallaber	W. Yorks. (joined at 15)	1915-1919 Sittles
Driver P. A. Mallaber	R.A.S.C. (joined at 17)	1914-1919 Sittles
Pte. J. E. May	R.A.S.C.	1916-1918 Alrewas
Sgt. R. S. G. Nettleton	1/6th N. Staffs.	1914-1919 Fradley Jntn.
Cpl. P. B. Powell	Royal Warwicks.	1912-1918 Alrewas
Pte. B. Salt	Lancs. Fusiliers	1917-1919 Alrewas
Sgt. T. G. Shemmonds	Royal Warwicks.	1916-1919 Alrewas
Pte. G. Smith	11th A. A. Company	1915-1918 Alrewas Hys.
Driver R. E. Statham	Royal Field Artillery	1915-1919 Alrewas
Pte. W. Storer	7th Berkshires	1880-1916 Alrewas Hys.
L/Cpl. W. Stubbs	1/6th N. Staffs.	1915-1919 Alrewas
Gnr. F. Taylor	Royal Artillery	1916-1919 Alrewas
Gdsmn. R. G. Taylor	Grenadier Guards	1915-1919 Alrewas
Pte. E. E. Thomas	Kings Own RoyalLancs.	1915-1919 Alrewas
Sgt. E. G. Thomas	Kings Own Royal Rifles	1915-1919 Alrewas
Pte. S. Titterton	Kings Royal Rifles	1915-1917 Alrewas
A/C G. Warrilow	R.A.F.	1916-1919 Alrewas

Sgt. T. Wassell	Middlesex Regt.		1914-1919 Wychnor
Pte. F. Watson	12th Lancers		1915 1919 Alrewas
Driver J. Watson	R.A.S.C.		1915-1919 Fradley
Cpt. A. G. Webb	1st London Scottish		1917-1919 Alrewas
Sgt. H. J. Whitfield	Tank Corps		1914-1919 Alrewas
Pte. G. Whitfield	3rd 5. Staffs.	(killed)	1914-1918 Alrewas
Pte. W. H. Whitfield	Grenadier Guards		1914-1919 Alrewas
L/Cpl. A. Whittingham	Notts. and Derbys.		1917-1920 Fradley Jntn.
L/Cpl. J.W.Whittingham	R.A.S.C.		1918-1919 Fradley
Pte. J. W. Williams	R.A.S.C.		1918-1919 Alrewas
Pte. E. Wilson	3rd Manchesters		1915-1919 Sittles Farm
Gnr. A. Yates	Royal Artillery		1915-1919 Fradley Jntn.

The Second World War

The Second World War involved or affected the whole nation in some way, and Alrewas was no exception; and the construction of the huge airfield at Fradley emphasised the reality of the war. In spite of the anxiety about those absent on active service, despite the worries of rationing and shortages, the difficulties caused by the blackout restrictions, and the lack of transport, the people on the home front here, were soon efficiently organised for the war effort. A Civil Defence unit was quickly formed under Mr. Egerton Orme, for defence against the threatened air attack, and wardens were trained in First Aid, and in precautions against gas or fire bomb attack. During the long winter nights of the enemy blitzes on Midland industrial centres, these men spent many cold hours patrolling the dark lanes of their various sections. A Local Defence Volunteer company soon came into operation (later, of course, the Home Guard) under its officers Major F. R. Durose, Captain F. Kidd and Lieut. A. Myrtle, with N.C.O's including Sgt. Major "Dick" Cluley, Sgt. Frank Turner and Corp. T. Griffiths. It included in its ranks, veterans like Nelson Ball and George Thomas, who volunteered for duty despite being physically handicapped by wounds received in the First World War. The Auxiliary Fire Service had been formed early, before the outbreak of war, and amongst its early leaders was Mr. J. Hickson, who was badly injured in a later fire incident. A Red Cross Unit and Women's Voluntary Service company came into being under the leadership of Mrs. Egerton Orme, who was later appointed Township Leader.

From the school, Mr. J. R. McKnight ran an Air Training Cadet Corps, as well as a Gardening Guild to assist in the "Dig for Victory" campaign. During the long and difficult years of the war, two exceptional people deserve a special mention. They were Doctor A. Russian and Nurse Cluley. Their practice covered Alrewas, Fradley, Orgreave, Fradley Junction, Croxall and Edingale, and often meant during the winters, long, tiring calls in appalling and dangerous conditions, which must, at times, have brought them to the point of utter exhaustion. Nurse Cluley was also the district midwife, and was a tremendous help in her unstinted attention to her patients.

Despite the wartime strains and difficulties the people of the Parish found time, energy and enthusiasm to work together to provide funds for local and national needs, and during the years between 1939 and 1949, four major collective fund-raising efforts were made.

The first, held in August 1939, just before the outbreak of war, was a Carnival to provide funds for the Parish Church Tower Fund. The committee was representative of a wide spectrum of village interests, and consisted of Mr. Egerton Orme in the chair, Secretary W. Taverner and Treasurer Mr. A. E. Stott, with Messrs. H. Garland, W. J. Shaw, W. G. R. Arblaster, R. W. N. Dawe, W. E. Ward, J. R. McKnight, C. J. Woodburn, R. N. Stubbs, T. Shemmonds, N. Ball, R. S. Nettleton, W. Fisher, F. R. Durose, A. Grundy, H. G. Taylor, W. E. Foden, J. Hickson, R. J. Barker, G. Garratt, E. G. Thomas, Rev. W. D. Boone, Dr. A. Russian, Mrs. Foden, Mrs. Barnes, Mrs. G. Maddocks, Mr. and Mrs. J. Bannister, Mr. and Mrs. J. T. Leavesley and Miss Hellaby.

The work began in May and, after several months, an extensive programme of events had been arranged to be held in the Paul Pry field (the old venue for Alrewas Show and the Football Pitch). It began with a Procession, which was begun by the crowning of Molly Shearer as Carnival Queen attended by her Maids of Honour, Nancy Leavesley, Stella Salt, Nada Randall, Phyllis Tipper, Ruby Hickson and Gwen Choun. The Heralds in attendance were Margaret Shemmonds and Pearl Hickson, with train-bearers Betty Mallaber and Marjorie Collingwood. The bearer of the crown was young Master Geoffrey Mallaber.

Following this, sheep dog demonstrations were held with sheep provided by Mr. Geoff. Hill, then jazz bands, children's sports, a gang show with glamour girls, a gymnastics display, a fire-fighting demonstration by the newly-formed

Alrewas A.F.S., and finally a boxing tournament, background music throughout being provided by Burton Silver Prize Band. At the same time, there was bowling for a pig, a raffle for a fat lamb, ice cream and sweet stalls, etc. It proved a most successful day, and realised a profit of £174. 10s. 2½d., which brought the year's total for the Tower Fund to the huge sum of £640. 13s. 3d.

On 17th September 1942, a meeting was called in the Village Club (now the Scouts' H.Q.) to consider joining in the National Spitfire Fund Appeal. Mr. J. E. May addressed the meeting and made the successful proposition that the chair be taken by Mr. R. W. N. Dawe, Mr. W. Taverner agreeing to act as Secretary. The meeting heard and appeal by Mr. Ward Jackson of the R.A.F., stressing the importance of the Spitfire Fund, and appealed for all possible assistance; and it was decided to call a public meeting in the Oddfellows' Hall on the 10th September.

This well-attended meeting was addressed by Wing Commander Hesketh, who took the opportunity to thank the people of Alrewas for the hospitality shown to the R.A.F. personnel who were billeted on them from the Aerodrome at Fradley. He spoke of the work and the needs of the Air Force, and wished the Alrewas appeal every success.

After Mr. J. T. Leavesley had agreed to act as Treasurer, a model Spitfire was auctioned, and raised £3. 2s. 0d., and a subscription list from the meeting raised £71. 17s. 0d.

A committee was appointed consisting of Messrs. J. E. May, T. Shemmonds, F. Brooks, S. Walker, W. E. Ward, C. Lamley, Miss Hellaby, J. Bannister, R. S. Nettleton, F. Haskew, A. E. Scott, J. R. McKnight, W. J. Shaw, F. Kidd, C. J. Woodbum, Egerton Orme, F. Durose, J. Collins, W. Foden, H. G. Taylor, Mrs. Lloyd Parton and Mrs. Dawe with Mr. R. W. N. Dawe as the Chairman. The next meeting allocated collecting districts to committee members for house to house collections and collecting boxes were to be put in public houses and shops, and Mr. S. Walker volunteered to make collections at functions at the Village Club and the Oddfellows' Hall. In three short weeks, the Spitfire Fund benefited by £233.

On the 18th September 1944, the Red Cross Committee called a village meeting with the object of arranging a Winter Fair in aid of the Red Cross Fund, and it was agreed to hold it on 2nd December. A committee was elected with Mr. Egerton Orme as Chairman, Mr. W. Taverner as Secretary and Treasurer

Miss W. Fidler. A powerful committee consisted of Mesdames Barnes, Durose, Leavesley, Kidd, Randall, Raworth, Dawe, Stott, D. Shaw, J. Shaw, Powell, Bannister, Myrtle, May, Taverner and Miss Hunter, with Messrs. J. T. Leavesley, W. E. Ward, J. R. McKnight, A. Shearer, J. Shaw, P. Coates, W. Fidler, 3. Hickson, F. R. Durose, R. W. N. Dawe, A. Stott, D. Shaw, R. J. Barker, A. Myrtle, T. Shemmonds, J. Todd, C. Lamley and W. Constable with T. G. Durose and P. 0. Young as Hon. Auditors.

Between September and November a whole train of events was laid down. An extensive list of stalls, catering arrangements, raffles, competitions, miniature bowling, darts, etc. Stalls were allocated to various sections of the Parish to sell toys, cakes, fancy goods, pound goods, produce, books and hardware, while Fradley was to arrange for a miscellany stall. There would be a fortune teller, a huge rabbit pie, raffles,.etc. A dance was arranged for 30th November for which Colonel James Kilean had agreed to provide the 10th Replacement Depot Band, and a whist drive and dance was to be held in the schoolroom at Fradley on 24th November.

The Fair was an outstanding success, most of the money being earned from donations of £56. 9s. 6d., Fradley Whist Drive and Dance £30. 5s. 3d., Alrewas Dance £33. 3s. 7d., the Draw £235. 15s. 0d., Fradley Stall £103. 4s. l0d., Alrewas Fancy Goods £137. 5s. 0d., Produce Stall £51. 3s. l0d., Potatoes £40. 8s. 6d., and refreshments £27. 9s. 0d. After deducting expenditure, the Committee was able to make a donation to the Red Cross of £1,000. 4s. l0d.

It was stated in the local press that never before had such a sum been raised in Alrewas, largely due to the co-operation and organising abilities of the committee members and to the generosity and goodwill of the people of the Parish.

Victory celebrations were held in 1946, with sports on the Cricket Field, with beer and refreshments, while two sittings for teas were held, one for the pensioners and partners, and one for the children between the ages of three and fourteen three months. A free dance was provided for the young people to be held in the Oddfellows' Hall. Mr. W. E. Ward was chairman of the committee and Mr. Bev Rhodes was appointed Treasurer, with Mr. W. Taverner as Secretary.

From 1944 onwards, the Parish Council was considering some ways of welcoming home and thanking the returning service men and women, and in

1946, steps were taken to make these early ideas into reality.

In August, a Public Meeting was called, and representatives of the village organisations were elected to form a committee. It was composed of: —

British Legion	— Mr. A. Shearer	Cricket Club	— Mr. E. G. Thomas
Women's Section	— Mrs. L. Bannister	Unionists	— Mrs. Cartwright
Village Club	— Mr. S. Walker	Bowling Club	— Mr. C.J. Woodburn
Women's Inst.	— Miss Hellaby	Parish Church	— Rev. F. Hodge
Football Club	— Mrs. Payne	Nursing Assoc.	— Mr. J. T. Leavesley
Methodist Ch.	— Mr. W. Constable	Home Guard	— Maj. F. R. Durose
School	— Mr. J.R.McKnight	W.V.S.	— Mrs. E. Orme
Parish Council	— Mr. W. E. Ward	Oddfellows	— Mr. C. Lamley
Civil Defence	— Mr. E. Orme	Alrewas Show	— Mr. J. Swinfield

It was proposed and agreed, that the Parish Council be responsible for the event, supported by the appointed committee.

A register of the returning services personnel was to be compiled by Mr. McKnight to include those from Alrewas and Orgreave. A house to house collection by the British Legion Women's Section was to take place, and an entertainment committee arranged whist drives, dances, raffles, draws, etc.

In December, it was decided to raise sufficient funds to give a dinner to each of the service men and women with their partners, to provide a free drink, a mounted commemorative scroll, and a gift of £2 to each. Following the house collection, the fund stood, as was announced by Treasurer W. Constable, at £250. A draw in March raised a further £32, in which a bottle of whisky was won by Mr. G. Duggins of the Black Horse, Edingale, and a bottle of sherry by Mr. H. Moreby of the George and Dragon. (Coals to Newcastle, as the Chairman remarked!)

The final Dinner and Concert was held on 9th April 1949, in the Oddfellows' Hall. The quotation from F. Garratt Ltd., of Lichfield to provide a dinner consisting of: Soup—Ham, Tongue and other cold meats—Salad and Pickles —Rolls and Butter—Fruit Tart or Trifle with Cream—Pastries—Cheese and Biscuits—Tea or Beer, stated that all this was to be supplied with waiting services, at a cost of four shillings (20p) a head, and it was enjoyed by a full representative village gathering. A concert followed the meal, with artistes provided by Home, Thompson Ltd., the music shop in Burton.

Mr. Ward made the speech of welcome to the guests, and the toast to "Our Guests" was given by Major F. R. Durose who said—quoted entirely— "It is an honour and a pleasure for me to say a few words of welcome to all those here tonight who have served in His Majesty's forces. Words are a poor medium to express the deep gratitude we feel, and it is a pleasure to see you all back in Alrewas after the years of separation.

"We at home, thought of you unceasingly while you were away, doing your hazardous tasks in many parts of the world. One hundred and thirty went from Alrewas, and sadly four of these-.--Sgt. Walter James Carr, Pte. Geoffrey Pickering, Pte. John Hancock and Pte. John Bosley—gave their lives, and I ask you to stand in silent tribute to their memory. "You have had experiences which we at home could only read of, and I sincerely hope the renewal of your home lives will be happy and congenial. "I trust that if at any time, we who have worked on the Welcome Home Committee, can be of any assistance to you in any way, in the years that lie ahead, you will not hesitate to come to us. Our help in your future lives is one expression we can make of our thanks to you for your past service to us and to your country.

"I trust that our efforts to entertain you this evening will show some of our appreciation, and that you will enjoy this entertainment we have provided for you.

"I now propose a toast—'To those who have served in His Majesty's forces, here with us tonight'."

A reply, on behalf of the guests, was given by ex L.A.C. Leavesley L.

The list of guests accepting the invitation as listed on the Secretary's minutes were: —

Driver S. Orme	Cpl. T. W. Cooper	L/Cpl. S. Ward
Gnr. C. Bancroft	Tpr. S. Kent	Pte. K. Ward
Pte. G. H. Fletcher	Cpl. F. Walker	Cpl. G. F. Smith
Cpl. S. A. Smith	C.P.Off. C. Wood	L.A.C. B. May
Cpl. W. Kilsby	Pte. C. Horsley	Pte. A. Clews
Cpl. A. E. T. Bailey	Pte. F. E. Dolman	Pte. A. C. Venables
Sgmn. R. Lovatt	Pte. W. H. Jones	Fus. W. C. Smith
Coder C. Hall	L.A.C. T. Hart	Cpl. A. L. Edwards

Capt. J. Bannister

Cpl. A. V. Smith

Sgt. R. J. Buckley

Sgt. J. W. Lister

Cpl. W. Fisher

Bdr. A. G. Heathcote

Sgt. J. W. Payne

Pte. C. W. Dainty

Pte. F. S. Dakin

Marine W. Thorpe

Pte. A. E. Peach

Rfman. A. J. Middleton

Capt. R. N. Stubbs

Pte. J. T. Swinfield

Bdr. J. Taylor

Cpl. N. G. Ward

Pte. G. H. Edwards

Sgt. T. E. Shuker

Cpl. A. R. Jeffs

Driver A. Millington

AC/i F. Kent

Pte. C. E. Heathcote

Pte. V. E. Heathcote

Fus. W. Heathcote

Pte. S. Simnett

AC/2 C. Thorpe

Sapper P. Burton

Sgt. E. Moore

In addition to this list, came a further supplementary list of: —

L/Cpl. H. Daniels

L.A.C. H. G. Burton

A/B R. W. Gould

Sapper J. Rayson

Gnr. B. Gilson

Pte. C. Bostin

L.A.C. C. Hackett

Pte. T. Durose

Sgt. F. Randall

Capt. J. Platt RAMC

L.A.C. E. Walker

Pte. P. J. Pither

Cpl. E. H. Goring

Pte. W. H. Dicken

L.A.C. L. Leavesley

Pte. F. H. Harvey

F/Sgt. A. Venables

L.A.C. A. J. Smith

Gnr. F. Durose

Gnr. E. Tranter

F/Sgt. R. White

L.A.C. R. Raper

Sgt. A. W. Corbett

Gnr. L. R. Povey

L.A.C. A. M. Cooper

A/B R. Randall

Bdr. C. R. Walker

Gnr. G. T. Walker

Pte. W. Prince

Wren E. Peach

A/W B. Sharp WAAF

L.A.C. H. D. Hunt

These lists may not be complete, in which case we apologise for unavoidable omissions, for events and people of forty years ago.

CHAPTER 26

The changing village

The forty years from 1945 to 1985 have seen greater changes in the village of Alrewas, than had occurred in two thousand years. The end of the war saw the implementing of the welfare state, and the nationwide crusade to create a better life for the people, in housing, welfare, medical care, education and in leisure activities.

As early as 1944, the Parish Council was considering the need for the provision of a Community Centre and Playing Field facilities. On 15th June 1944, a meeting of representatives of all village organisations was called by the Council, and a resolution was carried, agreeing with the principle of the need for the provision of a Community Centre. At this meeting, Mr. T. Houghton, the representative of the Oddfellows' Society, presented a letter from the Manchester Unity of Oddfellows Committee, offering to sell the Alrewas Oddfellows' Hall to the village for £1,500. By 1946 grants from the Education Authority, collections, events, raffles, etc., had realised the required sum and the legal transfer was completed, and the Oddfellows' Hall became Alrewas Village Hall. Eventually, the representative committee became the Village Hall and Playing Field committee, and the search for a suitable site for a playing field began. The first options were the Oddfellows' Hall field (now the site of Inge Drive and Deepmore Close) and the Pony Field (now the site of the new British Legion Headquarters). While this was under consideration, Mr. P. Mallaber offered to release over nine acres of Walk Field, including the Cricket Ground, for £3,000 and again the village found the money with the help of grants. The agreement for the sale contained a clause that, if necessary, vehicular access could be claimed from the Navigation cottages area, across the playing field to the house (The Nook) in Dickinson's Alley, at that time the property of Mr. John Mallaber of Manor Farm. This provision was eventually taken up by Mr. Mallaber, but the Parish Council was anxious to prevent the agreed access from cutting across the playing field and football pitch. To avoid this, and yet still provide the legally agreed access, the Council agreed to surrender the small north west corner of the field, which had always been difficult to maintain, and to allow a vehicular access across it from Chase View Road. An agreement specified that there should always be easy access across it, along the public footpath, from Chase View Road and the playing field, to Main Street. The arrangement solved a problem, but was the later cause of some misunderstanding and ill-feeling between later occupants of the house, and the residents of Chase View who claimed the impeding of their right of way to Main Street.

Many changes occurred during the period which were merely cosmetic, improving, modifying, or enlarging existing features or facilities. Many old and delapidated properties were restored by their new owners, and have improved not only the occupied properties, but the general appearance of the village.

The Churchyard was levelled and re-seeded at the instigation of the Parish Council, and paid for by a levied rate, since it was considered that nearly all parishioners of all denominations will eventually have an interest there. The interior of the church was altered to give better acoustics, by removing the screen and opening up the Chancel, and carpet tiles quietened the rear of the church, while removal of rear pews enabled greater usage of the west end for meetings, coffee service, etc.

The Methodist Church put in a great effort and raised money to enlarge the chapel and add a schoolroom, which today provides accommodation for Alrewas Nursery School, infant welfare, Boys' Brigade, Club meetings, Council meetings, etc., as well as a summer centre for cyclists competing in road-racing trials on the A38. The new infant and junior school in Furlong Lane, with its extensive playing field, replaced the old school, and two old building firms' yards have been taken over, Kent's in Main Street as a chocolate factory, and W. E. Ward's White Hart Works as a car park and Motel, attached to the George and Dragon. One striking change has been the change of usage and clientel at the local public houses. These, before the war, were the smoke-filled meeting places of the local males, sharing local gossip and indulging in quiet games of darts or dominoes. They were places in which no lady ever ventured. Nowadays, they have been improved out of all recognition, serving cooked bar-meals at lunch, and evening meals for all who want them, and ladies are equally welcome and ample car parking attracts diners from more distant places than the Parish boundaries.

They have become popular and eminently respectable.

Beyond the village, the river has been deepened, its course from the Swarborne confluence diverted, and the old flood gates near to the mill have been demolished, completely changing the appearance and character of that part of the river.

A new sodium lighting system replaced the old, expensive and inefficient street lights, and the village is now well-lit at night. Later, most of the high tension and telephone poles were removed and the cables put underground, and new gas pipes have been installed to avoid any threat of leaks by fracture.

Bus shelters were provided in Fox Lane and near the Post Office, but unfortunately, misuse and vandalism have necessitated their removal.

By the early 1950's, work was in hand to convert the A38 into a dual carriageway. Old bridges were removed, and a new wider bridge constructed over the river. The old Paul Pry Hotel vanished, and the Transport Authority refused to consider the local request for a roundabout at the junction with A513, the road from Tamworth. The hold up of traffic at the junction was to lead eventually to the recent construction of the fly-over, and the by-pass, to lighten, too, the traffic passing through Alrewas Main Street, which had made crossing the street a really dangerous hazard.

These then, were some of the changes made to existing features. The greatest effects were to be the replacement of fields, crofts and gardens by new housing estates.

First came the Council estate at Anson Road, and then soon after, Oakfield Road with its island of bungalows designed to accommodate the elderly villagers. Fox Lane and Somerville followed the same pattern, the elderly being provided with a warden and a communal centre. After this, estate followed estate, and at the same time small plots from former gardens and demolished property, were rapidly developed and dwellings sprang up on the most unexpected sites. The developers had, and seem still to have, a field day, for the process of building seems to continue on any piece of open ground. Suburbia appears to have buried the old village and fragmented what was a tightly knit community, a fragmentation which begins at the school level. The older children are now separated at eleven from the younger ones, and mixed at the Secondary School with pupils from the whole district of villages, hundreds in number, and divided into many groups, so that the bond of belonging to a particular village is weakened. In former times all Alrewas children were together, from the age of five to fourteen or fifteen, which formed a great sense of awareness of belonging to the youthful village community.

To many of the elderly Alrewas folk, the transformation of their village has been sad and bewildering, but they realise the inevitability of change, and the right of other people from outside to live here and enjoy this attractive village. Many of the new residents are already well-assimilated into the Alrewas community, bringing enthusiasm and fresh ideas to the local clubs and societies, and making a useful contribution to the life of the village which provides for the welfare and social life of the people as it always appears to have done. It now has its Parish and Methodist Churches, its Women's Institute, British Legion, Cricket Club, Football Clubs, Agricultural Show, Fireside Club, Darby and Joan Club, Nursery School, Pre-School Playgroup, Mothers and Toddlers Club, Church Youth Group, Scouts, Guides, Boys' Brigade, Floral Art Club, Drama Society, Bowling Clubs, Angling Society, Civic Society, and maybe others, but sufficient in number to cater for the needs of the village, and the variety of interests of the villagers.

CHAPTER 27

Alrewas Cricket Club

Cricket in Alrewas, as an official club game, began in the early 1870's with the founding of a Cricket and Tennis Club. The site of this first club was along what is now Oakfield Road, then a public footpath across several narrow pasture fields. There was no pavilion, but in those days most of the players arrived at the ground already dressed for play, any necessary privacy having to be provided by nearby hedges.

By 1879, a new ground had been acquired, this time where the present ground is situated, and in 1881, a formal agreement was drawn up on 25th July, between the lord of the Manor, the Earl of Lichfield, and Alrewas Cricket Club, and the Club has been in continuous existence on that site since then. The agreement was for a seventy yards square area of Walk Field, and as with the old site, was part of the ancient open arable field known originally as the Great Furlong. The whole area of this field, from Walk Field to the Rykneld Street, and from Main Street to Daisy Lane and beyond Somerville Road has been divided into narrow eleven yards wide arable strips, which eventually created the waving surface of the permanent pastures of later years. This switch-back effect was a great source of enjoyment to speeding child cyclists crossing Walk Field to the cricket ground, but a cause of embarrassment to outfielders playing cricket. The wicket square was levelled to allow the laying down of playing pitches, with posts and wire to protect it from cattle and horses. Some of the terms of this agreement laid down by the Earl of Lichfield are of interest and worthy of inclusion.

1. To limit the trespass to an acre of ground, say seventy yards square, and not to graze it.
2. To strictly prohibit intoxicating drinks of any kind on the ground, or to be sold or given from any adjacent property abutting upon Walk Field.
3. To prohibit and prevent all betting and swearing on the ground.

   The rent was fixed at five shillings per annum, the agreement being signed on behalf of the Club by the Vicar, Rev. W. A. Webb, who was President, Joseph Cartwright, who was Captain, and it was witnessed by J. W. Williams and T. G. Smith.

   Shortly afterwards, a pavilion was erected, largely through the generosity of Mr. E. Houghton, and Mr. Joseph Cartwright of Alrewas House, who owned the Steam Mill on the canal side near to Gallows Bridge.

   A tennis club was formed, with two levelled tennis courts north of the cricket pitch, and the whole area of just over two acres, was then fenced with iron railings, which were provided by Mr. H. B. Whetstone of Alrewas Mill. Thus the present ground was established.

   Among the players of those days were J. W. Williams, H. H. Brierley, J. Stanley, S. Smalley, C. E. Arnold, R. W. Adamson, S. Nettleton, F. Sherratt, F. Barrett, A. J. Selvage, A. W. Millett, G. H. Job, F. Deans, E. H. Mallaber, Rev. W. A. Webb, Dr. Norton, Rev. W. Inge, Capt. Occlestone, and J. Hodson, with J. Watson, C. Woodburn and J. Cartwright.

In 1903, Alrewas produced its own newspaper called "The Intelligencer" which contained records of Alrewas cricket matches, in which the scores were often very low, due no doubt to primitive batting techniques and indifferently prepared pitches. One can imagine though, that trains or horse-drawn vehicles brought back very happy cricketers from Lichfield, Burton, Abbots Bromley Hoar Cross, Barton, Walton or Shenstone, and other nearby villages. In 1904, Alrewas played the Arcadians from Birmingham, winning by 129 runs to 75, but in victory the locals were thrilled by an innings of 44 not out, and by the bowling of a stripling opponent named R. T. Foster, who was later to play for England. Brooks and Inge scored 73 runs for Alrewas on that day. In those untroubled days, the local gentry, vicars, doctors, schoolmasters, etc. were mostly active members of the club, but even so, one entry contains a lament (often repeated by later Captains) from R. W. Adamson, an all-round sportsman—"We should have played Rugeley on 23rd June (1904), but were unable to raise a team. I don't know what their various excuses were, but I believe it is not the first time we have failed them. I envy those members who can get away regularly, and I should want some better excuses than some have, for not playing every match, were I in their shoes'

Some exceptional results are worthy of note. At Walton, Alrewas were dismissed for four runs, but in the return match, Alrewas returned the compliment, dismissing Walton for the same low score. In another match, Stanley and Barrett (licensee of the George & Dragon) dismissed Rugeley for seven runs. In 1897, the fixture list included matches against Albion Brewery, Allsopp's Offices, Theological College, Winshill St. Marks, and Tamworth Athletic. On 8th May, in that year, playing against Bass and Co., Alrewas made 107 to their opponents 13, and against the Theological College on 15th May, Alrewas won by 70, making 103 to their opponents 33. Other matches were against Lullington, Fazeley, Abbots Bromley and Catton, during June 1897. After the First World War, the club grew, and earned a strong reputation in local cricketing circles under the captaincies of men like Doug Shaw, Nelson Ball, Cyril Palfreyman and Bill Harris. The administration of the club in the 20's was in the capable hands of Mr. C. Styne, Mr. Egerton Orme, and Mr. George Thomas, who for so many years contributed so unselfishly to the Club as secretary, treasurer or chairman. He is still remembered by older residents as a strict and outstanding umpire, always an inspiration in his wide loyalty to Alrewas, but never favouring its players in his interpretation of the game. In the 10 years before the Second World War, under the shrewd captaincy of Jim Norbury, the club had many happy and successful seasons, culminating in 1937 with the winning of the newly-begun Chauntry Cup Competition, when Lichfield were defeated in the final, umpired by R. M. K. Foster and "Tich" Freeman, national cricket celebrities. The club was rich in young talent in the years before the war, George and Ernie Heathcote, Geoff. Watson, Mike and David Potter, Ron Walters, Jack Whitfield, Harold Pepper, Alf Cliffe, Tom Smith, Joe Thompstone, N. Stubbs, Ron Lovatt, Howard Hoskisson, etc. Came the Second World War, and in the last match, the opposing team was captained by "Dusty" Rhodes, who was to become a great player and an even better known test umpire.

During the war years, the club was kept alive largely through the hard and patient work of Mr. Geoff. Watson and Mr. George Thomas, so that when the peace came, the club once more took its place as an important parish amenity.

For many years, the club was under the watchful and benevolent eye of its president, Mr. Egerton Orme, and in 1947 the Orme Knock-out Competition was conceived, for a trophy donated by the president. Over the ensuing seasons, the competition has provided the village, players and spectators, with interest and enjoyment. The work of re-adjustment in the early post-war years was carried out under the efficient secretary-ship of Mr. K. Howkins, ably supported by the treasurer, Mr. W. Simpson, who were largely responsible for the club's sound financial position, by the formation of the weekly Tote.

During this period a strong team was built round such players as George Burton, D. May, Roger McGibbon, Jim Fox, Frank Harrison and experienced pre-war players, with a new crop of talented youth coming along, who were to be the backbone of a great side in the 50's. The club was captained by N. Stubbs at that time, who had helped to develop natural talents shown in the school by Michael Watson, Peter Watson, Ian Kirkland, John Fox, John Stubbs, Malcolm Harcombe, Dick Jones, Brian Elton, Graham Toft, who were a few years later, under Mr. Geoff. Watson's captaincy to be the foundation of a most successful sequence of years, when the team could hold its own against the best teams in the midlands. He was to be followed as captain by his nephew Frank Watson, who became a most successful long-serving groundsman.

Some of the best and most enthusiastic members of the club have been the loyal and contented players in the second eleven, who really enjoyed their cricket. Over the years, many names of these popular members come to mind, like Tom Shemmonds, Jack Jones, Eric (Nurker) Jones, Vic Heathcote, Fred Sherratt, John Potter, Dennis Collingwood, Tom Mansell, Harold Weaver and his son Brian, Bill Simpson, Tom Green (later of First Team class) Jack Lister, Basil May, Stan Orme, Aden Fletcher, Dick Woodburn, Frank Kent, Bert Pitt, Ernie Gray (also a scorer for the club), Fred Short, etc.

Loyalty is the mainspring from which a club derives it's success, and over the years there have been many loyal members who have served the club over long periods, like Tom Shemmonds, Nelson Ball, Jack Jones, George Thomas, Geoff. Watson, Bill Simpson, Tom Green, Frank Watson, Roy Walker, 'Jacko' Bladen, George Burton, Ken Howkins, to mention but a few.

By 1967, the old pavilion was quite inadequate. A new tea-hut had made the provision of teas on the ground possible, instead of as in the past trooping to the Navigation Inn or to Whitfield's shop (later the premises of Mr. W. Simpson), but accommodation was very cramped, in fact the standing joke was the possibility of having one's leg in someone else's trousers while dressing! We cannot do better than quote the account of the conception and construction of the new pavilion by the then secretary, Mr. Mark. Homan.

"There is only one thing special about the pavilion . . . we built it. It's a home-made job, but we are proud of it.

It all started almost by accident. The Parish Council had just bought half of Walk Field for village recreation and agreed to lease the ground to the cricket club when the "new hut", as it became known, came on to the market. Although it was not new, it was ideal from the club's point of view, as it was just within the limit of the Club's finances at the time. Our thanks must go to the Parish Council for it's co-operation, and the quickness with which the Councillors appreciated what we were doing for the village, and in particular to Mr. R. N. Stubbs as Clerk of the Council, whose skilful negotiations with the Club Chairman, R. N. Stubbs, smoothed out all the differences.

The new hut, which stood in Post Office Road, was dismantled, and at this point the real club spirit began to show. Once the inside walls and lining has been removed, it took just three week-ends of real team to unbolt the sections, transport them across the village, and re-erect the building again, all 950 square feet of it. It only took one more week-end to re-roof it in a hurry under threat of wet weather, the work going on by car headlights after dark, in a freezing mist. The weather broke next day, and it rained incessantly for several weeks. At this stage, just when we needed encouragement, we noticed the truth of the saying that God and people help those who help themselves. Vice-presidents, some of whom hadn't been seen for years, came forward with donations, the ladies Committee made a great success of a Christmas Whist Drive, and when the Chairman and I went to Edgbaston, the Midland Cricket Club Conference recognised our application for a grant, largely because of the members own contribution to the work. We also received much help in kind. Mr. Woolley lent us a tractor and a cement mixer. Mrs. Rowe lent us a tractor and trailer. Mr. Birkenshaw, the Lichfield District Surveyor who resided in Oakfield Road, gave much free advice on siting, and in particular on digging a hole for a septic tank, that would satify the authorities, and Leavesley's lent a crane to lower the huge concrete pipe into the hole to form the tank. Richard Hill (the finest vice-president a club could wish for) produced flooring sections for the verandah, and fibre board to augment our battered supply. Materials came from several unexpected sources; the members knocked down a barn to provide rubble, and Frank Watson obtained timber for us from the demolition of the Railway Station.

It is amazing what a variety of talent can be found in such a small club. The plans for the enlargements, etc., were drawn up by the architect (Brian Elton), assisted by the surveyor (John Homan), and by advice from absolutely everybody. The Clerk of the Works (Ian Kirkland), advised on building, though the joiners (Peter Watson and Malcolm Harcombe) didn't always agree with the advice. Once the walls were re-lined, we found that everyone could paint. Of course, not everyone was given top coats to do, but everyone painted something. John Watson painted on his days off, the schoolmasters painted in the holidays, the Green family painted en masse, and everyone indeed joined in.

The old tea hut was duly taken down, re-erected alongside the new hut, partitioned, and converted into changing rooms, a verandah was constructed along the front, and batsmen now had to climb the pavilion steps after making a 'duck'. The kitchen was expertly laid out by Malcolm, Peter and Ian, under guidance from the ladies, who deserve an even better one. We couldn't manage without the ladies... . . thank you, Joan Green for the tea and coffee throughout the winter. It was then discovered that the club had no electrician and apparently no bricklayer. The first problem was solved by the generous work of Mr. Geoff. Harvey, and the second brought back two former players, George and Ernie Heathcote. Their brickwork formed the cloakroom section, and linked the other units, opening into changing rooms and clubroom. Anyone who has dug five feet under Alrewas knows that there's water there. Anyone who has dug ten feet, knows that there is a lot of it. Much can be achieved by a good pump, and the example of a chairman who rolls his sleeves up and grabs a shovel, and in very little time, the amphibious mole unit, Tom Green (who was also groundsman), Malcolm Harcombe, Peter Watson and Ian Kirkland, with various assistants, had the job done.

The rest was finishing touches, but by this time, the hut and the tea hut had become the Pavilion, and the space next to the kitchen had become the bar, and the club as a social, as well as sporting centre, came into being.

On 29th April, 1967, the pavilion was officially opened by Rachel Heyhoe, who at Mark Homan's instigation, brought the England Ladies' team to play Alrewas. The team was welcomed by the President, Mr. Egerton Orme, and an excellent and enjoyable match took place, just won by the Club. The club team consisted of Frank Watson, Captain, George Burton, Tom Green, Mark Homan, Bunny Johnson, Dick Jones, Ian Kirkland, Ron Rowe, John Stubbs, Graham Toft and Peter Watson. It carried a number of reserves to share in the game, Geoff. Watson, Brian Elton, Fred Short, Norman Hunt and Malcolm Harcombe, with Scorers, Pam Dolman and Ken Howkins.

The ladies' team consisted of in batting order, Sheila Plant, Enid Bakewell, Rachel Heyhoe, Edna Barker, Audrey Disbury, Lynne Thomas, Pam Cram, June Moorhouse, Lesley Clifford, Carol Evans and Jean Clark.

Unfortunately, after a few seasons, the new pavilion was burnt, the cause of the fire not being really established, but very quickly it was rebuilt and is now a major contributor to the sporting and social life of the village. The ground has been levelled and the club now has an excellent ground as well as a fine pavilion, large enough to hire out for social functions.

A new crop of fine cricketers, many with familiar names like Neil and Mark Burton, Frank Watson's sons, Roy Walker's son, and other cricketers' offsprings are carrying the old club into the future. Cricketers' wives are often a great support to a club, and Alrewas owes much to the work of Mrs. Geoff. Watson, Mrs. Tom Green, Mrs. Fletcher, Mrs. Bladon, etc.

Long may the old club flourish!

CHAPTER 28

Extracts from Parish Magazines 1888-1897

September 1888—Mothers' Meeting Excursion
On Tuesday, 21st August, the members of the Mothers' Meeting drove in a brake to Shugborough Park. They arrived about two o'clock and were met by Lord and Lady Lichfield, who took them into the house and gave them full liberty to roam about the gardens, where there were plenty of seats and shelter, both being very welcome on account of a sudden and heavy shower. The Vicar of Great Haywood very kindly arranged a special service in the Church, which all attended. It had been intended to go on to the Chase, but the unsettled weather made all very glad to accept the kind proposal to stay at Shugborough. A very good tea was provided through the kindness of Mrs. Bird, Miss Bird, Mrs. Follows, Miss Bond, the Vicar, Mrs. Turner, Mrs. Powles and Mrs. Webb. Every one enjoyed the excursion thoroughly, and it is hoped it may be the first of many.

New members will receive a hearty welcome any Tuesday afternoon in the Parish Room (The Church House attached to the old Vicarage) at 2.30 p.m.

December 1888
Our Wake Feast, which originally took its rise from the Dedication Festival of the old Parish Church, has once more come, and we are glad to think, passed happily. The church as usual, took an active part in providing innocent amusement and recreation. The customary Tea and Dance was held in the School on the Monday, and a concert, in aid of the Working Mens' Club, on the Tuesday.

At the former, this year an unusual but pleasing episode took place. On behalf of the parishioners, Mr. Bird publicly presented the Rev. W. A. Webb, who has now left us for his vicarage at Wall, with a number of gifts, as a token of the affection and regard which he has so deservedly won. These consisted of a clock, a lamp; a gold Albert chain, and a purse of 26 sovereigns. Mrs. Follows, on behalf of the women of the Mothers' Meeting gave Mrs. W. A. Webb a "Ladies Companion".

Offertories for Nov. 11th—£1. 9s. 3¾d

February 1890

In Memoriam William Bond, aged 85 Extract from the Vicar's sermon.

"The close of one such truly Christian life it has been your privilege and mine to see, in him who has been on this very day, called to his rest. In the venerable William Bond, Alrewas has had these many years, a bright example, a noble benefactor, and a faithful friend. No one knows all that he has been, both to my predecessors and myself. It was always a refreshment when cast down, wearied and perplexed, to go to his house and simply to look upon his calm, trustful face. And no one will know till the last great day, the good he has done among his neighbours, and for the Church of God. And now, we shall see that "crown of glory", his hoary head, among us no more, but his memory, God grant, will long be evergreen.

Sunday School Treat Holy Innocents' Day falling on a Saturday, the children had their annual tea on St. John's Day instead, and enjoyed their happy evening. The prizes were distributed by Miss Bond, Mrs. Bird and the Vicar sending a supply of crackers. The Fradley children had a similar happy meeting on Monday, January 19th.

February 1890 It is done at last! The beautiful old screen is now standing in its place, the admiration of all who have seen it. And now, the work of bringing back the old tower to its original beauty is accomplished, and better still PAID FOR, now a matter of satisfaction and thankfulness to all of us, and so felt our Bishop in dedicating the work on January 5th to the glory of God.

It may interest our readers to know what has been expended on the church since the Rev. W. R. Inge commenced the restoration of the Chancel in 1877.

It is as follows:—

Restoration of Chancel	— £1,791
Erection of Organ and expenses	— 415
Alteration to Pulpit	— 4
Restoration of Tower with removal of Gallery and new Porch	— £1 029
New clock (Three dials)	— 140
Making a total of	— £3,379

Trip to Blackpool The ringers and members of the choirs of both churches had their Annual Excursion on July 11th. The day was spent at Blackpool and we hope it was a pleasant day to all. The collections for the Choir Fund at Fradley Church will be on Sunday, August 3rd.

Mothers' Meeting November 1890
On September 23rd, the members of the Mothers' Meeting drove in brakes to Rangemore. Here they were shown round the gardens and park, and then sat down to a very good tea, kindly provided by Mrs. Bird (of Orgreave Hall), who also paid half the expenses of the brakes.

Glee Class A Glee Class will be held in the Schools on Monday evenings at 7.30. A small subscription will be paid by members. The first meeting will be on 17th November, 1890.

Flower Show A public meeting will be held on Tuesday, November 18th at 6.30, when all who are interested in the well-being of the Show are earnestly requested to attend. It would be a matter of the greatest regret to the Committee, if, through lack of interest, this old and valued show should have to be given up.

March 1892
Extract from the Vicar's letter.
"I cannot close my letter without expressing my grateful thanks to Mr. and Mrs. Gilbert-Smith for collecting subscriptions to supply soup and beef-tea to many of our parishioners during this most trying time of sickness. Never was

kindness of this description needed, or, I believe, more appreciated and I am truly thankful to them and to all who have assisted them. I trust, by the mercy of God, both those who have suffered, and those who are still suffering from this severe epidemic will soon be restored to health and strength'

Instruction in Cookery A class for "High Class" Cookery will be held every Tuesday morning at 11 o'clock, at 1 shilling per lesson; and at 3 o'clock the same day, an instruction will be given on Cottage Cookery, at 1½ pence per lesson, in the old Parish Room.

May 1892

The Vicar desires to acknowledge his own obligation, and to express the thanks of all who received soup during their recent illness, to Mrs. Charles Dolman, who was good enough to make it every day for seven weeks, at so much personal inconvenience and trouble.

June 1892

The Annual Parish Tea will be held on Monday, June 13th at 5 o'clock. After tea there will be a service in Church and on re-assembling in the Schoolroom, there will be a Vocal and instrumental concert by members of the choir and others. Tickets for the tea may be obtained from district visitors or from the Post Office, price 6d.

July 1892

Mothers' Meeting Outing On Monday, July 25th, the members of the Alrewas and Fradley Mothers' Meetings and Bible Class had their annual excursion. Upwards of fifty drove to Tutbury Castle in brakes. Mrs. Bird and Mrs. Fox met them there, and a good tea was provided by Mrs. Turner, given by Miss Bond, Mrs. Follows, Mrs. Shaw, Mrs. William Shaw and Mrs. Webb. Mrs. Crossman helped to defray other expenses. Most of the party went over the Tutbury Glass Works and all spent a very happy and pleasant afternoon.

November 1892

Extract from the Vicar's letter.

"I would remind the young men of the Parish, that they will find a comfortable room, and be able to spend a pleasant social evening, at the Working Mens' Club, at very small cost. I cannot think that any good can be attained by standing at street corners, as I see so many young people doing. It seems to me such an absolute waste of time, and must be very uncomfortable, and altogether an unprofitable way of spending time, so I hope that many will take advantage of the Working Mens' Club, (now the Scout Headquarters) where to say the least, they will find a much pleasanter way of spending an evening'

December 1893

The Coal Club This Club closes for this year on December 18th, and the coal will be distributed to the members between that date and the end of the month. In the face of what is likely to be a trying winter, to our poorer brethren, we venture to express the hope that we may receive many new subscribers to this most useful club; and also, that those who have assisted us in the past years will continue their valued help, and should they find it possible, in the midst of so many calls on their generosity to increase their subscriptions. There can be no doubt of the usefulness and benefit of a club like this, and in helping it, we have the satisfaction of knowing that we are helping those who, at any rate, are trying to help themselves. Miss Bond will be glad to receive subscriptions. The Club will be re-opened for the New Year on Monday, January 1st at 4 o'clock.

1897

"The Concert held on December 14th, 1896 on behalf of William Statham, realised a sum of £4, which has been forwarded to the Secretary of the Institution of the Blind at Nottingham, to be used for his benefit. Our thanks are due to those who so kindly gave their services on the occasion, more especially to Mrs. Kay, Miss Worthington, Mr. F. Oakley, and Mr. Cresser, who came from a distance to help. W. Statham desires to return his grateful thanks to all for helping him in his necessity'

April 1897

The Parish Bier The new wheeled bier has now come to hand, and is ready for use. A charge of is 6d will be made for the use of it, and will be paid to the Churchwardens to be kept as a Repair Fund. A further charge of 1 shilling will be made within a mile radius of the Parish Church, is 6d within two miles, and 2s 0d beyond two miles, for taking the Bier to and fro and for keeping it clean. This will be paid to the Sexton.

Appended is the Balance Sheet of the account as it stands

	£	s	d
Received from Sales of Work and Wake Tea	15.	9.	9.
Donation from Miss Abell	2.	0.	0.
Total recepits	£17.	9.	9.
Paid to Mr. Robinson for Bier	£19. 10. 0.		
Balance due to Mrs. Webb	2.	0.	3.

In June 1897, the Vicar's letter referred to the Queen's Diamond Jubilee, stating—"Her influence for good over her people on account of the love and purity that have always reigned in her court and home, has been inestimable. Whilst our Sovereign is the most queenly of women, she is also the most womanly of queens.

"On June 22nd, amid the shouts of rejoicing thousands, amid the blare of trumpets, the steady tramp of glittering regiments passing in review before the royal standard, all hearts will be beating for one exalted personage—all eyes will be turned upon one queenly figure in the sunset of life—gracious, dignified and calm'

It is hoped that these few extracts from Parish Magazines will give some glimpses into the life of the village, as it was nearly a hundred years ago, centred mainly round the Parish Church.

CHAPTER 29

Alrewas Sunday School in the 1890's

The first Sunday Schools of the late 18th Century, were, for all denominations, created to teach the fundamentals of education and religion to the children of the working classes in towns and country. By 1870, the provision of the Education Act catered for the education of the nation's children, and the role of the old Sunday schools had changed to a voluntary one catering mainly for religious education on a sectarian basis.

In Alrewas, as in most of the country in the late 1800's, the Sunday School became an important voluntary institution, instructing and influencing a large number of children, keeping them occupied for a large part of both mornings and afternoons on most Sundays of the year. The school, under the superintendant, Mr. W. H. Brierly, was run on efficient lines, the registers being marked each morning and afternoon, a dot signifying present and an 'a' denoting absence, and the teachers' section was marked too. It was from these registers that the attendances were totalled at the end of the year to decide on the allocation of the books which were given as prizes, and also to qualify pupils for attending the Sunday School Treat in the summer.

In 1890, the school had eighteen teachers, with 101 children attending, ranging in age from four to fourteen. Some teachers took morning school only, as did Miss Harris, Miss Draper, Mr. Sellick, Mr. Selvage, Mr. Thomas Stubbs, and Miss M. Durose, while others, like Mr. C. Colman, Miss Dolman, Miss Bean, Mr. W. Williams, Mr. T. Durose, Mr. Tillett, Miss Bishop and Mrs. Eggleston attended the afternoon classes. Some enthusiasts were prepared to go mornings and afternoons, as were Miss Johnson, Miss Turner, Miss Gray, Miss Lakin, Miss E. Gray and another Miss Durose.

Other teachers in those early days were Miss Bond, Miss R. May, Miss A. Powell, Miss D. Powell, Mr. Perry, Mr. Lord and Mr. W. Ryde. There are of course, too many children's names to include here, but many old Alrewas families are there, whose relatives still reside here, or have done until recently. Class 1 of 1893 contains such names as Harry Lindsay, Charles Woodburn, Ernest May, Will Meacham, Joseph Dolman, Edward Lakin, William Ball and George Ward.

The infants class of 1897 contained many names familiar to older Alrewas folk—Eddie Houghton, Nelson Ball, Leonard Ward, Tom Shemmonds, George Whitfield, Fred Bates, Tom Houghton, Fred Dolman, Harry Mallaber, Edward Budgeon, Edith Dolman, Maggie Bates, Nellie Mallaber, Daisy Whitfield, Bertha Dolman, Ada Ward, Dora Woodburn, Lizzie Smith, etc., and in the earlier class, Herbert and Nelson Gould.

In 1891, the following boys were excused school in the afternoon to attend choir practice in church—Ernest May, Randolph Draper, Henry Dumolo, George Cross, Will Meacham, Ernest Byrne, Harry Byrne, Fred Tipper, Clement Taylor and George Heathcote. The lists for 1891 contain the names of George Heathcote, Walter Heathcote and Ernest Heathcote, all three giving their names to the present well-known Heathcote brothers.

The register for Sunday school extends to 1901, after which it was used to record the names and attendances of members of the choir, first by Miss Bond and Mrs. Webb, the organists, and then by Mrs. Alice Ball who was organist and choir mistress for many years, and who eventually passed the register to Mr. Fred Durose, to whom we are indebted for its loan.

CHAPTER 30

Snippets from the district

It would be inappropriate to end this study without reference to one or two of the many interesting fragments of history contained in the long sagas of other local villages, some of which read like the fictional ingredients of historical novels. Handsacre and Mavesyn Ridware have the story of the rivalry between the Handsacre and Mavesyn lordly families, which ended in 1403. Sir Henry Percy, nicknamed Hotspur, had rebelled against the King, Henry IV, and Sir William Handsacre collected his vassals to join the King, while at the same time, Sir Robert Mavesyn, from his nearby manor gathered his men to join the rebel Percy. At some point on their journey to join the opposing armies, the two rival groups met, and to avoid unnecessary bloodshed, the two rival knights met in single combat. Sir William was slain in the fight and Sir Robert continued his march to Shrewsbury, where in the ensuing battle, he too was killed. The sequel was not a continuation of the feud, for Sir William's son, instead of seeking to avenge his father's killing, fell in love with Sir Robert's daughter, the Lady Margaret Mavesyn, and thus ended the long quarrel between their families, by their marriage.

At the old village of Colton, the manor house was said to have been the scene of a murder in 1271. The crime was committed by a priest named John, who was the chaplain of Colton. He is alleged to have killed Christina, the wife of Nicholas de Colton, while interposing in a quarrel between her and a stranger residing at her house. Whether the lady was killed accidentally or not, John fled from the hue and cry that pursued him. He escaped, but had to endure outlawry, all his goods and chattels being confiscated. As was the custom at that time, when an assassin escaped, the entire village was held responsible and punished by having to pay a heavy fine. Later, another murderer is said to have claimed sanctuary in the church, which brought a further punishment and burden to the villagers.

Elford has a long history, and is associated with many noble families, the Ardens, the Campvilles, Pipes, Lathams, Staffords and Vernons. In the middle of the 15th Century, the lord of the manor was Sir John Stanley. In the church, there was a small table tomb carved in hard gritstone, on which was carved the figure of a child. In the child's left hand was a ball, and the right hand pointed to the little boy's temple, thus signifying the cause of his death. He was killed by being struck on the head by a tennis ball, while he was watching what was then an indoor game. He was the grandson of Sir John Stanley, and the last male heir of that branch of the family.

Wolseley Bridge and the nearby Wolseley Arms at the junction of the Stafford and Stoke roads, are well-known by many local people, but few realise that the old Wolseley Hall and nearby estate was the original home of one of the oldest and most celebrated families in England. Their ancestors can be traced back to Edric Wolesley, a Saxon noble, who had large possessions in the country before the Normans came. The family has a distinguished military and diplomatic record. In the 17th Century, Sir Charles Wolseley married Mrs. Anne Fienes, the daughter, of Lord Say and Seale, who bore him ten daughters and seven sons. The fourth of these sons eventually became the third baronet, Sir William Wolseley, who spent much time in foreign travel. While in Egypt, a seer prophesied to him that he would meet his death by drowning, and he was so impressed by this that when he returned to England he travelled the overland route across Europe, a long and dangerous undertaking. Years later, in 1728, when he was 69 years old, he was returning in the evening from Lichfield with his suite, in a chariot pulled by four Arab horses. On the way, there occurred a violent thunderstorm, accompanied by torrential rain, and as the chariot was crossing a stream over the road at Longdon, a nearby mill dam burst. An immense flood of water burst down the stream, just as the vehicle was crossing. Caught in the rushing torrent, the vehicle was overturned and it, the four horses, Sir William and his suite, were washed away and drowned. One of the postillions survived the tragedy, for after being carried a hundred yards downstream, he saved himself by clinging to the boughs of an apple tree in an orchard, until the rush of the torrent subsided. A hundred years later, the armour plate of the chariot was found buried near the scene of the disaster, and was later mounted in the Hall.

Kings Bromley's long history began when it became the summer seat of Leofric, the Earl of Mercia, and his better-known wife, Lady Godiva. Later, in the 17th Century, the Manor was the home of the Lane family, one of whose members was Jane Lane, who took her place in history by bravely assisting in the escape of Charles Stuart after his defeat at Worcester in 1651. One quaint bit of Bromley history from the Parish register in the 17th Century, relates a remarkable case of longevity in a lady named Mary Cooper. She not only attained a great age, but saw her descendants to the sixth generation, all living at the same time. It was claimed that after a new birth in the family, she was able to say to her daughter, "Rise daughter, go to thy daughter, for thy daughter's daughter hath got her a daughter".

The Tale of Tommy Bond

Only a few of the oldest parishioners will remember hearing the account of the callous and brutal murders which occurred at Orgreave around the end of the last century. This is the true story as it was handed down by old villagers.

There was a farming family living at Orgreave at the time, consisting of a Mr. and Mrs. Bakewell and their son, and they carried farm produce to Lichfield regularly, to sell it at the market there. One day, after returning from a very profitable sale, they were surprised in their cottage by an intruder armed with a gun. It was a local man named Tommy Bond, who demanded the surrender of the money which he knew that they had brought from the market. On their refusal of the demand, Bond shot and killed Mr. Bakewell, then killed the son, and to silence the wife's cries, he shot her too. He then carried out his intended robbery, left the cottage and made good his escape. His departure was seen by a young Mr. Walter Heathcote, who saw him throw his gun into a nearby coppice, from where it has never been found.

Unfortunately for Bond, his third shot had struck Mrs. Bakewell a glancing blow on the substantial bones of her corset, deflecting the bullet, and only causing a slight wound and severe bruising. She soon recovered and was later able to provide the police with the information which identified the murderer. Immediately, a warrant was issued for the arrest of Tommy Bond, and his description was widely circulated throughout the country.

Some time later, a policeman in Nottingham, who was shaving at home, looked through the window and saw the wanted man passing by in the street. Without hesitation, he rushed out, went after Bond and arrested him. After trial and being found guilty, Tommy Bond was hanged for his crime.

CHAPTER 31

Into the 21st Century

In the twenty five years since the completion of the Alrewas bypass, the purpose of which was to reduce the flow of heavy traffic through the village, and also provide an uninterrupted crossing and interchange with the A38, the pace of change has gone on relentlessly at an ever increasing rate.

In some ways the construction of the bypass has left the village more isolated, cut off from the Croxall Road that led to Tamworth, cut off from the part of Fox Lane that led to Lichfield and from Daisy Lane that connects the village to Fradley. These roads and lanes of course still exist on the other side of the A38 and the A513, but are no longer the natural extensions of the village, which used to provide the escape directly into the countryside, especially for children.

The provision of the bypass has however led to different pressures on the village; the village fields and farms, which spread from the edges of the village, were disrupted. Small areas of land between the village and the bypass were not useful agriculturally and in consequence were sold to developers who built houses on them. Somerville Road had a group of large houses placed opposite the old people's bungalows. The truncated Daisy Lane had large houses, built opposite the row of houses, which once had a view out across the fields. The Cricketers filled the space between the cricket pavilion and the bypass, though the sports facilities that were promised by the developers when seeking permission to build never materialised. The field on the eastern side of Fox Lane, at the point where it joins the bypass was the possible site for a new village hall, but again this never materialised, the land was covered by houses, now known as Mellor Drive. The bypass also had the effect of isolating the remaining farms in the village. No longer could the cows walk from the fields down Fox Lane to be milked at Home Farm, and it was not so easy for the cows at Manor Farm to get from the fields to the farm buildings, even though they had an underpass beside the canal to some of their fields. Though Tom Mellor from Essington Farm could still be seen driving his tractor along Fox Lane to his fields on the other side of the bypass this did not continue for long.

Gradually the nature of farming was changing nationally with the trend towards larger farms and larger herds of cattle. The effect was felt in Alrewas. Home Farm was the first to turn its farm buildings into accommodation joining the movement that had begun to spread across the nation for "barn conversions", thus Swallow Close and Heron Court were created. The farm buildings at Manor Farm being developed in the same way followed this soon after. Fortunately the planning authorities in both cases insisted on the retention of the historic farm buildings, incorporating them into the designs of the new houses. Essington Farm ceased to be a working farm with the death of Tom Mellor, but at the time of writing remains uninhabited. The developers who wish to build on the adjoining land on the river side of Dark Lane have been frustrated by the District Planning Authorities, supported by a large portion of the Alrewas population.

For a variety of reasons shops and businesses closed, and once again developers were quick to see the possibilities of conversions or the building of more houses. The moving of the school from Mill End Lane to Furlong Close removed the passing trade from the two shops that were close to Kent's Bridge, and both closed. Bisbel closed its electrical business in the village and houses were built on the site in Park Road. Johnson's Haulage business operating out of Furlong Lane closed and a large bungalow was built on the premises. The Claymar Motel behind the George and Dragon, in what had once been a builder's yard, ceased trading and its accommodation units were converted to private housing together with some new building. The British Legion Club moved its location to what had been the Tree Café at the end of Wellfield Road, this released land for building and also gave the opportunity for some of the residents of Wellfield Road who had long gardens, to shorten them so that a sizeable development now known as Poppy Gardens could be built. Such has been the frenzied approach to development that any piece of land that could support a house has been considered, resulting in houses appearing in what had been large gardens, and demolition of properties to replace one house by two or more. One such development saw the demolition of "Southlands" on Daisy Lane, to be replaced by six large houses. In addition there have been many properties which were of a modest size that have been extended, rather than the occupants leaving to find a larger house elsewhere, creating "life style" improvements to their properties, which would have been beyond the wildest dreams of the villagers of the mid twentieth century.

One effect of this change and development is that Alrewas is now seen as a desirable location to retire to, or for an upwardly mobile professional to have as an out of town base from which they can commute to work. This has had a dramatic consequence for the price of housing in the village so that there is little that the first time buyer with a modest income can contemplate.

As the housing in the village has increased there has been a need for more school places in our primary school, with the constant addition of classroom space, first as temporary classrooms in the form of huts to be replaced with permanent buildings when it was seen that the numbers were not likely to decline again. The steady core of teachers who have stayed at the school for long periods of time has indicated the settled and congenial nature of the school and has served to provided continuity. The school has also had some good leadership through its head teachers, who have gradually raised the standards of achievement within the school, so that at the time of writing it was adjudged to be one of the best within Staffordshire. While there has been a decline in pupil numbers in many parts of the country, this does not seem to have affected Alrewas where the maximum number for the school is the normal situation, and in some years is over ridden. The school has maintained the policy that there should be a place for all children from the village of Alrewas and they should have priority over children who wish to attend from outside the village. In the early 1990s there was a move to sell off part of the school land for housing as it was seen to be surplus to requirements. Fortunately the shortsighted view that had been taken by the County Council was vigorously opposed and the plans were dropped so that the space needed by the since expanded school was preserved.

Once the children have graduated from the primary school they have to be transported to the secondary schools outside the village. The majority can be seen waiting in groups around the village for the coaches that transport them to the John Taylor High School at Barton under Needwood. A few travel to Lichfield to King Edward VI School, the Friary or Netherstowe schools. The John Taylor High School in recent years has achieved the designation of a specialist science school.

The recent years of affluence have meant that more households own cars and two, three or four car families are not unusual. In a village where the older houses were in terraces of small dwellings, or where the houses were placed in close proximity this has caused problems, so that residents have had to leave their cars on the road outside their houses. Those older houses which once were something of a small holding have some space beside the house so that cars can be parked off the road. Houses built post war seem to have been built with garages on the site, many of the houses being designed with integral garages; but there has been a trend in recent years to use the garage as a store room and leave the car outside, and again cars have spilled out onto the road so that our roads in the village have a cluttered aspect, particularly at weekends when many of the residents are not at work. Another phenomenon which has contributed to the present congestion in the village is what is known as the "school run" when some children are transported by car to be dropped off at school or to be collected at the end of school. It has been observed that for some, this journey has been as little as a quarter of a mile.

Government legislation enacted by Parliament has had significant changes to activities within the village and a change in the lifestyles of some. Licensing laws for the public houses have enabled a more flexible approach to opening hours, but the prohibition of smoking in enclosed public spaces has literally changed the atmosphere in the establishments. With the change in public attitude to 'drinking and driving' the licensed premises saw a falling off of their traditional trade and so to attract customers they have become places to eat and be entertained by visiting musicians, sometimes linked to theme nights. The first of the smoking prohibition acts drove the smokers from the areas where food was being served. The later one in 2002 drove them outside, so that groups of exiles became a common sight standing round the doorway of the pub as they satisfied their needs for a cigarette. Taking pity on the plight of their exiled customers some of the pubs have erected outdoor shelters which are not totally enclosed but do provide some protection from the elements.

With increased leisure, linked to affluence and lifestyle changes, the canal has seen an increase in traffic with more and more privately owned narrow boats travelling through Alrewas, supplementing the ones that can be hired from the holiday companies for a weeks cruising. Alrewas has become a preferred mooring for one or two nights with the close proximity of shops, pubs and a post office being significant attractions in addition to the picturesque nature of the village. In recent years there seem to have been many more occasions when after heavy rainfall in its catchment area, the River Trent was running at a high level. This has caused potential problems for the relatively inexperienced narrow boat sailor as they try to cross the river below the Alrewas Lock. No doubt with an eye on health and safety implications, when the crossing of the river looks to have potential dangers, the gates of the Alrewas Lock will be chained and padlocked by an official of British Waterways to prevent a narrow boat descending into the fast running floodwater.

The wide part of the canal below the Alrewas Lock, just before the junction with the river was always a convenient place to be able to turn the larger narrow boats to enable them to travel back again in the direction of Fradley Junction. On the occasions when the gates had to be locked for safety reasons, this meant that boaters were restricted to staying at Fradley Junction if they wanted to be sure of being able to return westwards along the canal, and it meant that Alrewas was no longer accessible.

To overcome this problem the Parish council agreed to the creation of a winding hole beside the Walkfields. This involved cutting a small semi circular piece from the bank of the playing fields to produce a wide point which would enable the longest of narrow boats to be able to turn on the canal. The edge of the playing fields at that point was planted with shrubbery to help restore the look of the bank after the work had been done.

Some years earlier there had been a move by a developer to create a marina on the Essington Farm side of the canal above the Alrewas Lock. There were many objections to the proposal, from local residents, the Parish Council and the District Council, and eventually the idea was dropped. However mooring places for the increasing number of narrow boats on the canal have been found along the bank side at Wychnor and the creation of a marina in the old gravel workings at Barton Turns, a short way along the canal in the direction of Burton on Trent.

As shopping habits have changed and out of town supermarkets have tended to entice trade away from small local shops, village shops have fought back with increased opening hours and ever-wider choices of goods on the shelves. Their strength has been the friendliness of the staff who seem know everyone, and their central position in the village, so that they are very accessible and the passing trade can be gained from those going to and from work together with the parents taking their children to school. For many years the loss of the Midland Bank in Main Street was felt to be an inconvenience, but in recent years this has been overcome by the installation of an ATM, the modern electronic cash point, in the wall of the Co-op.

There are times of the day and days of the week when this economic hub of the village becomes quite crowded with traffic, notably in the morning for a visit to the paper shop on the way to work, or a visit to the doctors' surgery. The Alrewas Fryer provides the attraction in the evenings with clientele coming from quite a distance, in the same way that the butchers shop is extra busy at the weekends with patrons coming from a wide area to buy local produce that they can trust. The little local shops which provided a small income for enterprising villagers selling sweets an items of haberdashery have long gone, but the enterprise is still there, with plants and flowers being offered for sale from the driveways of houses. One particular example can be found on the front wall of a house in Post Office Road where daily throughout the year jars of local home made jams, preserves and pickles can be purchased. These are all unattended with an honesty box for payment. It says much for the village that we live in is a place where this can happen.

In recent years the A38 running alongside the village has become a very important link in the nation's road network, not only linking major conurbations but also providing a traffic link between the M1 motorway and the M6. At times it seems to be treated by its users as if it were a motorway itself. The distribution industry has been well aware of its importance and in consequence either side of the village, on the site of the wartime airfield at Fradley, at Barton Turns and Burton on Trent, large areas have been covered by vast sheds in which all the items for modern living are momentarily stored before they are transported to the shops to be purchased by us. Those who live on that side of the village are well aware of the constant roar of traffic which continues both day and night with little respite except for a short periods at the weekend.

The Trent valley had deposits of sand and gravel laid down hundreds of thousands of years ago and these rich mineral deposits have been extensively quarried for the last fifty years. The archaeologists researched, excavated and recorded the pre Saxon village that was on Catholme before it was obliterated by the gravel extraction. Something that came as a real surprise was the uncovering of the well-preserved skull and partial skeleton of a woolly rhino in the Lafarge quarry at Whitemoor Haye, on the far eastern side of the Parish, together with the bones of bison, mammoths and reindeer. These finds brought archaeologist from around the country to the site, and the remains were transported to museums for conservation.

With the establishment of the National Forest Company in 1995, an area of 400 square miles was designated for regeneration as the National Forest. Alrewas found itself included in the southwest corner and this has come to have a significant impact on the area. The gravel companies, who were extracting gravel from the land, had laid upon them a requirement for the regeneration of the areas from which they had extracted minerals. The National Forest and the regenerated areas, intersected in the Trent valley. The Lafarge minerals company were working the land on the opposite side of the A38 to the village. After the sand and gravel had been extracted from the land to the north of the Croxall Road, it was restored by backfilling with inert material and then the topsoil was replaced. This piece of land was then offered to David Childs on a long lease of 999 years at a peppercorn rent to create the National Memorial Arboretum.

The 155 acres that was designated for the Arboretum was within the boundary of the National Forest and it was also within the boundary of the Lichfield District and these two organisations combined to fund the planting of the first 44,000 trees. The planting of the first whips started in 1997 and soon memorial plots began to appear. Funding from the Millennium Commission combined with donations from groups around the country, both military and civilian together with individual donations made the whole project possible. This funding enabled the first buildings to be constructed on the site; a visitor centre, restaurant and conference facility connected by a cloister walk to the chapel. The beginnings were slow and tentative but were supported by the Friends of the Arboretum, a group of local people from Alrewas and the surrounding area, who helped with the setting up of the enterprise in many ways, being able to turn their hands to almost anything that was required.

For quite some time few people seemed to know of the Arboretum until visits by members of the Royal Family, and particularly her Majesty the Queen, began to bring the place to the notice of a wider audience. The National Memorial Arboretum has gradually raised its profile as the years have progressed with more and more memorials and dedications being added, and by its tenth anniversary in 2007 the trees had grown to the extent that it now had the appearance of a well-wooded area. The original 44,000 trees has now expanded to 50,000 and of the 32 species of trees truly native to the United Kingdom the arboretum has all but one, the wych elm which has largely died out due to Dutch Elm disease. The number of memorials, some large plots others simple obelisks now numbers about 160. While visitor numbers had been steadily increasing over the years, a big step forward was experienced with the opening of the Armed Forces Memorial in 2007. This memorial honours the memory of the service men and women, who have died since the end of Second World War, and in particular the more than 16,000 who have lost their lives on active service, and whose names are inscribed on the gleaming Portland stone walls. Since its dedication by Rowan Williams, the Archbishop of Canterbury in the presence of Her Majesty the Queen, on 12th October 2007 the Arboretum has become a place of National Pilgrimage with visitor numbers climbing into thousands per month.

The regeneration of other gravel extraction areas comes under the umbrella of the Central Rivers Project. Here some of the workings have been restored as wildlife habitats, particularly for water birds, other are being developed as recreational areas with water sports in mind. Passing through the area is part of the projected long distance footpath from Birmingham to the Humber, crossing the River Trent by way of the new Mythaholme footbridge. Alrewas has become a gateway to this regenerated area and the National Forest and is truly on the map of the Nation's consciousness as well as the one produced by the Ordnance Survey.

At the end of chapter 27 Norman Stubbs commented on the effect that the transformation of the village had on the elderly Alrewas folk, particularly the ones who have spent all of their lives in the village. In addition he felt that the newcomers to the village would be able to add to the village life and that has turned out to be the fact. Many of the well established activities continue, though some, which depended for their existence on the enthusiasm of their leader have fallen by the wayside. Of particular note was the Scout and Guide Band which was the passion of Ron Chapman, and which introduced music to some young people who otherwise would have never had the experience of playing a musical instrument, let alone the opportunity to play in public. Remembrance Sunday parades have never had quite the same feeling about them since his departure. Other activities have been generated by some of the talented people in the village encouraging others to have a go and explore their own latent abilities. In 2006 this culminated in the Alrewas Arts Festival, for a whole week activity workshops took place throughout the village free of charge, where those who had a particular skill or talent shared it with others who wished to learn. These showed a wide diversity, which ranged from Narrow Boat art, painting roses and castles, and Wax Batik to Sugar Craft and Scriptwriting. Alongside these were performances of music, dancing and drama, together with exhibitions of art and photography in venues around the village. The highlight of the week was the Street Fair when Post Office Road was closed to traffic and the whole village seemed to come together in a joyful celebration. The week being finished off with an open air Finale Concert on the Walkfields. The success of the Festival suggests that it could become an established biennial event.

Alrewas started as a settlement at the crossing of two ancient track ways and the place where the river Trent could be forded. In the following centuries it expanded to be a sizeable, village and out on Fradley Heath a few scattered farms and dwellings appeared. When civil parishes were formed in 1894, Alrewas and Fradley were considered together as one entity with Fradley being the smaller partner. In recent years since the closing of the airfield at Fradley there has been development of industrial units and of estates of housing on the site, so that the combined areas of Fradley and Alrewas have become too large to administer effectively as one parish council. Fradley is now of a size where it can be a parish council in its own right, and in consequence the year 2009 will see the separation of the two parishes. From that point onwards Alrewas will become a separate parish which will also contain the hamlet of Orgreave.

There will be more changes in the future. Will the gravel extraction extend to the western side of the A38? Will the railway be reopened to passenger traffic, and the station be replaced? Will heavy goods vehicles be banned from travelling through the village? Will developers be permitted to build outside the present village boundary? Whatever changes, it is to be hoped that the village will manage to retain a character that will link back firmly to its long history.

Norman Stubbs born in the Potteries in 1911 came to teach in Alrewas in 1931. Except for a five-year break for army service during the war, he taught at the local Church of England School until 1957. He then moved to the John Taylor secondary School in Barton–under-Needwood, subsequently becoming Head of lower School until his retirement in 1976. During his younger days Norman was a keen sportsman, having played cricket for Alrewas and football for Deacons Works at Lichfield. This book is the result of the author's long felt wish to enable others to read and appreciate this district's ancient and historical background. After long study and research he has found the knowledge well worthy of recording and preserving. Norman died in November of 1996 and is buried in the Alrewas churchyard.

9780955668517